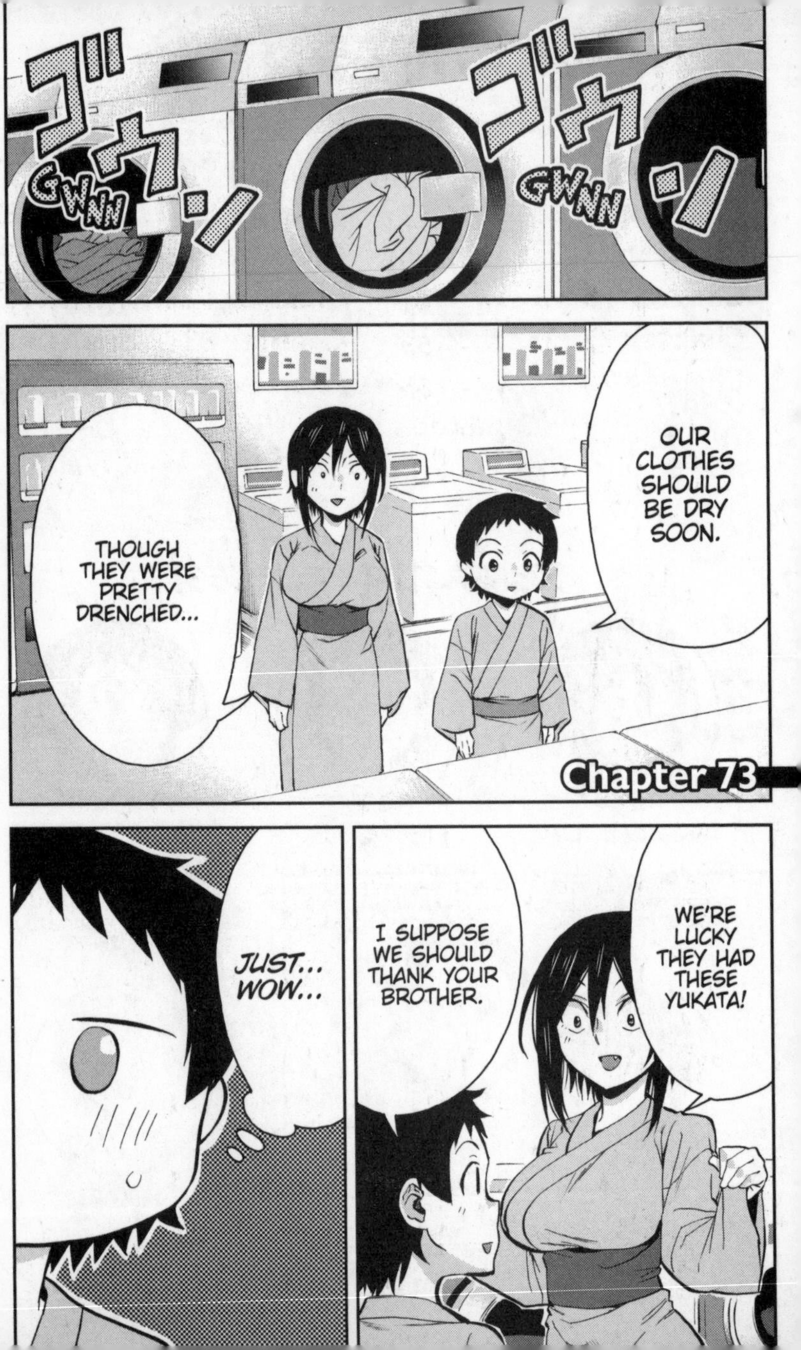
ゴウン
GWNN
ゴウン
GWNN
OUR CLOTHES SHOULD BE DRY SOON.
THOUGH THEY WERE PRETTY DRENCHED...
Chapter 73
WE'RE LUCKY THEY HAD THESE YUKATA!
I SUPPOSE WE SHOULD THANK YOUR BROTHER.
JUST... WOW...

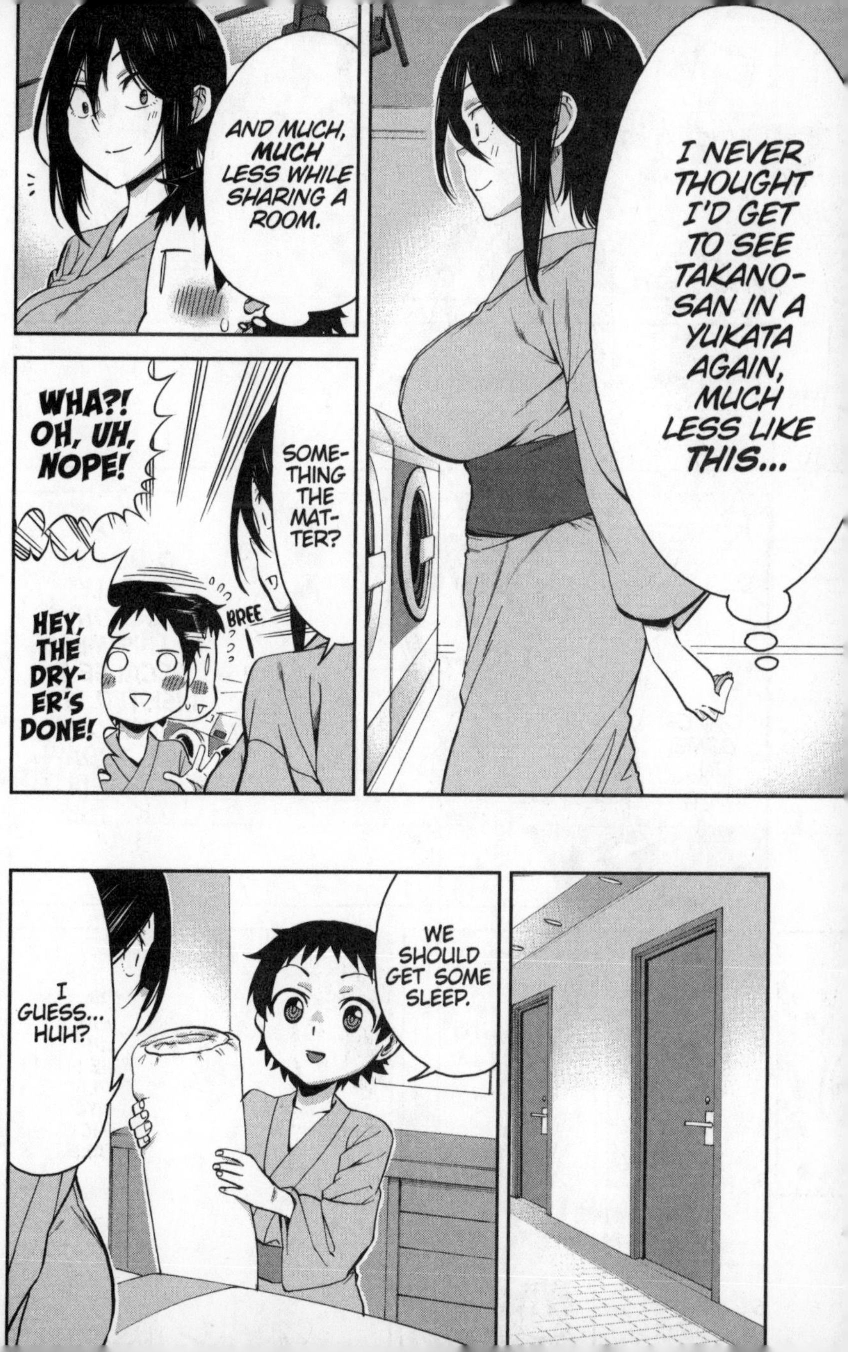
I NEVER THOUGHT I'D GET TO SEE TAKANO-SAN IN A YUKATA AGAIN, MUCH LESS LIKE THIS...
AND MUCH, MUCH LESS WHILE SHARING A ROOM.
SOMETHING THE MATTER?
WHA?! OH, UH, NOPE!
BREE
HEY, THE DRYER'S DONE!
WE SHOULD GET SOME SLEEP.
I GUESS... HUH?

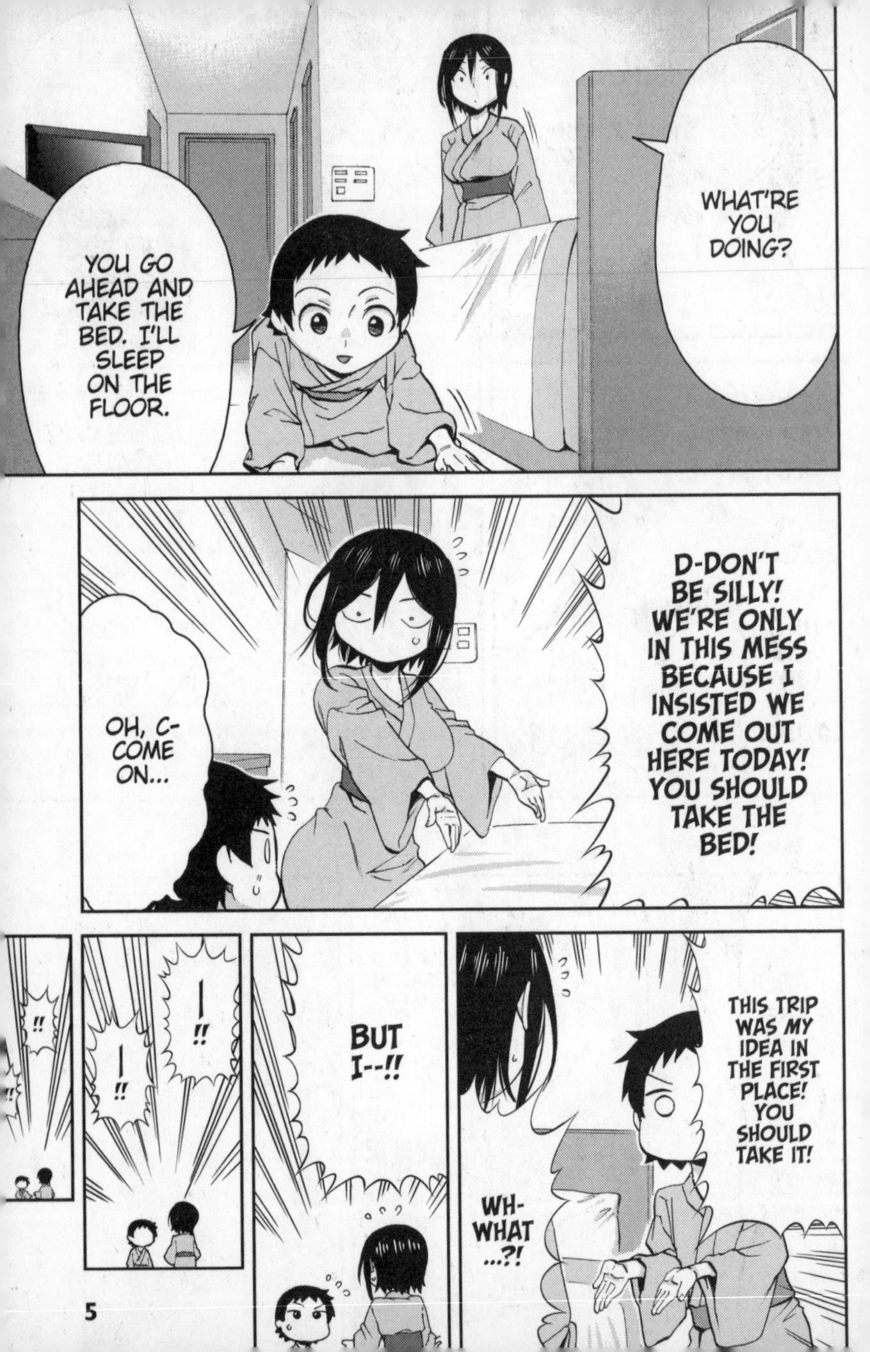
WHAT'RE YOU DOING?
YOU GO AHEAD AND TAKE THE BED. I'LL SLEEP ON THE FLOOR.
D-DON'T BE SILLY! WE'RE ONLY IN THIS MESS BECAUSE I INSISTED WE COME OUT HERE TODAY! YOU SHOULD TAKE THE BED!
OH, C-COME ON...
THIS TRIP WAS MY IDEA IN THE FIRST PLACE! YOU SHOULD TAKE IT!
WH-WHAT ...?!
BUT I--!!
—!!
—!!
!!

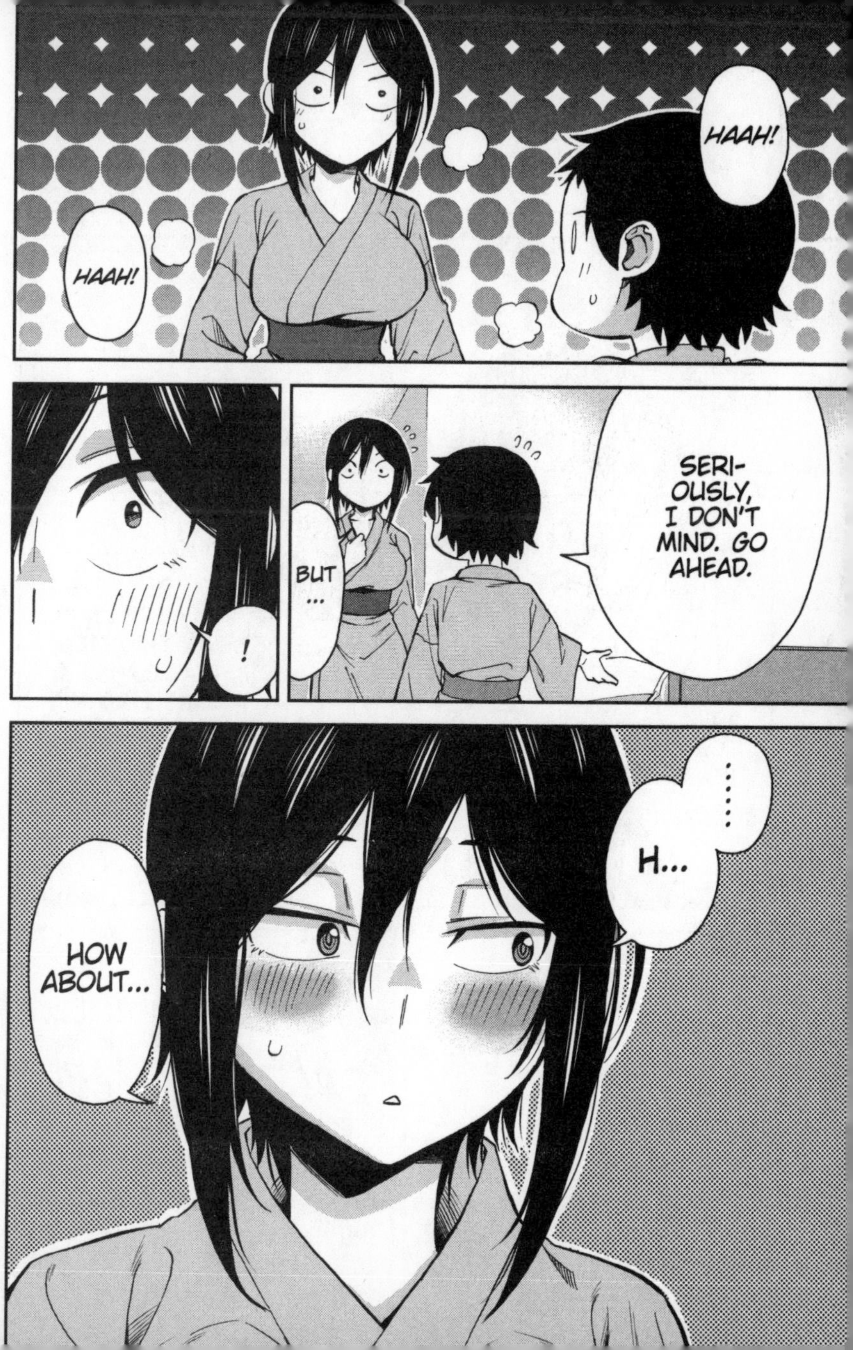
HAAH!
HAAH!
SERI-OUSLY, I DON'T MIND. GO AHEAD.
BUT ...
!
......
H...
HOW ABOUT...

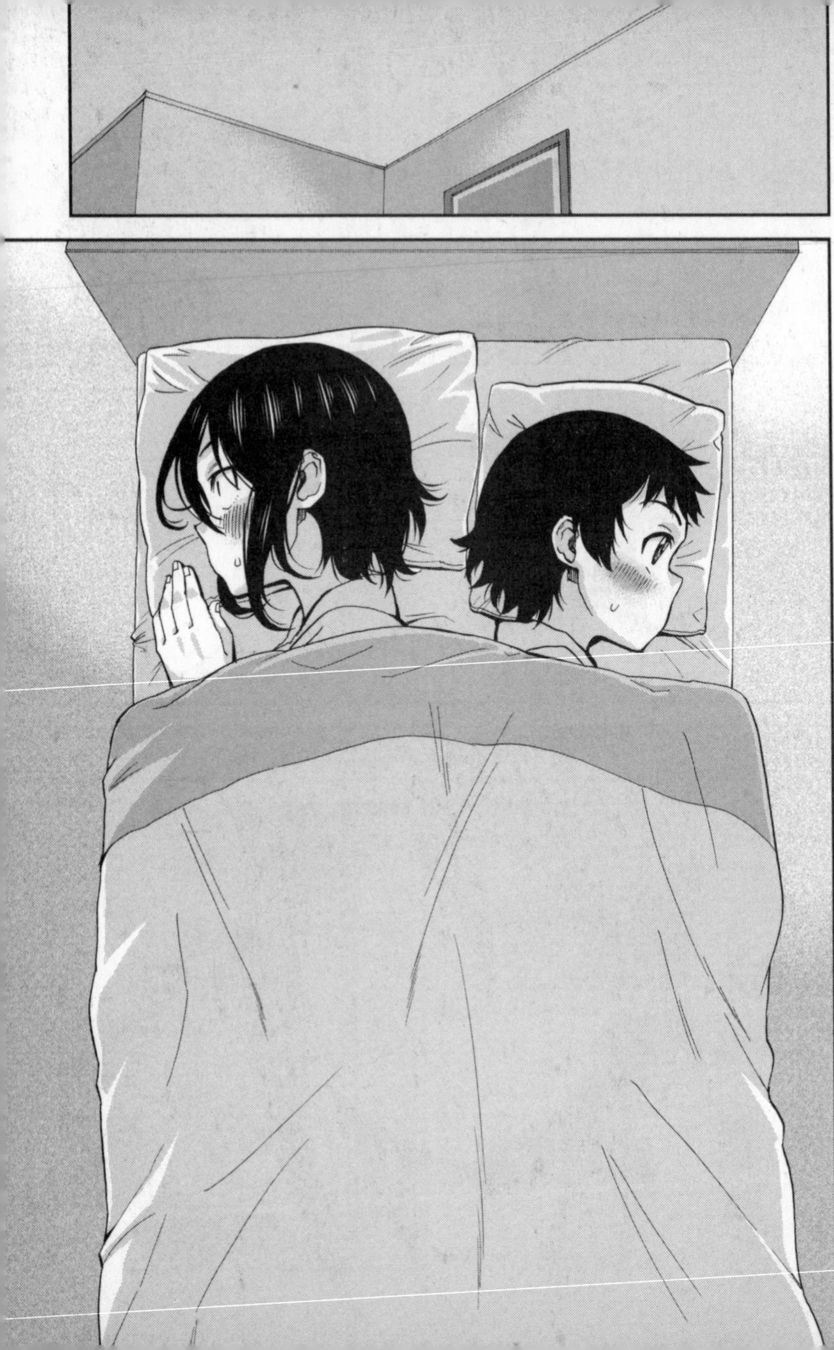

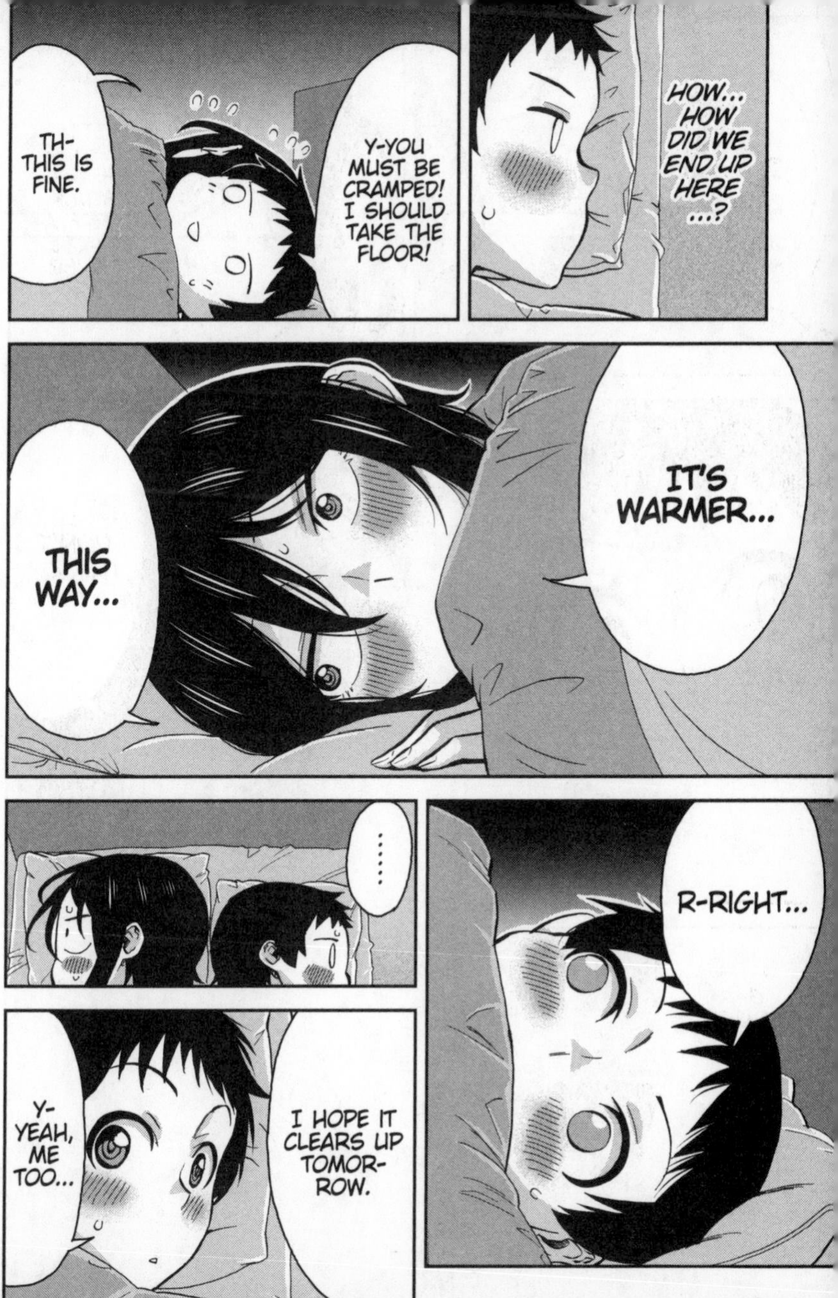
HOW... HOW DID WE END UP HERE ...?
Y-YOU MUST BE CRAMPED! I SHOULD TAKE THE FLOOR!
TH- THIS IS FINE.
IT'S WARMER...
THIS WAY...
R-RIGHT...
......
I HOPE IT CLEARS UP TOMOR-ROW.
Y-YEAH, ME TOO...

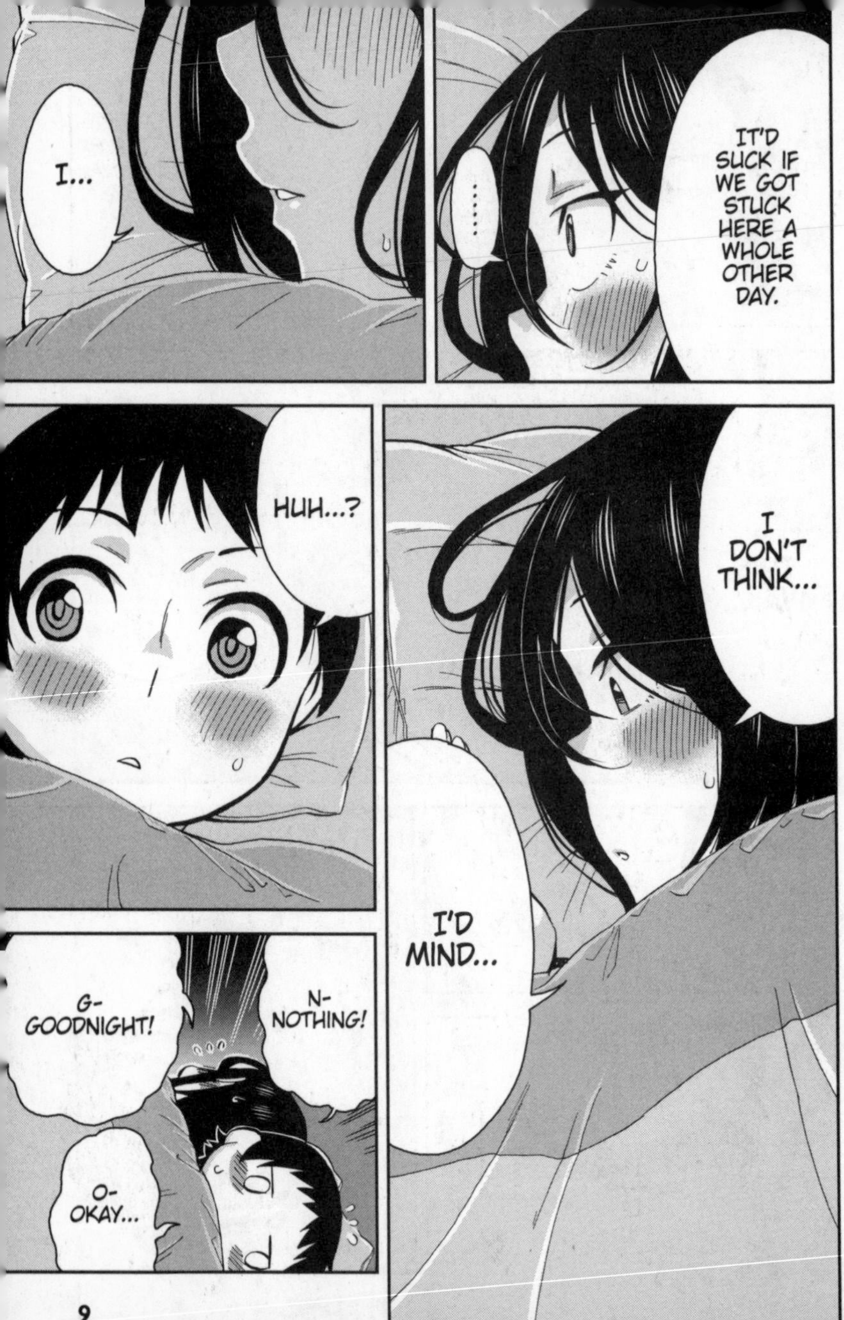
IT'D SUCK IF WE GOT STUCK HERE A WHOLE OTHER DAY.
......
I...
I DON'T THINK...
I'D MIND...
HUH...?
N-NOTHING!
G-GOODNIGHT!
O-OKAY...

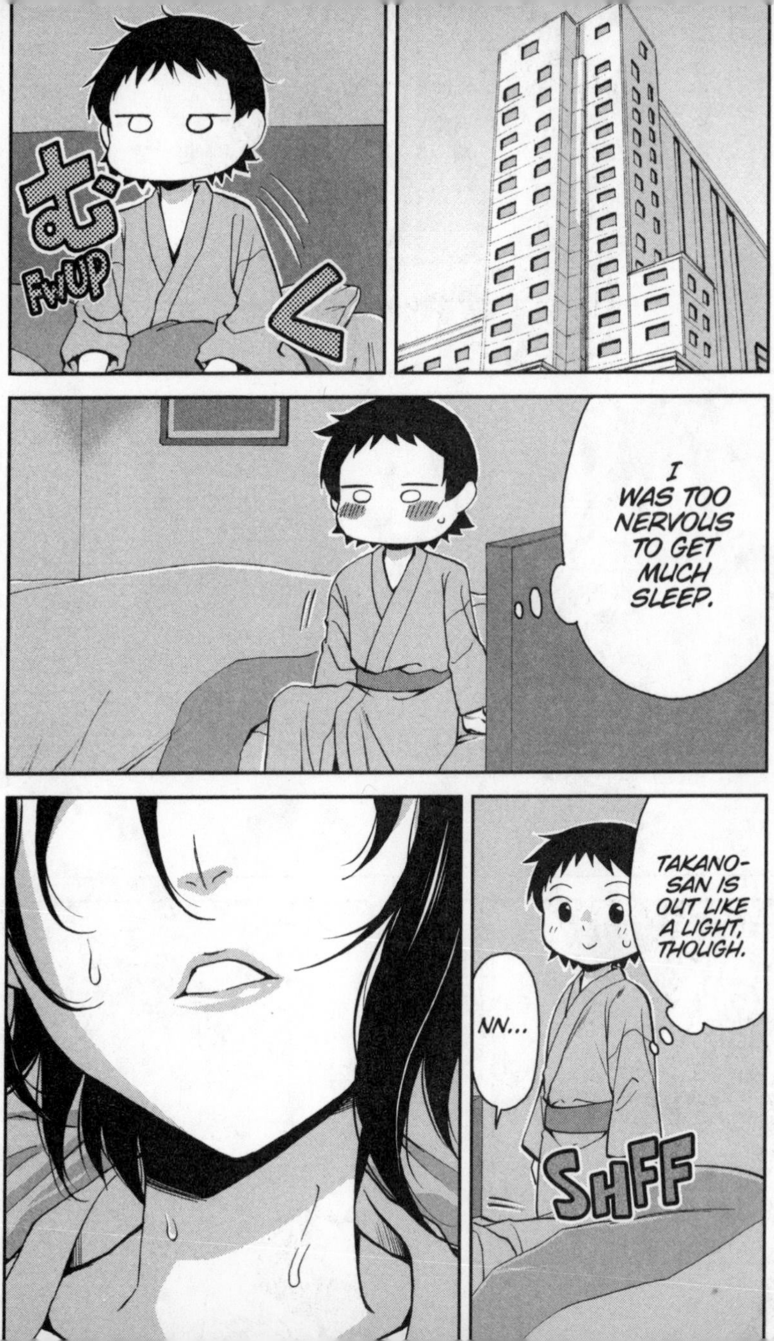
むく
FWUP
I WAS TOO NERVOUS TO GET MUCH SLEEP.
TAKANO-SAN IS OUT LIKE A LIGHT, THOUGH.
NN...
SHFF

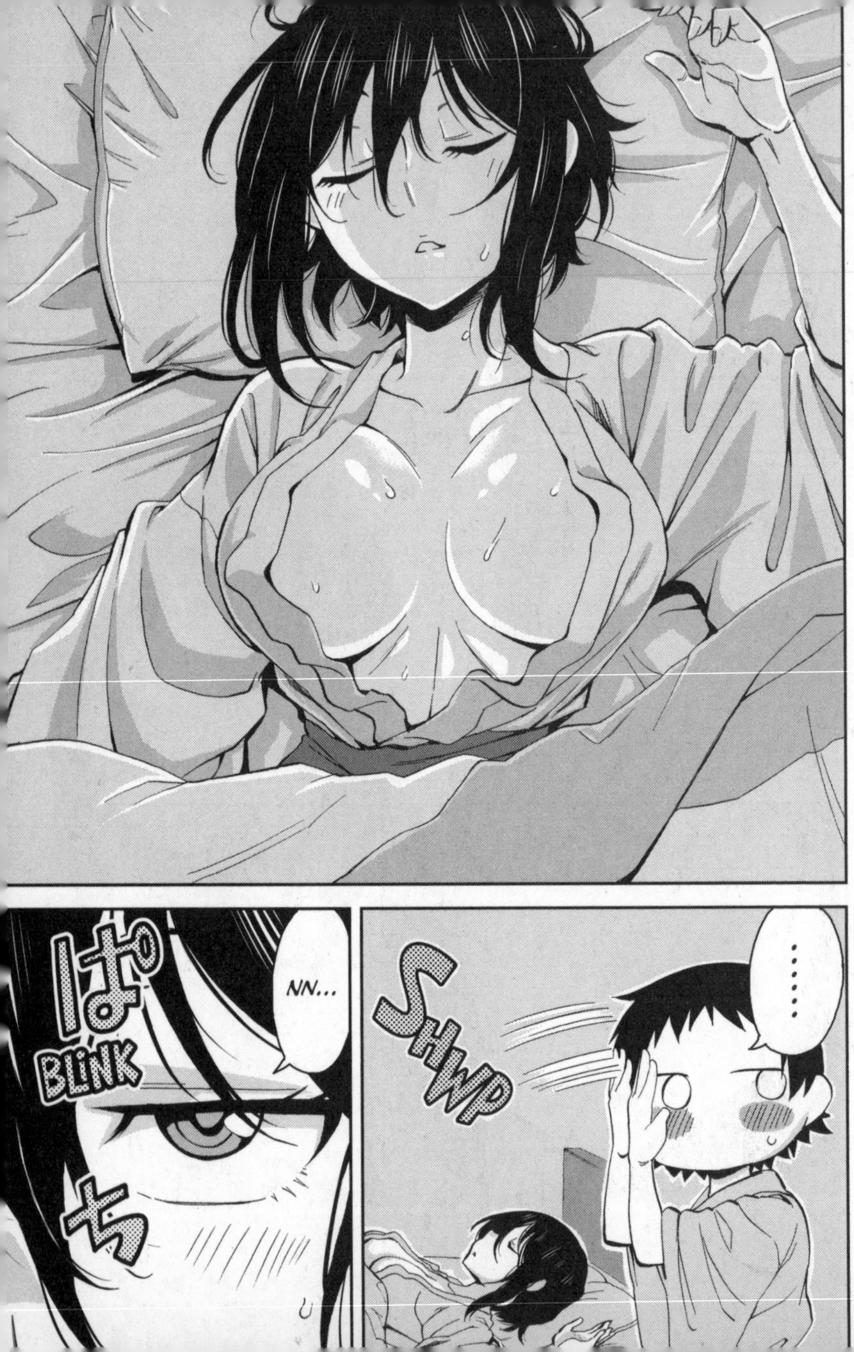
......
SHWP
NN...
ぱ
BLINK
ち

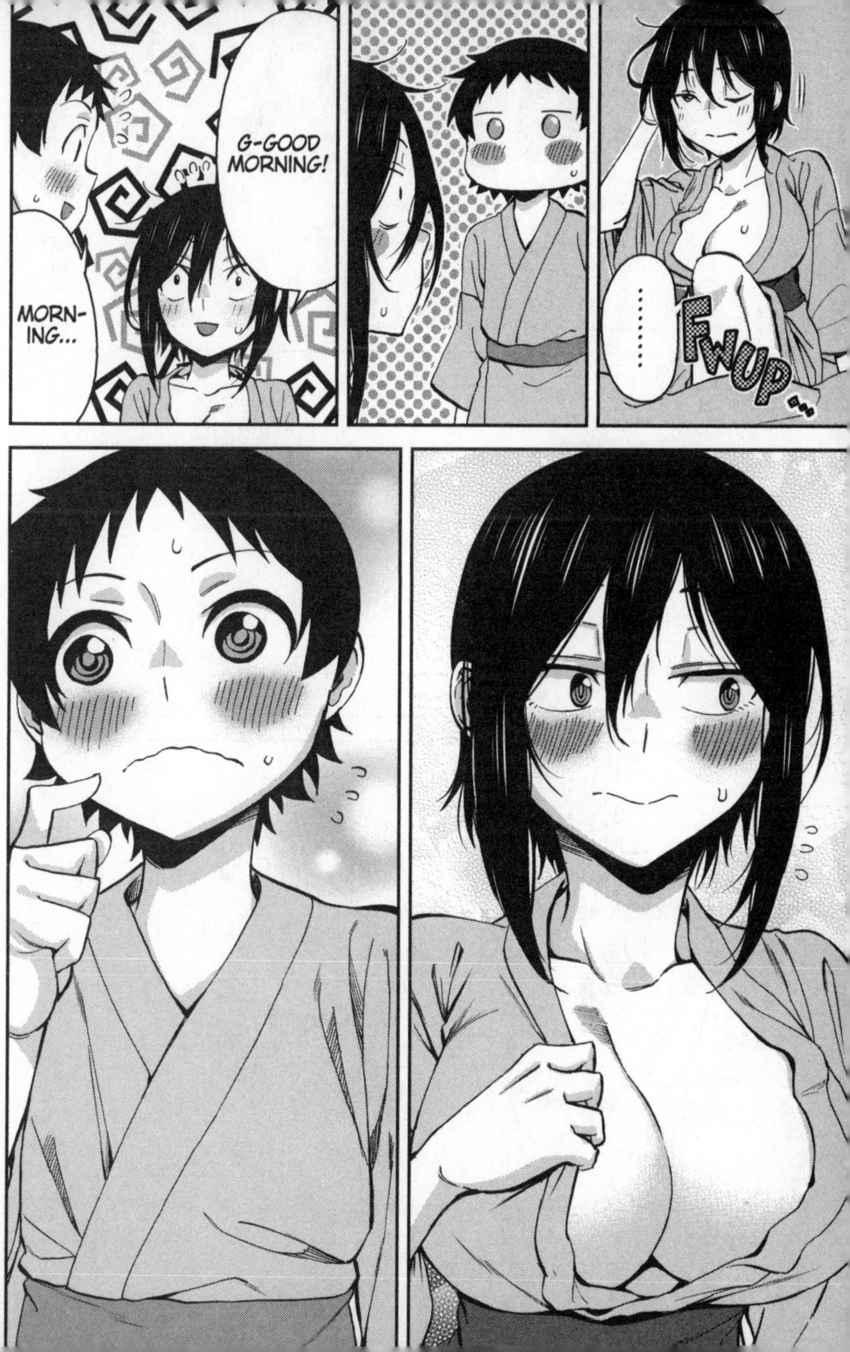
......
FWUP
G-GOOD MORNING!
MORN-ING...

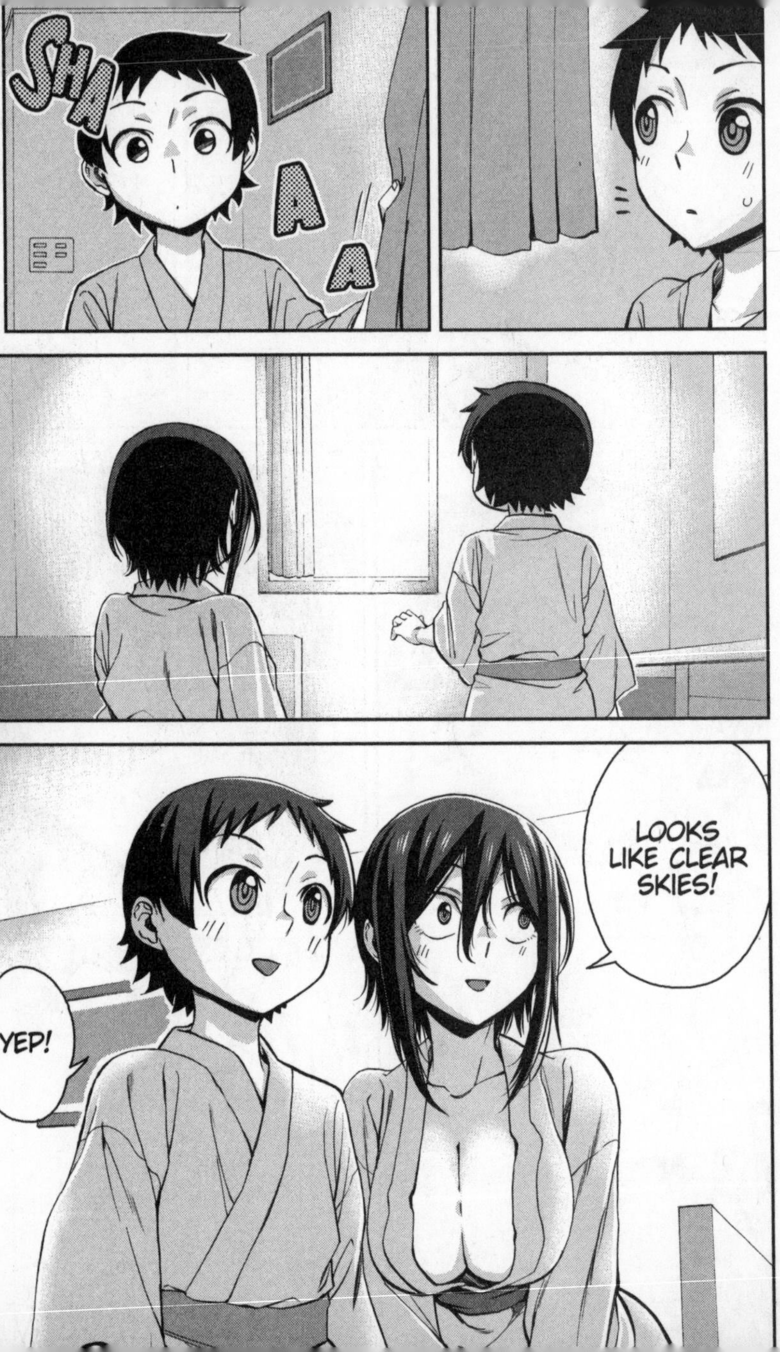
SHA
A
A
LOOKS LIKE CLEAR SKIES!
YEP!

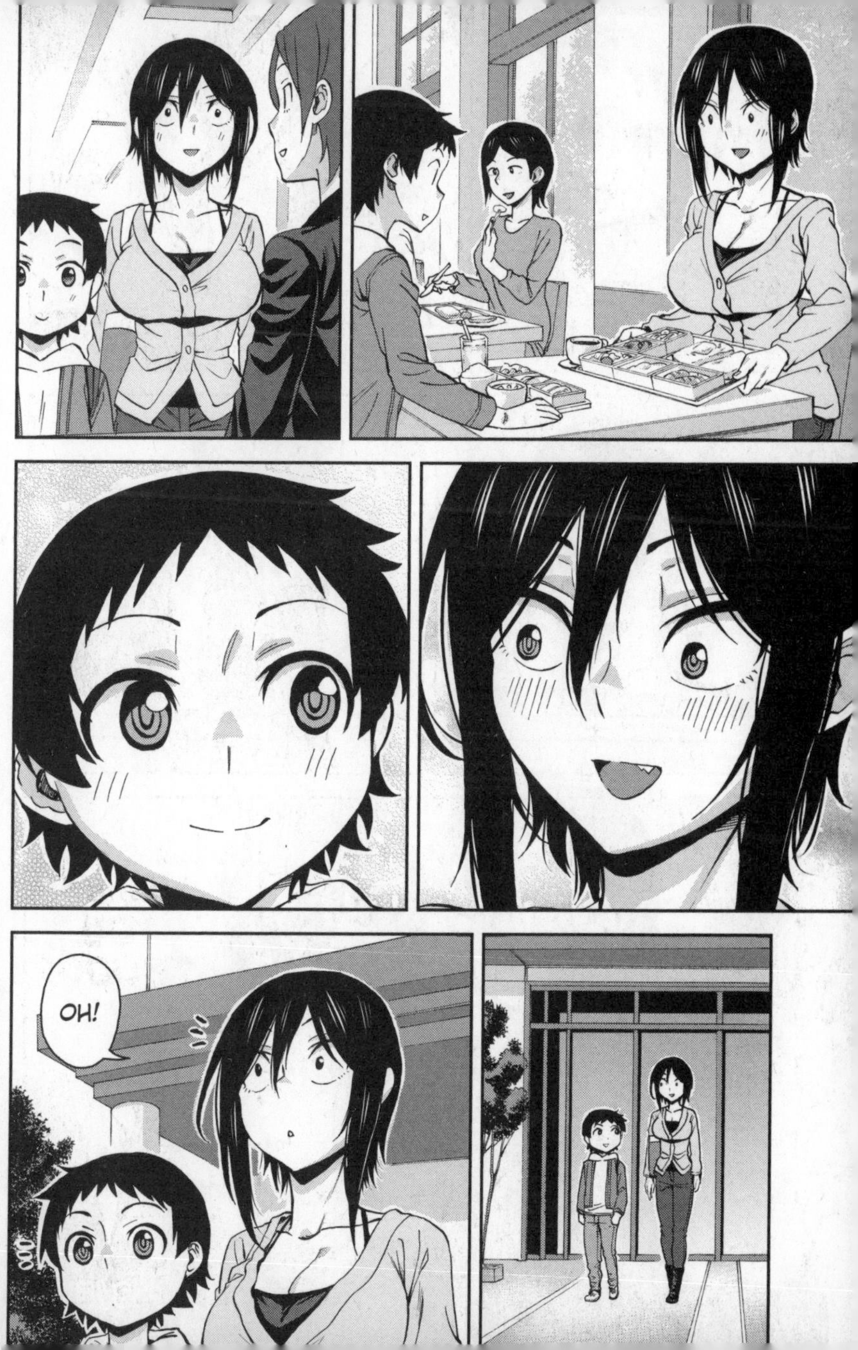
OH!

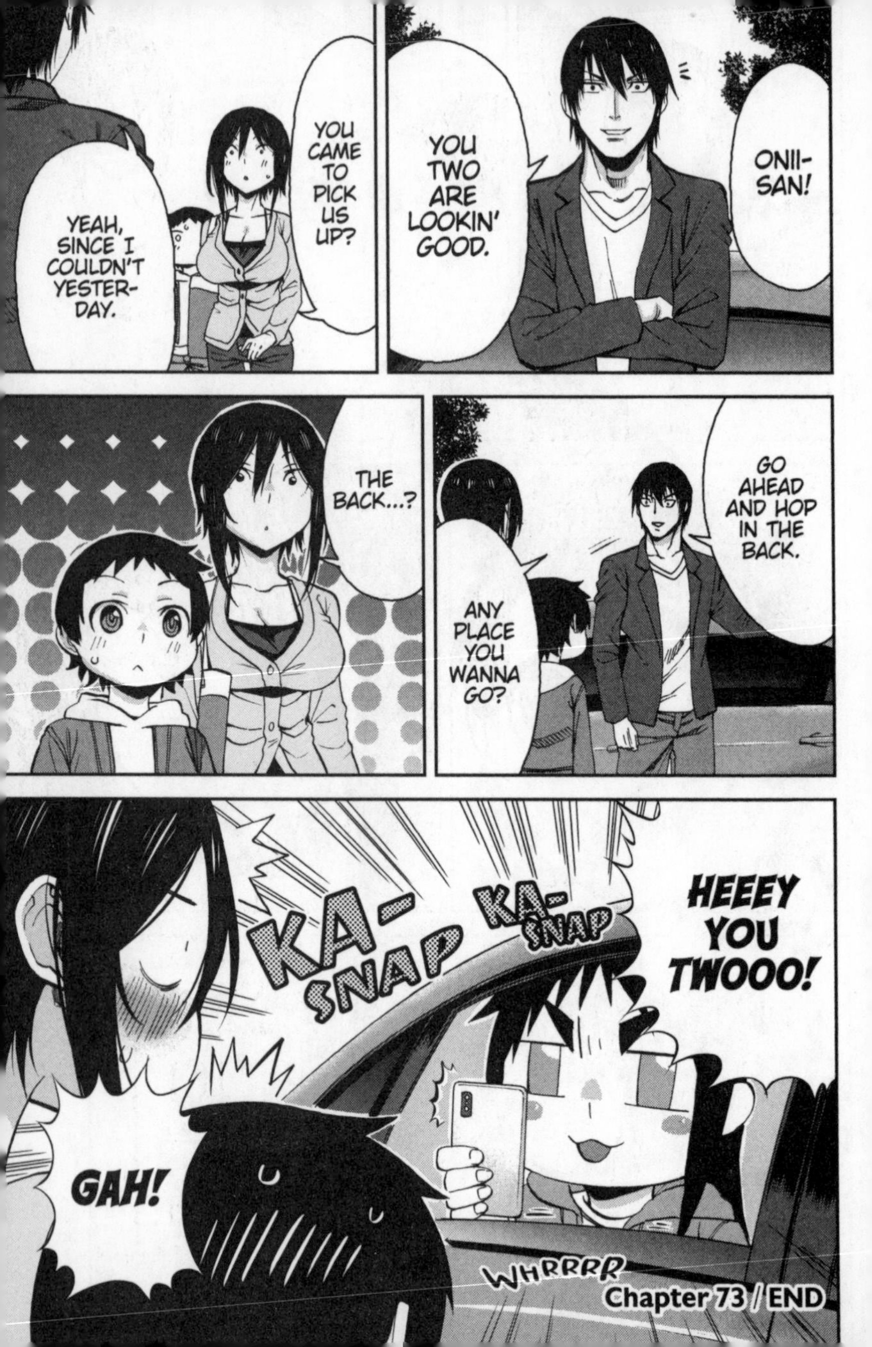

ONII-SAN!
YOU TWO ARE LOOKIN' GOOD.
YOU CAME TO PICK US UP?
YEAH, SINCE I COULDN'T YESTER-DAY.
GO AHEAD AND HOP IN THE BACK.
ANY PLACE YOU WANNA GO?
THE BACK...?
HEEEY YOU TWOOO!
KA-SNAP KA-SNAP
GAH!
WHRRRR
Chapter 73 / END

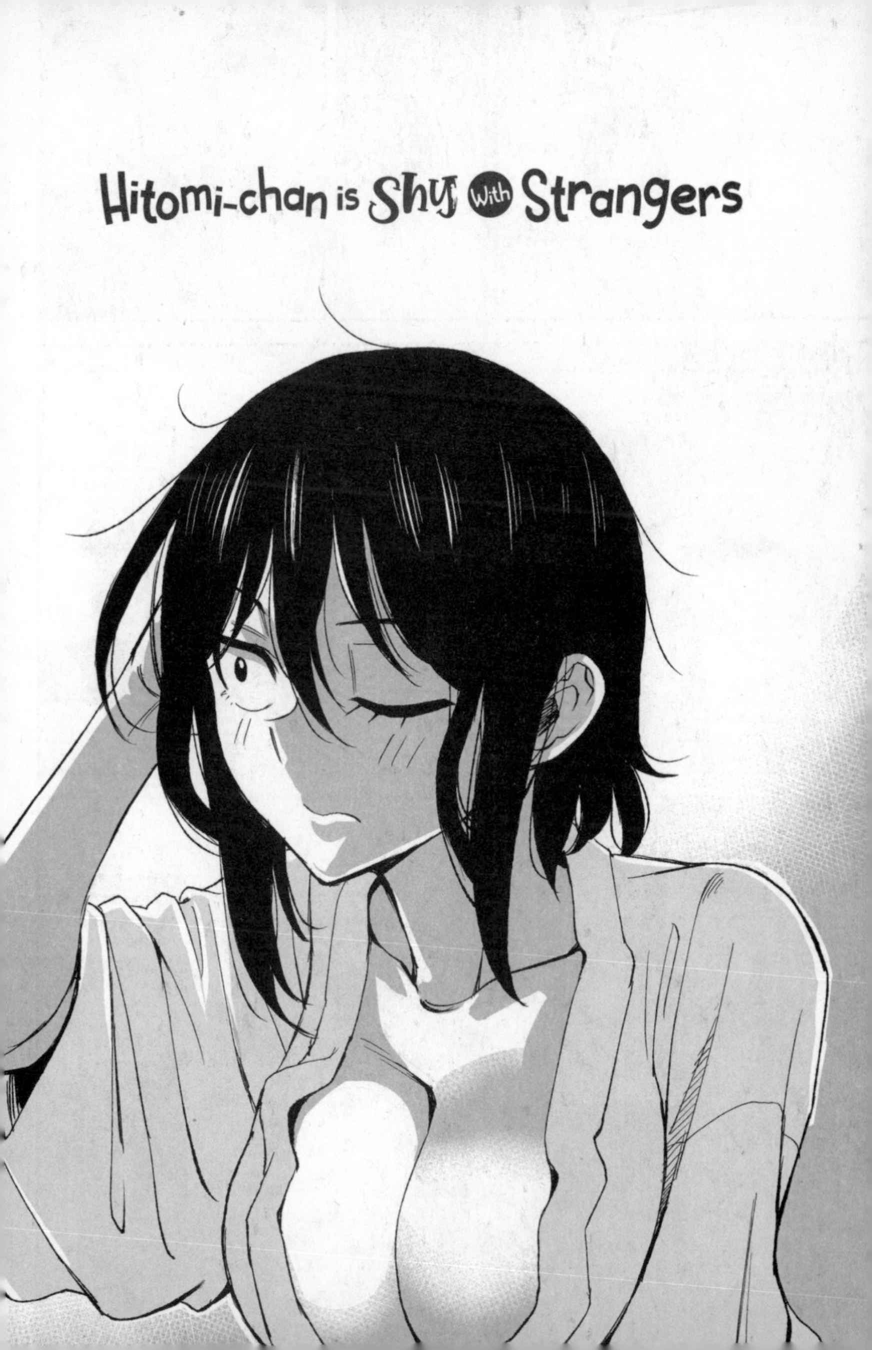
Hitomi-chan is Shy With Strangers

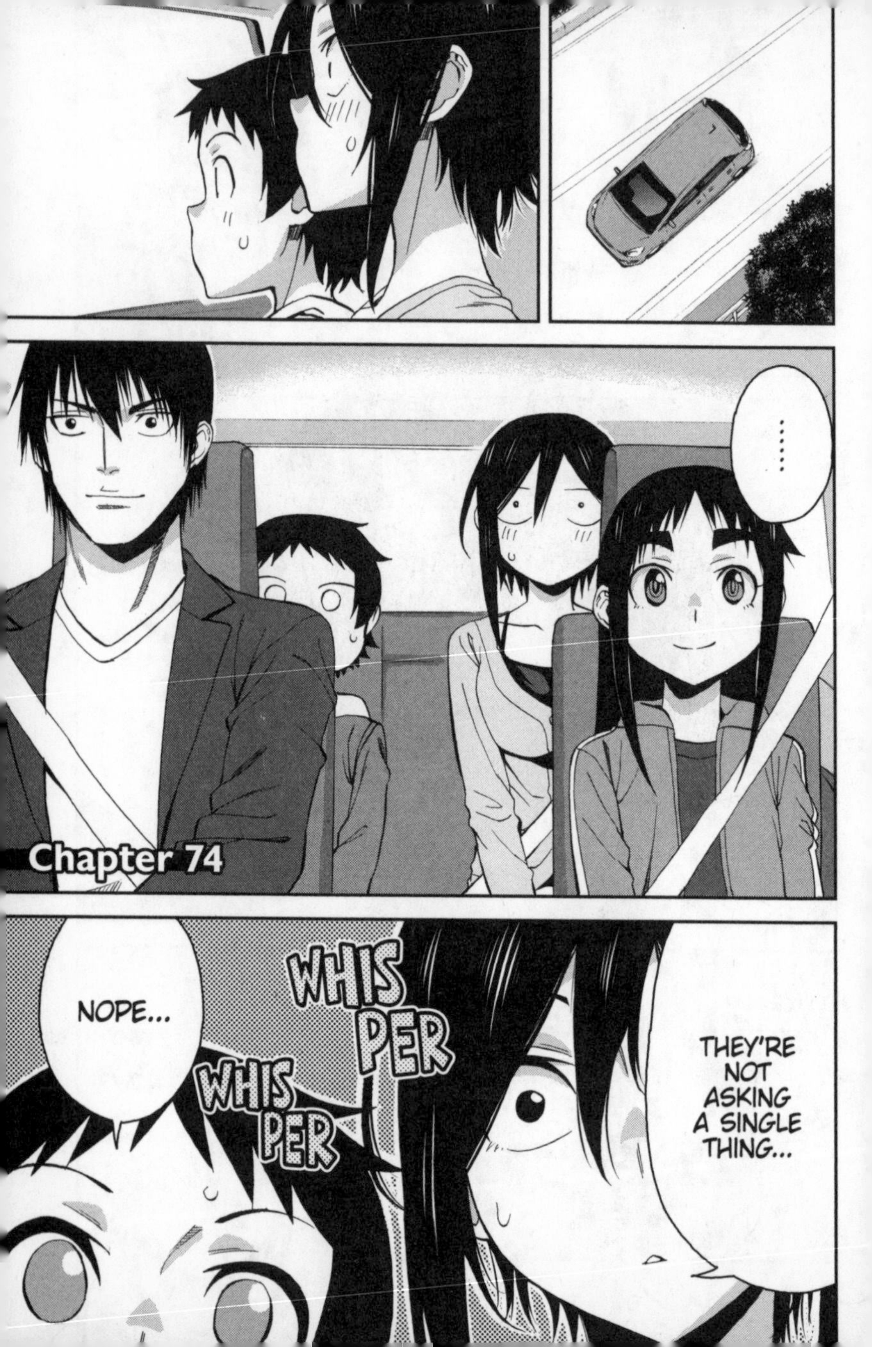
......
Chapter 74
THEY'RE NOT ASKING A SINGLE THING...
WHISPER
WHISPER
NOPE...

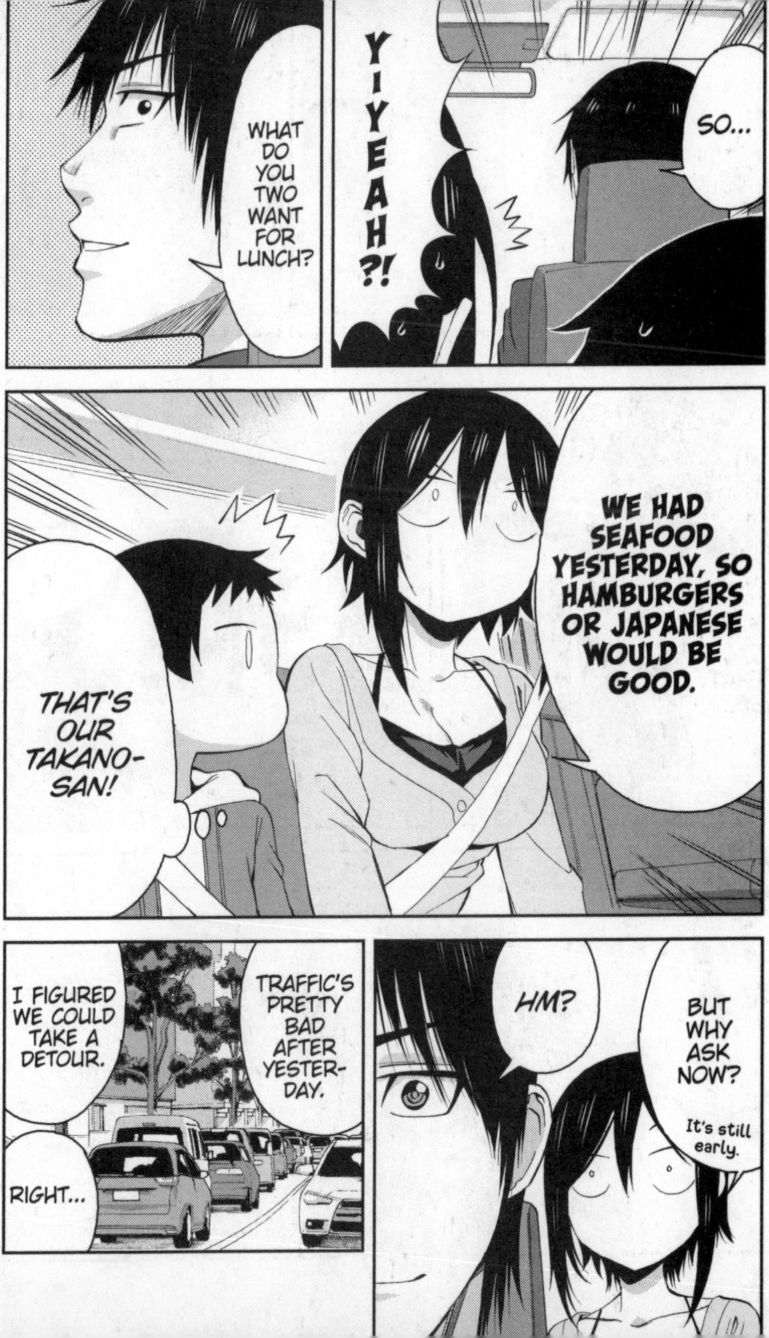
SO...
YIYEAH?!
WHAT DO YOU TWO WANT FOR LUNCH?
WE HAD SEAFOOD YESTERDAY, SO HAMBURGERS OR JAPANESE WOULD BE GOOD.
THAT'S OUR TAKANO-SAN!
BUT WHY ASK NOW?
It's still early.
HM?
TRAFFIC'S PRETTY BAD AFTER YESTER-DAY.
I FIGURED WE COULD TAKE A DETOUR.
RIGHT...

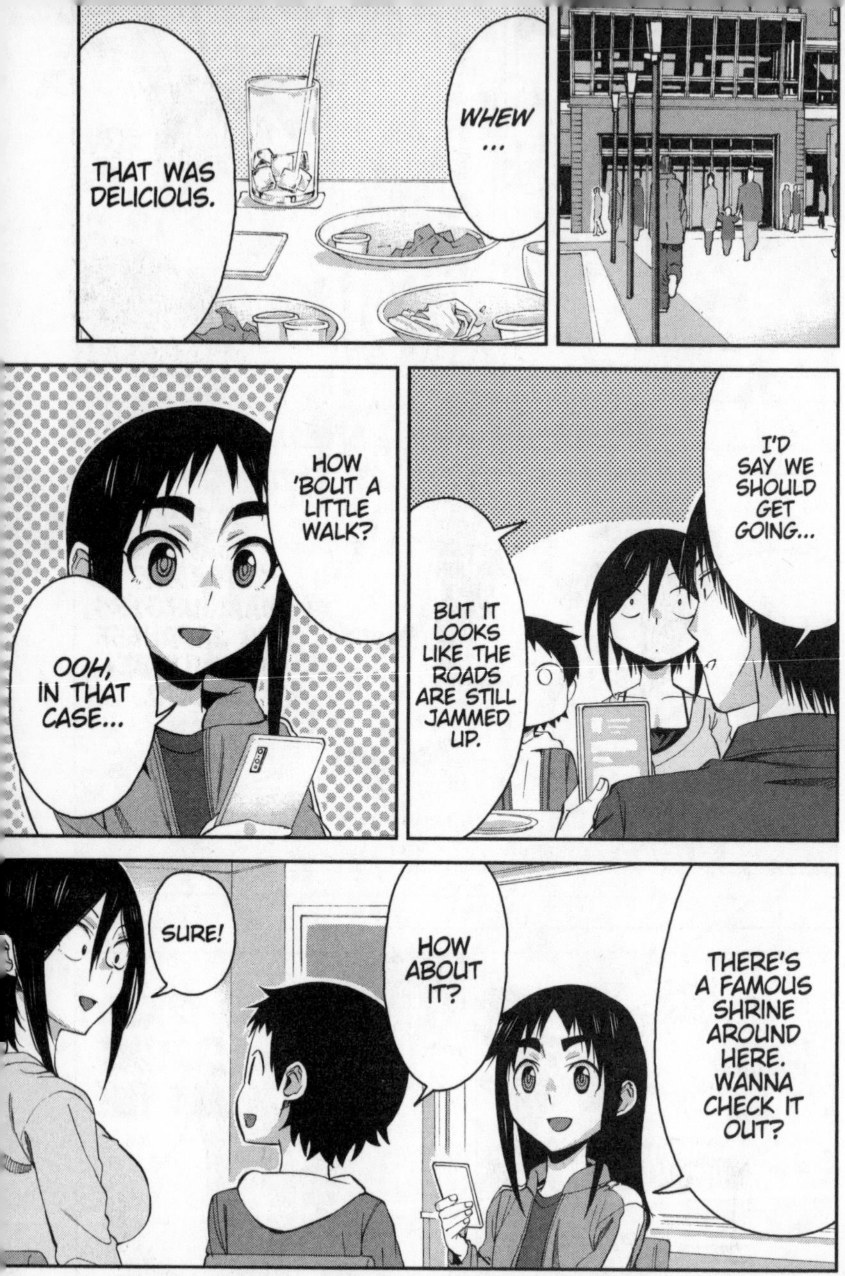
WHEW ...
THAT WAS DELICIOUS.
I'D SAY WE SHOULD GET GOING...
BUT IT LOOKS LIKE THE ROADS ARE STILL JAMMED UP.
HOW 'BOUT A LITTLE WALK?
OOH, IN THAT CASE...
THERE'S A FAMOUS SHRINE AROUND HERE. WANNA CHECK IT OUT?
HOW ABOUT IT?
SURE!

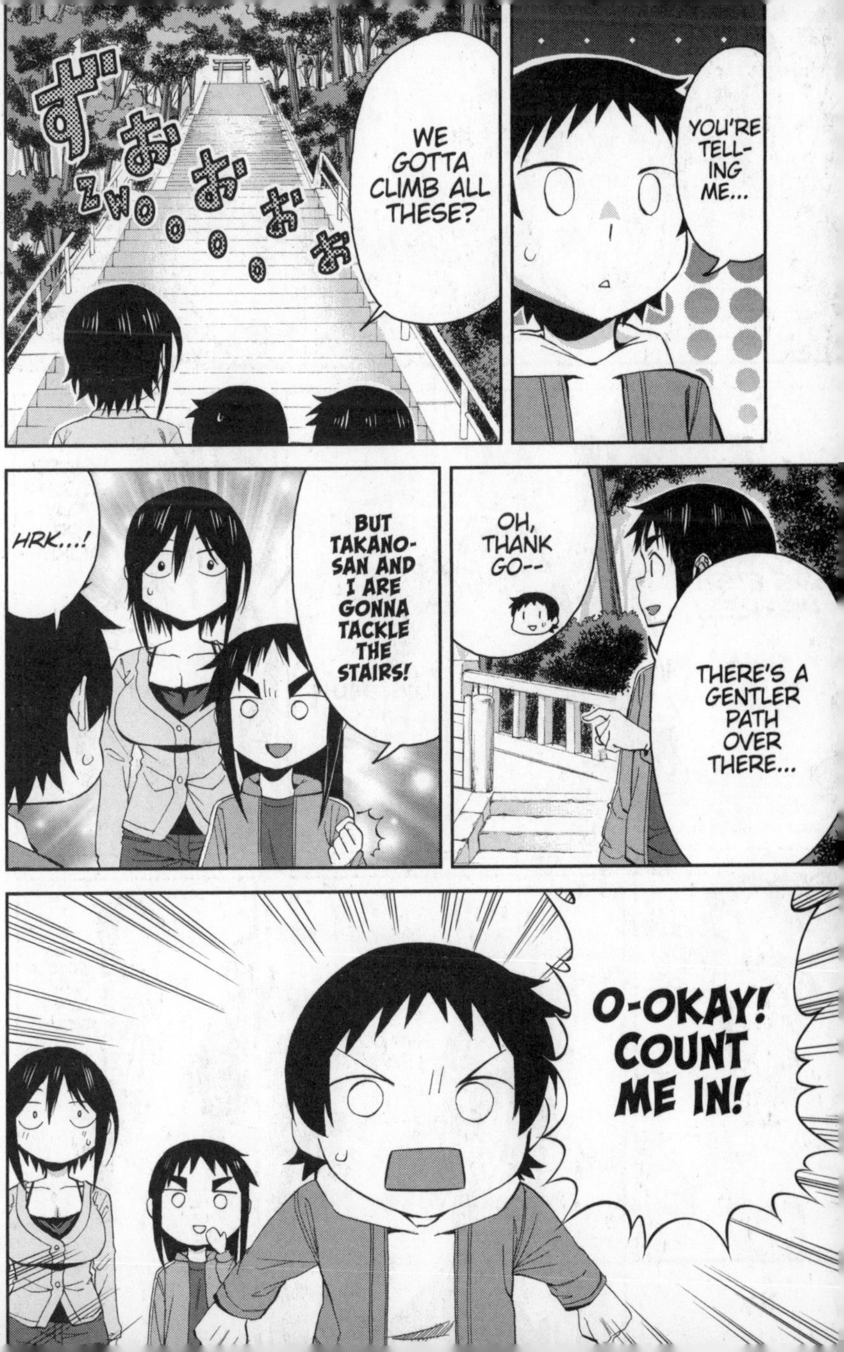
YOU'RE TELL-ING ME...
WE GOTTA CLIMB ALL THESE?
ZWOOOO
OH, THANK GO--
THERE'S A GENTLER PATH OVER THERE...
BUT TAKANO-SAN AND I ARE GONNA TACKLE THE STAIRS!
HRK...!
O-OKAY! COUNT ME IN!

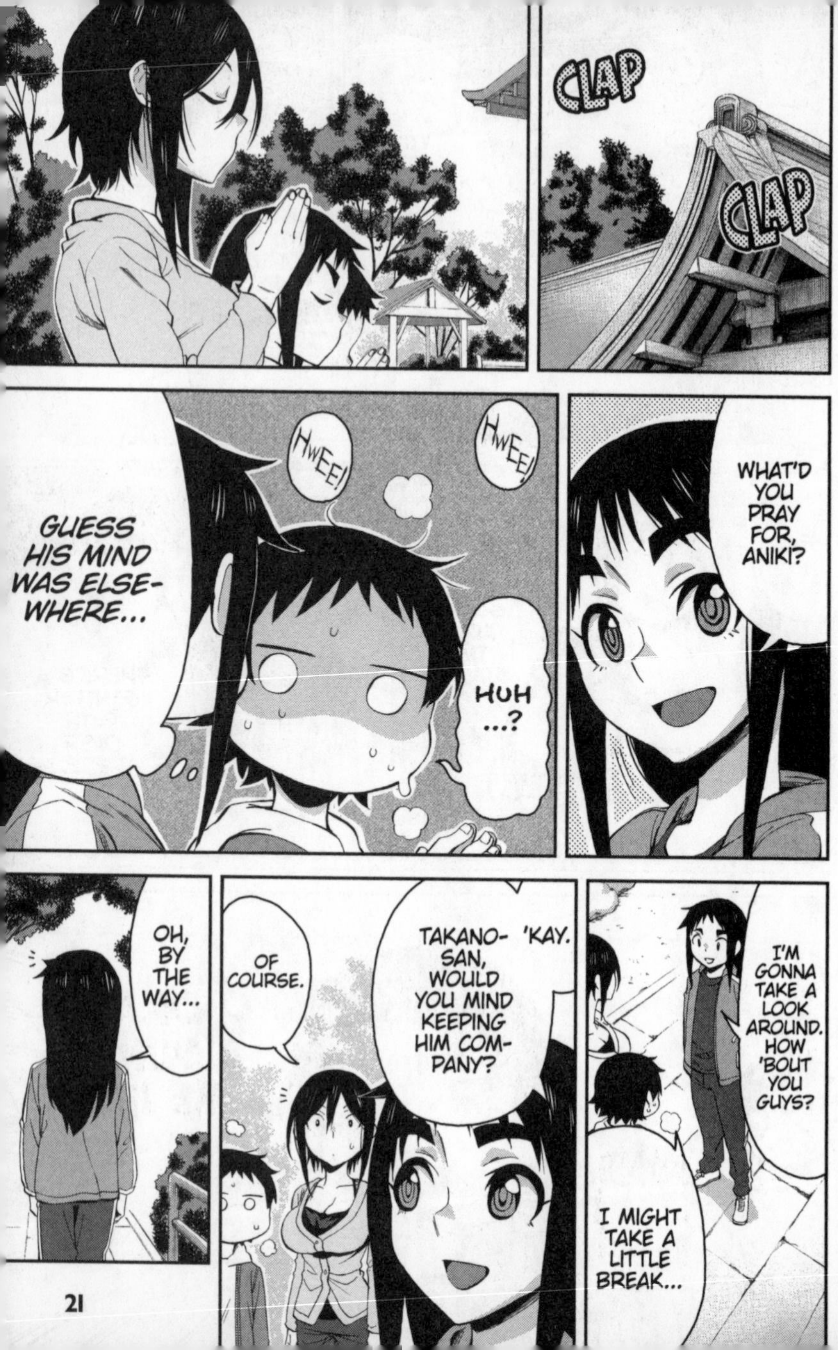
CLAP
CLAP
WHAT'D YOU PRAY FOR, ANIKI?
HWEE!
HWEE!
HUH ...?
GUESS HIS MIND WAS ELSEWHERE...
I'M GONNA TAKE A LOOK AROUND. HOW 'BOUT YOU GUYS?
I MIGHT TAKE A LITTLE BREAK...
'KAY. TAKANO-SAN, WOULD YOU MIND KEEPING HIM COMPANY?
OF COURSE.
OH, BY THE WAY...

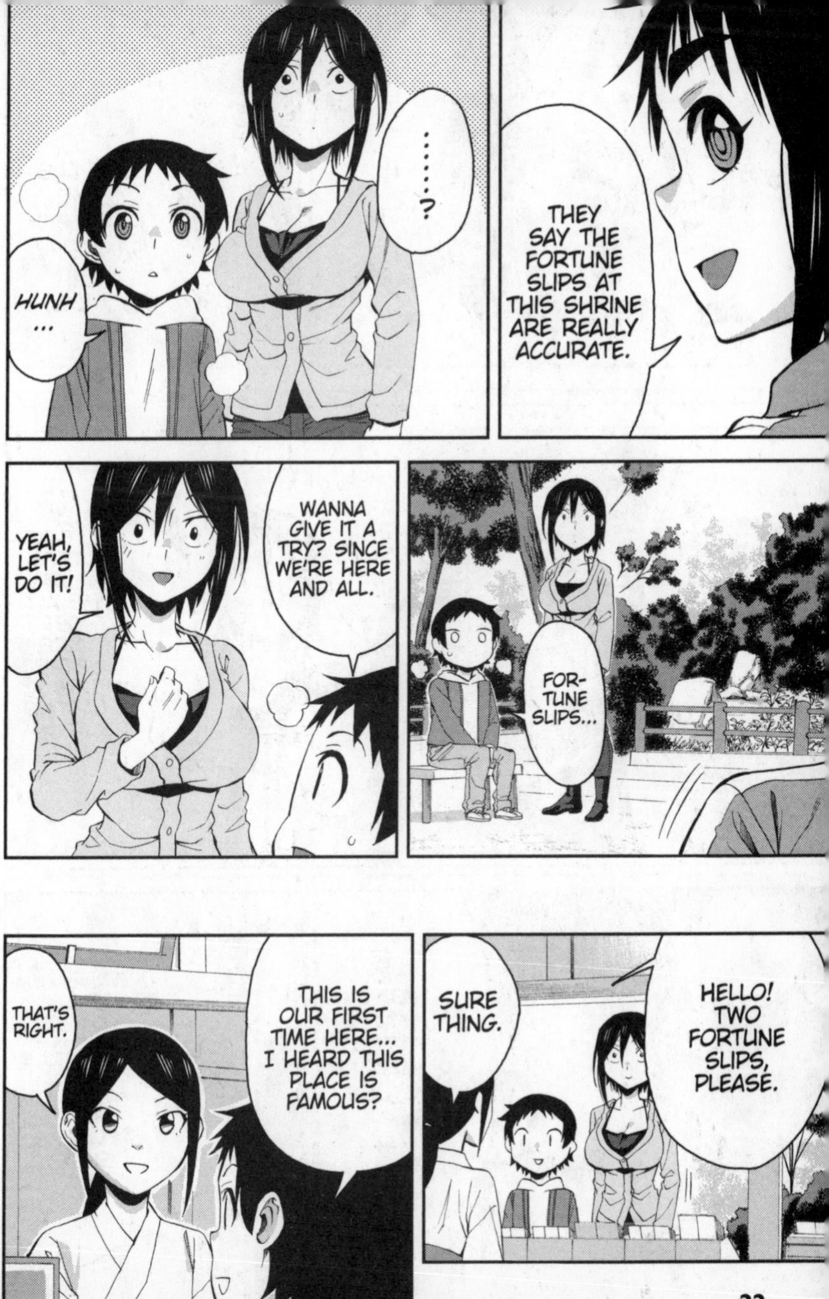
THEY SAY THE FORTUNE SLIPS AT THIS SHRINE ARE REALLY ACCURATE.
......?
HUNH ...
FOR-TUNE SLIPS...
WANNA GIVE IT A TRY? SINCE WE'RE HERE AND ALL.
YEAH, LET'S DO IT!
HELLO! TWO FORTUNE SLIPS, PLEASE.
SURE THING.
THIS IS OUR FIRST TIME HERE... I HEARD THIS PLACE IS FAMOUS?
THAT'S RIGHT.

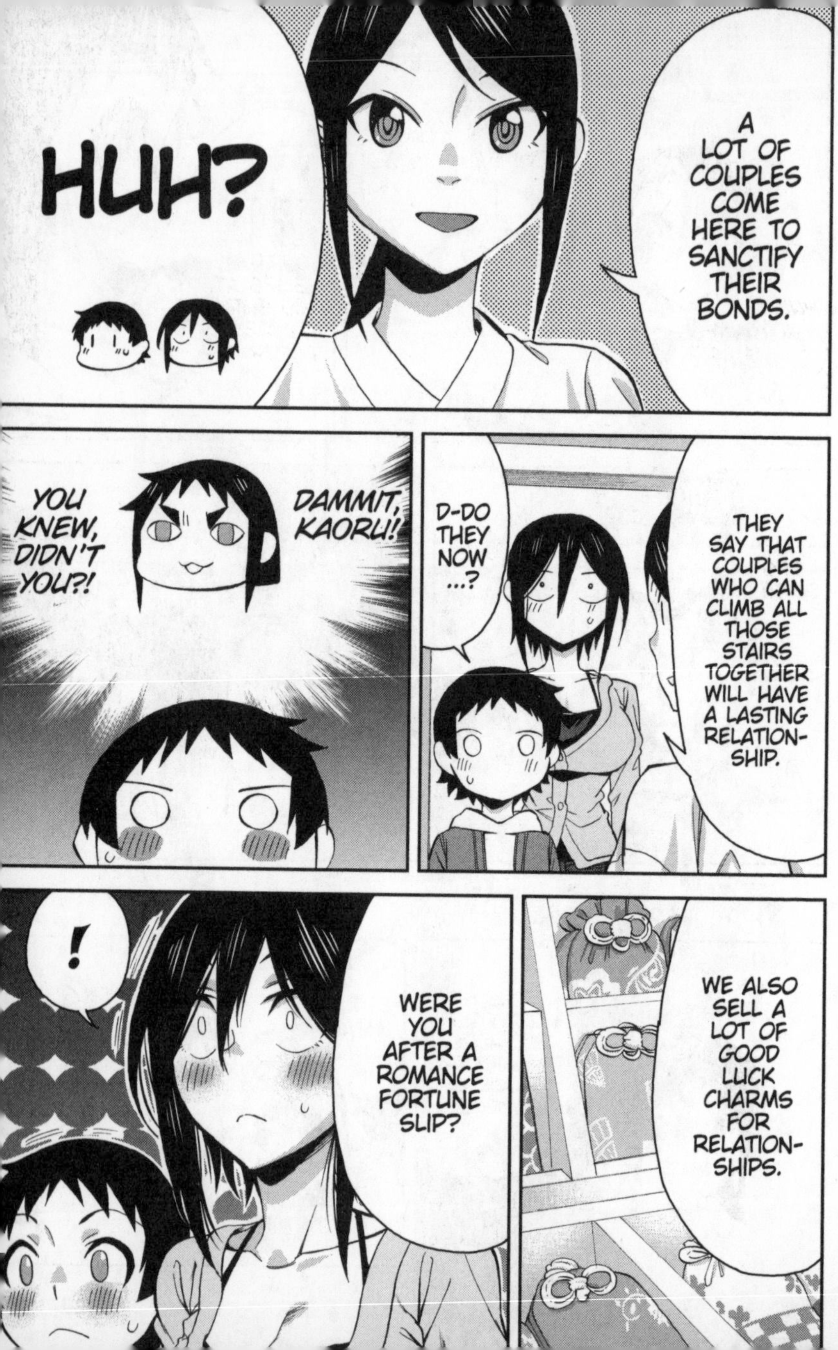
A LOT OF COUPLES COME HERE TO SANCTIFY THEIR BONDS.
HUH?
THEY SAY THAT COUPLES WHO CAN CLIMB ALL THOSE STAIRS TOGETHER WILL HAVE A LASTING RELATION-SHIP.
D-DO THEY NOW ...?
DAMMIT, KAORU!
YOU KNEW, DIDN'T YOU?!
WE ALSO SELL A LOT OF GOOD LUCK CHARMS FOR RELATION-SHIPS.
WERE YOU AFTER A ROMANCE FORTUNE SLIP?
!

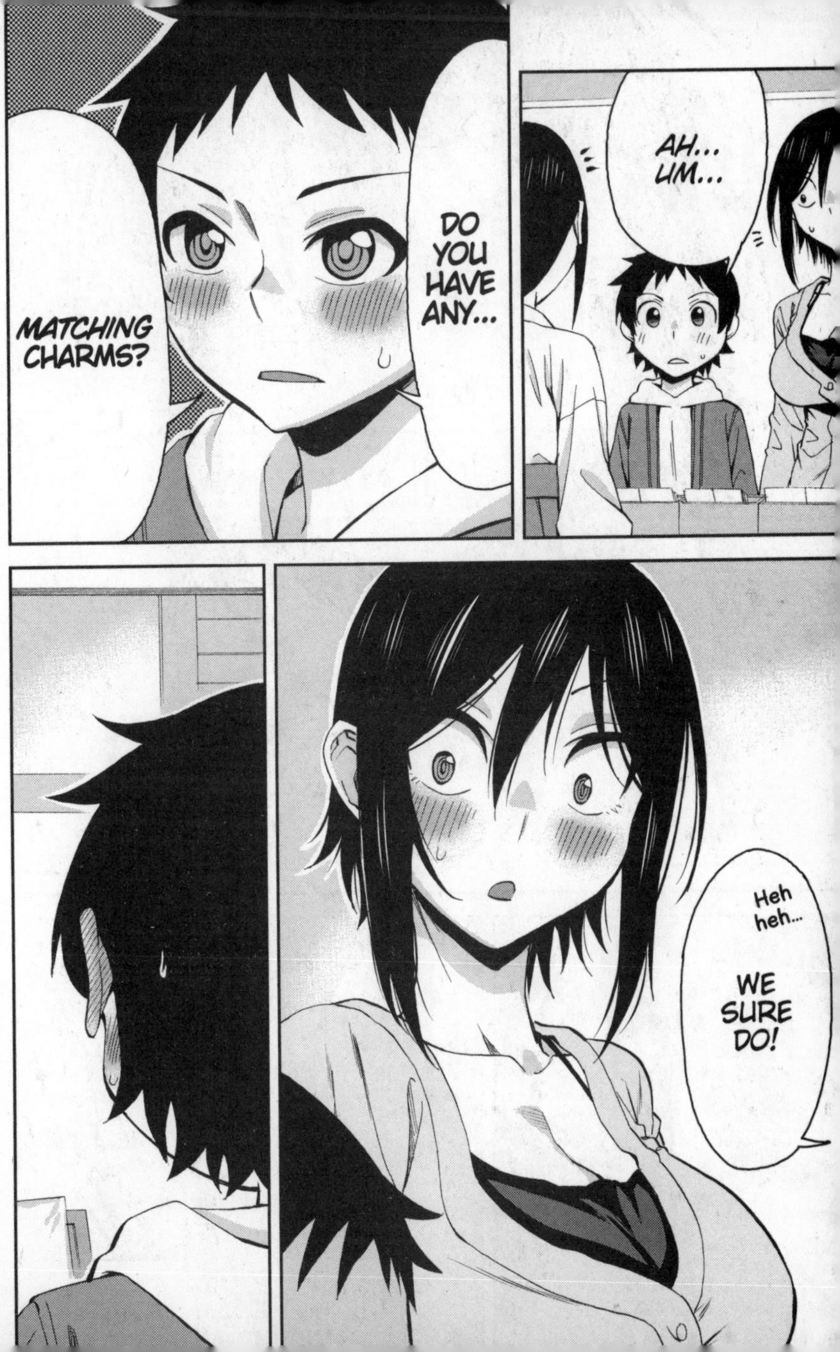
AH... UM...
DO YOU HAVE ANY...
MATCHING CHARMS?
Heh heh... WE SURE DO!

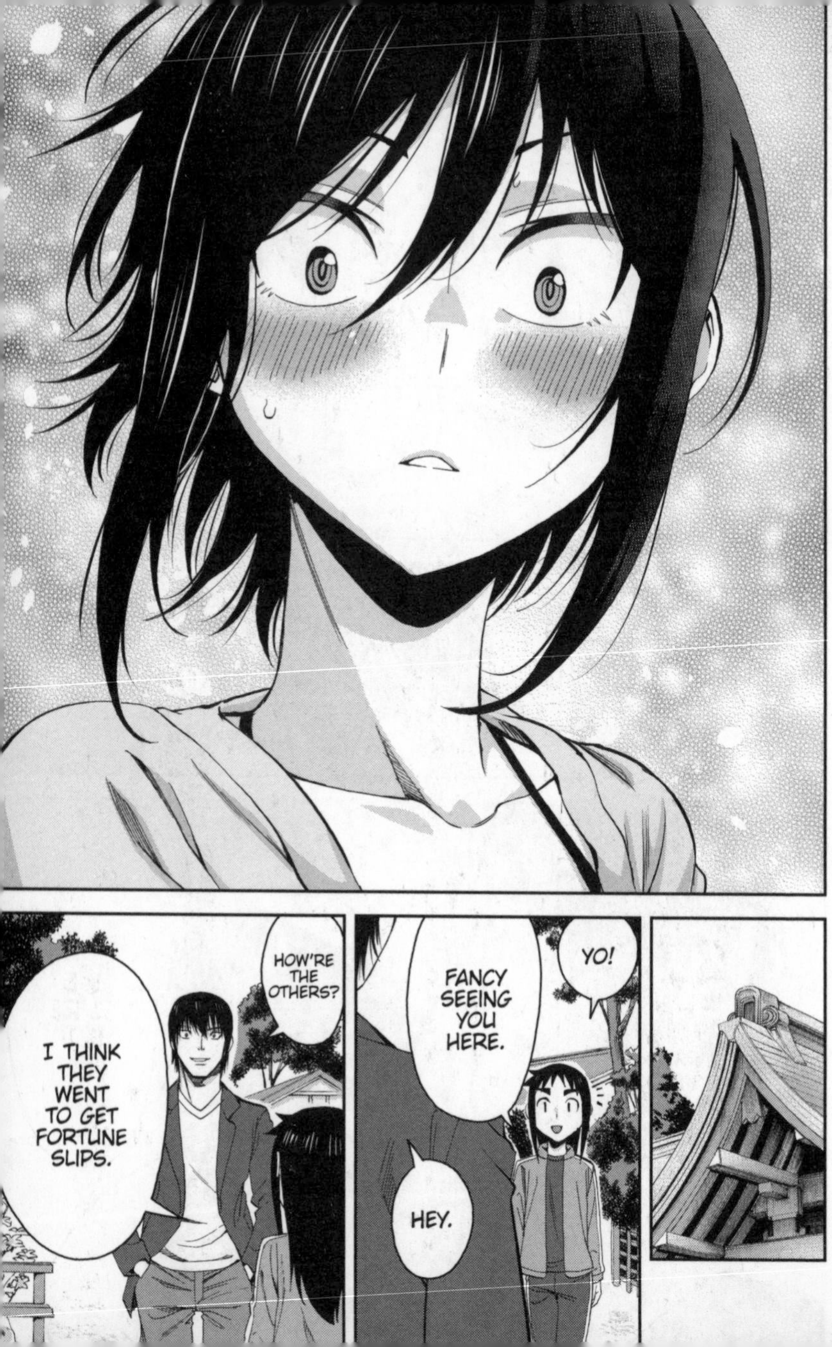
YO!
FANCY SEEING YOU HERE.
HEY.
HOW'RE THE OTHERS?
I THINK THEY WENT TO GET FORTUNE SLIPS.

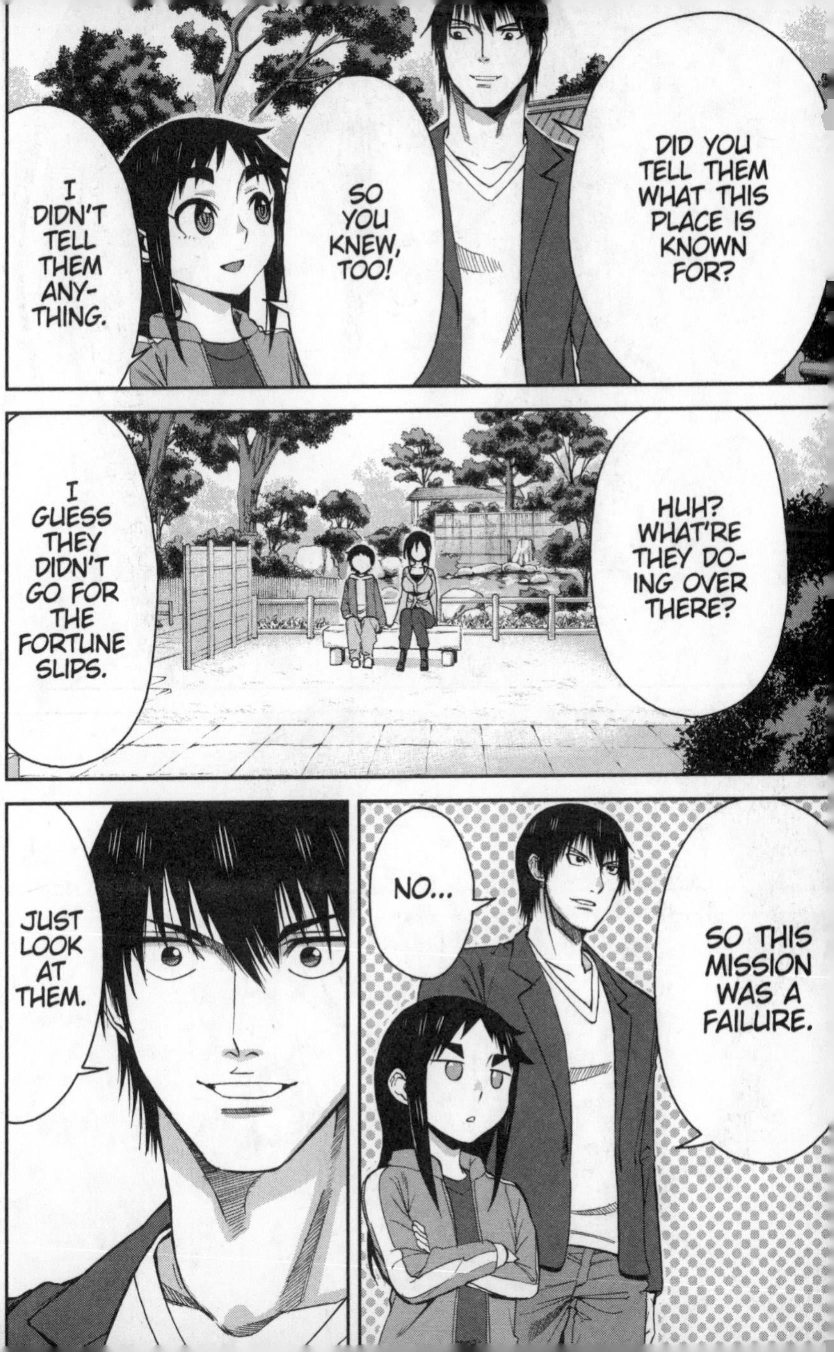
DID YOU TELL THEM WHAT THIS PLACE IS KNOWN FOR?
SO YOU KNEW, TOO!
I DIDN'T TELL THEM ANY-THING.
HUH? WHAT'RE THEY DO-ING OVER THERE?
I GUESS THEY DIDN'T GO FOR THE FORTUNE SLIPS.
SO THIS MISSION WAS A FAILURE.
NO...
JUST LOOK AT THEM.

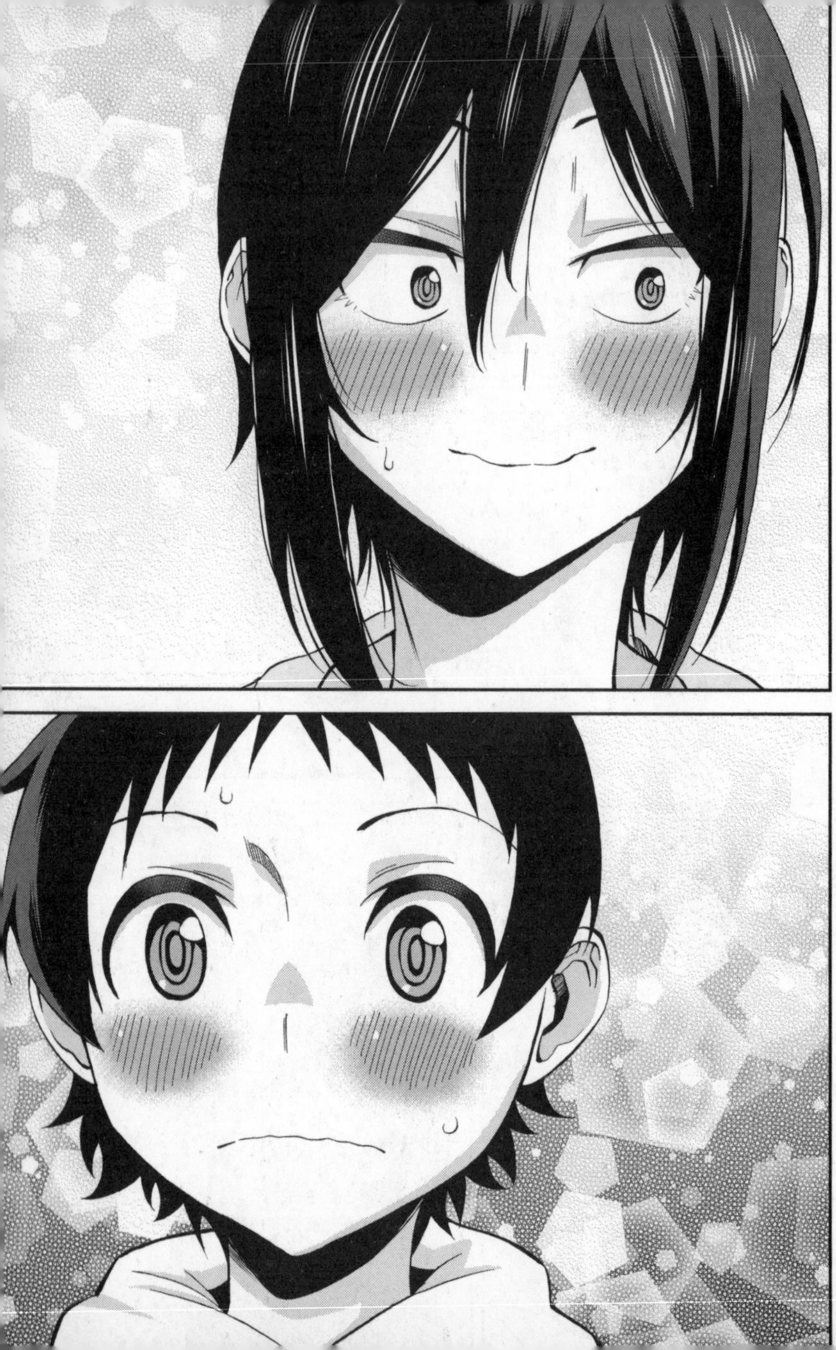

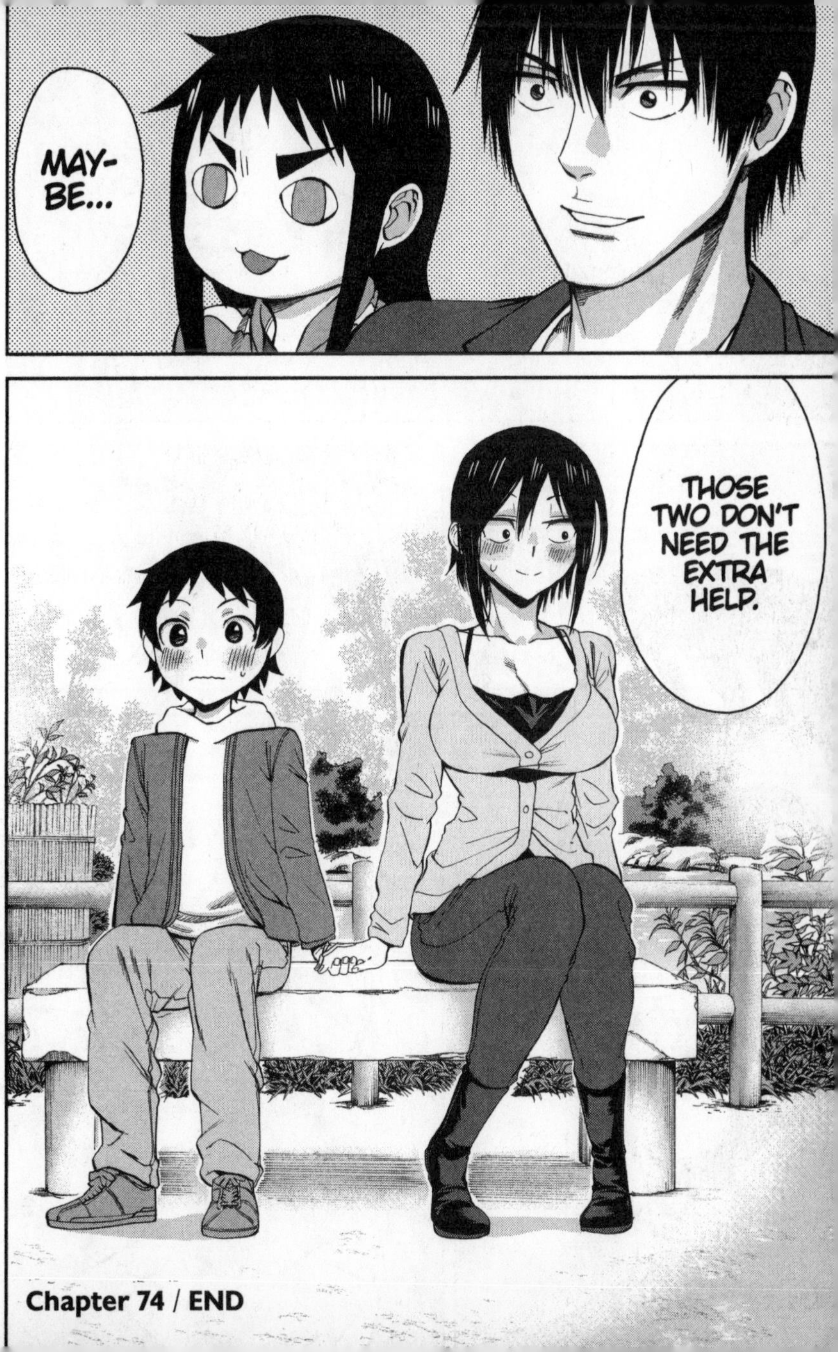
MAY-BE...
THOSE TWO DON'T NEED THE EXTRA HELP.

Chapter 74 / END

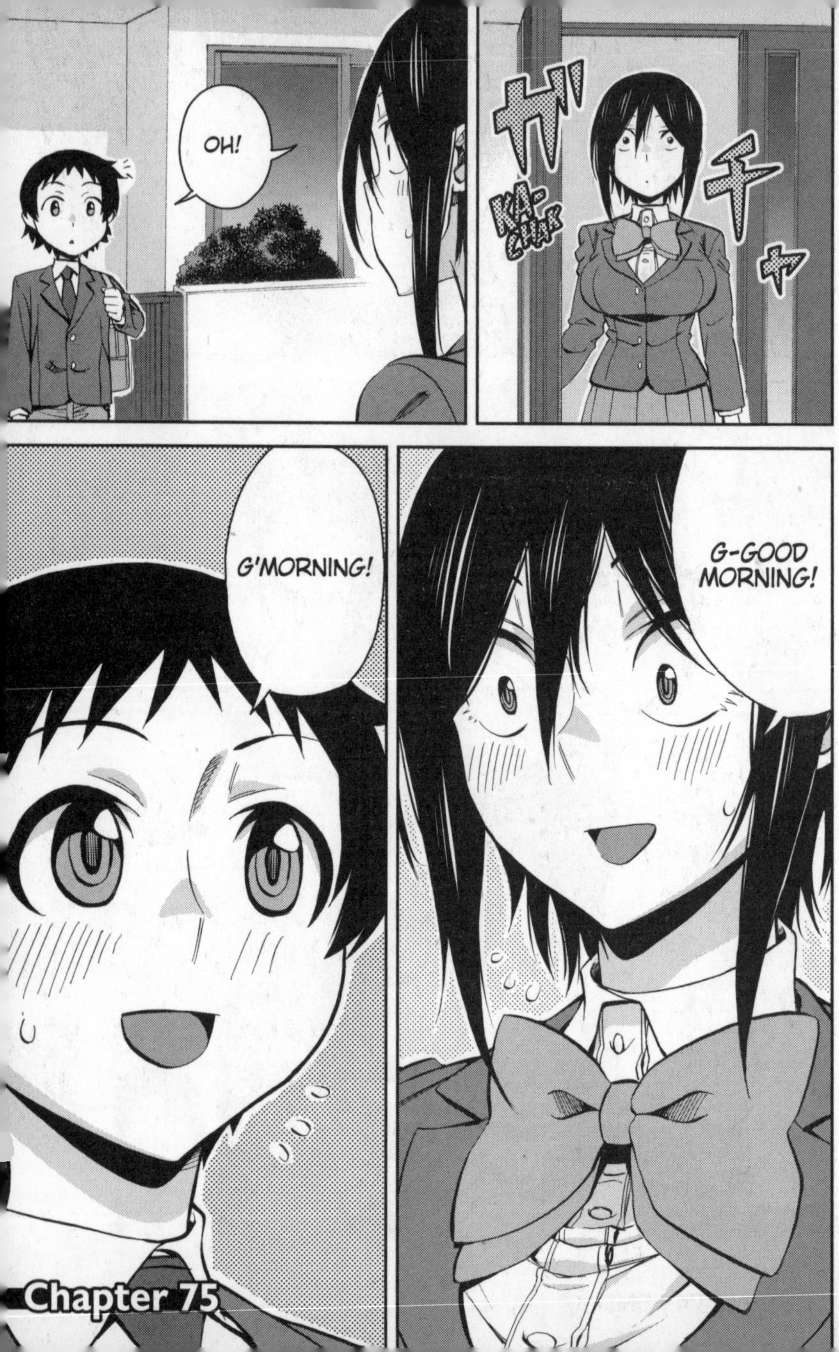
ガチャ
KA-CHAK
OH!
G-GOOD MORNING!
G'MORNING!
Chapter 75

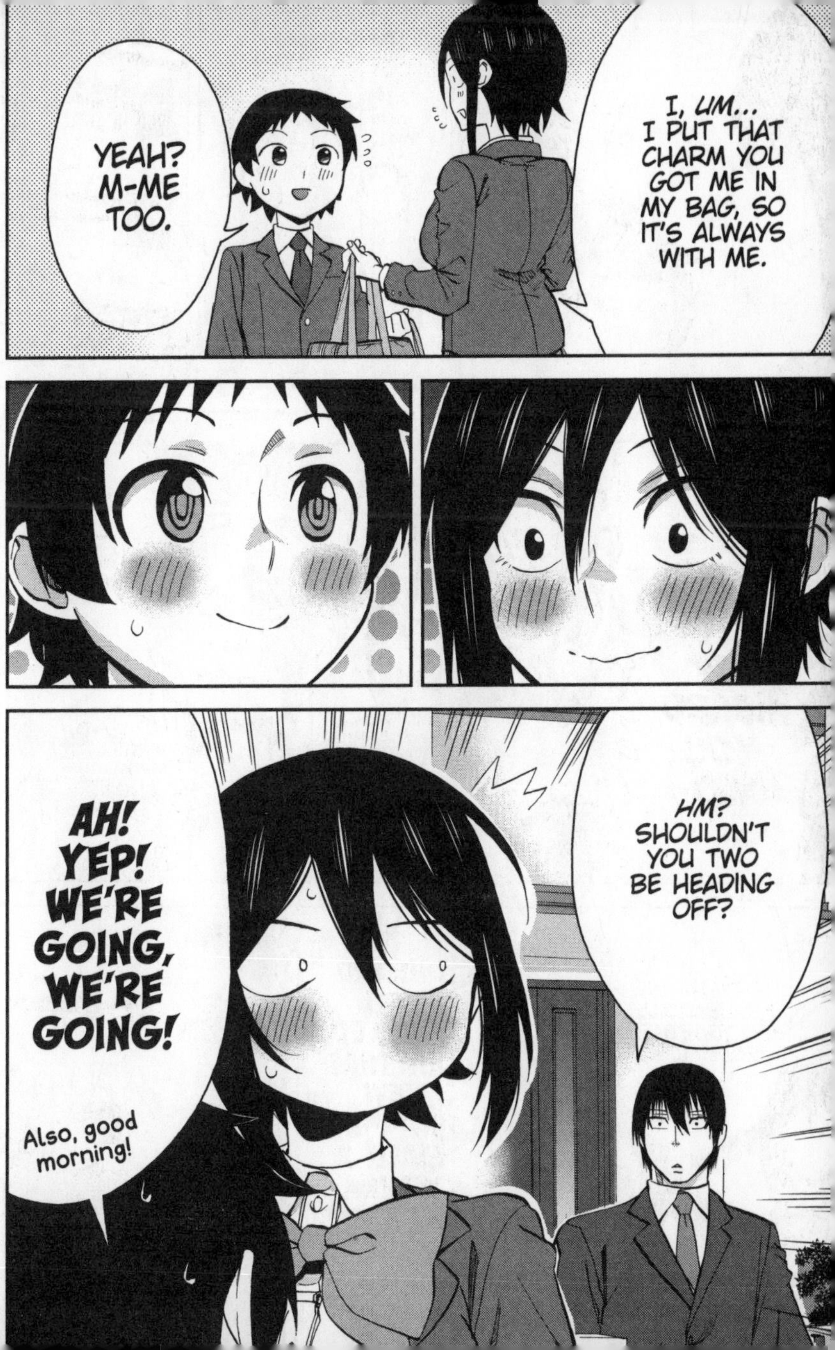
I, UM... I PUT THAT CHARM YOU GOT ME IN MY BAG, SO IT'S ALWAYS WITH ME.
YEAH? M-ME TOO.
HM? SHOULDN'T YOU TWO BE HEADING OFF?
AH! YEP! WE'RE GOING, WE'RE GOING!
Also, good morning!

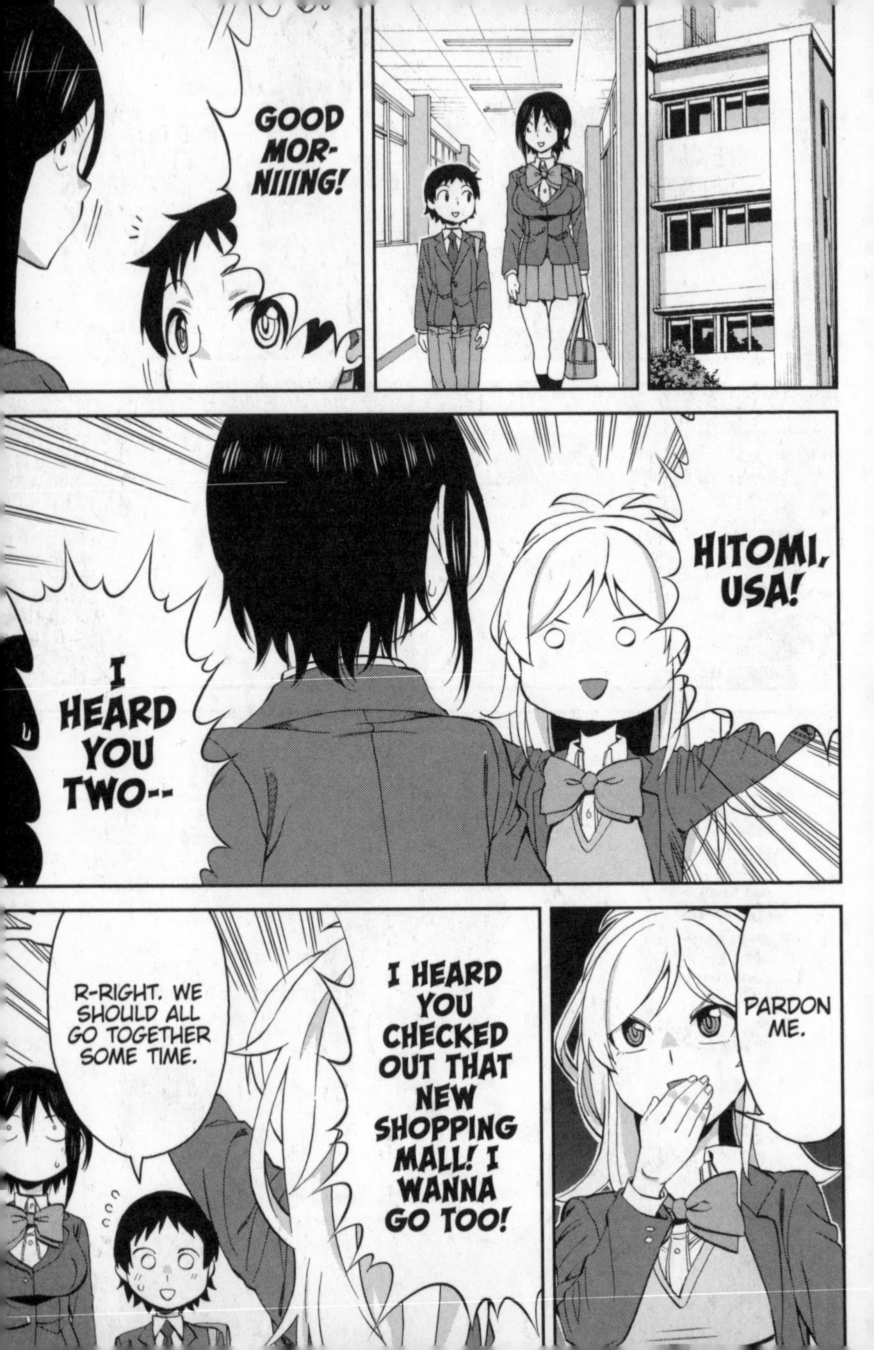
GOOD MOR-NIIING!
HITOMI, USA!
I HEARD YOU TWO--
PARDON ME.
I HEARD YOU CHECKED OUT THAT NEW SHOPPING MALL! I WANNA GO TOO!
R-RIGHT. WE SHOULD ALL GO TOGETHER SOME TIME.

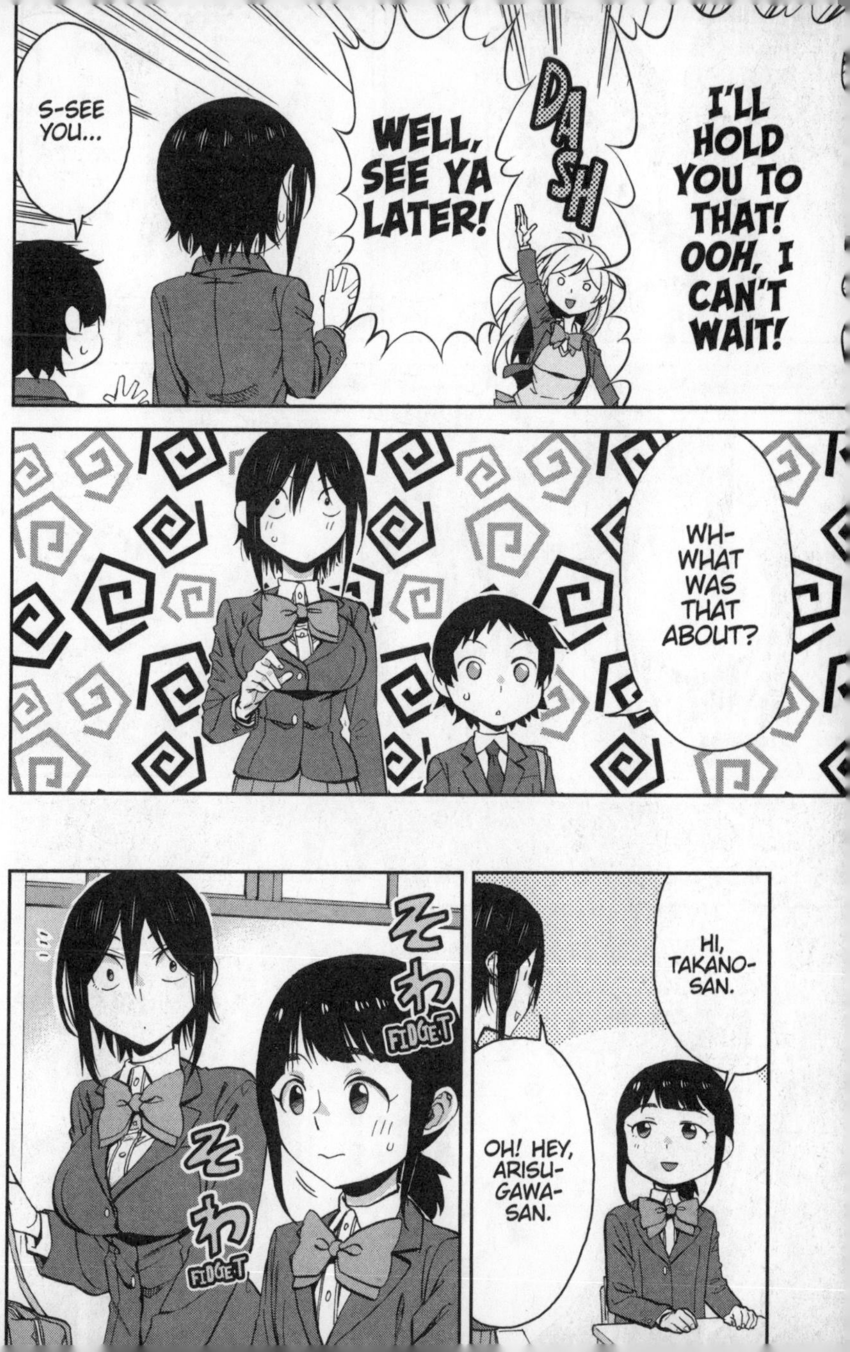
I'LL HOLD YOU TO THAT! OOH, I CAN'T WAIT!
DASH
WELL, SEE YA LATER!
S-SEE YOU...
WH- WHAT WAS THAT ABOUT?
HI, TAKANO-SAN.
OH! HEY, ARISUGAWA-SAN.
そわ FIDGET
そわ FIDGET

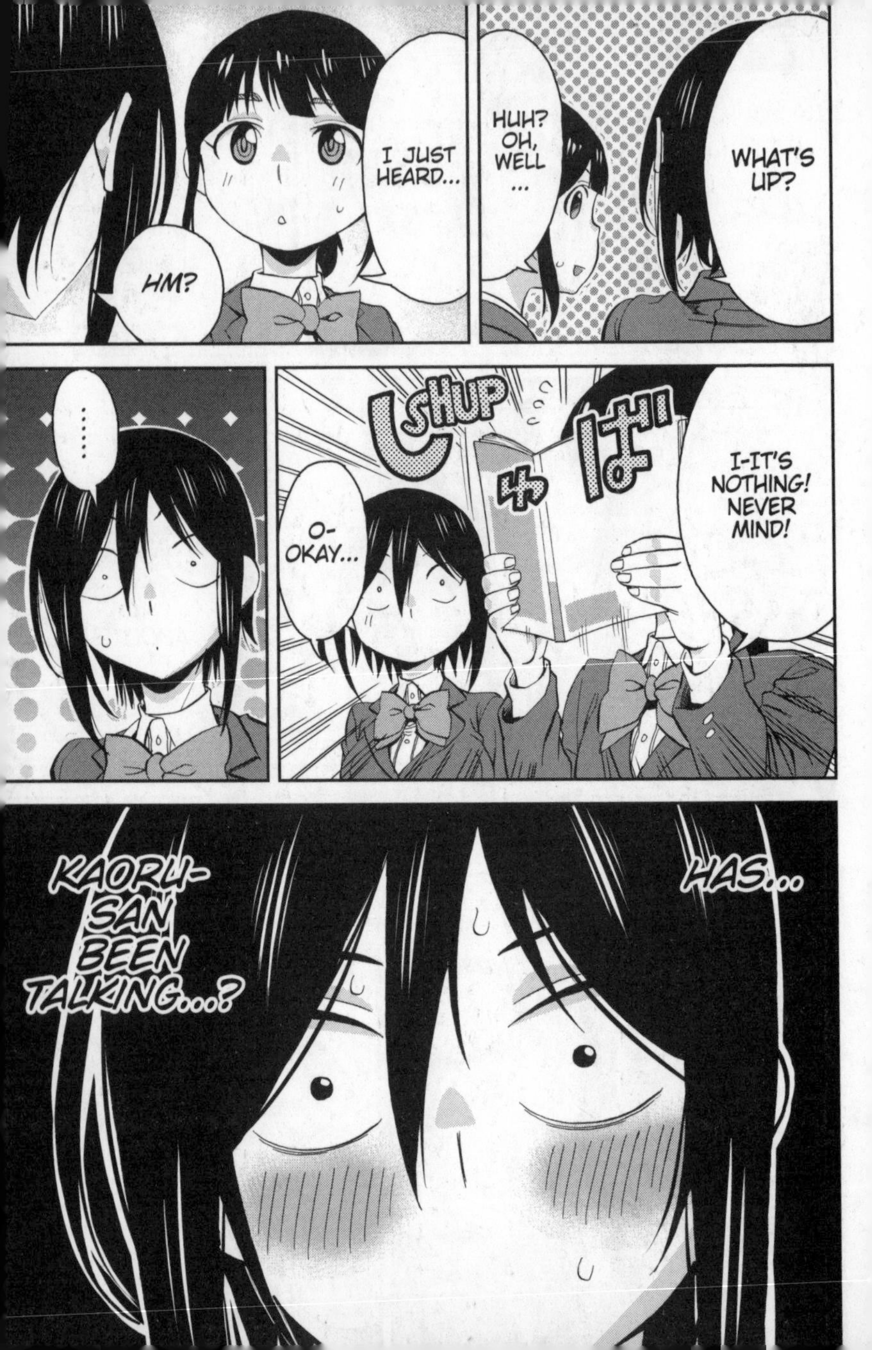
WHAT'S UP?
HUH? OH, WELL ...
I JUST HEARD...
HM?
I-IT'S NOTHING! NEVER MIND!
SHUP
しゅば
O-OKAY...
......
HAS...
KAORU-SAN BEEN TALKING...?

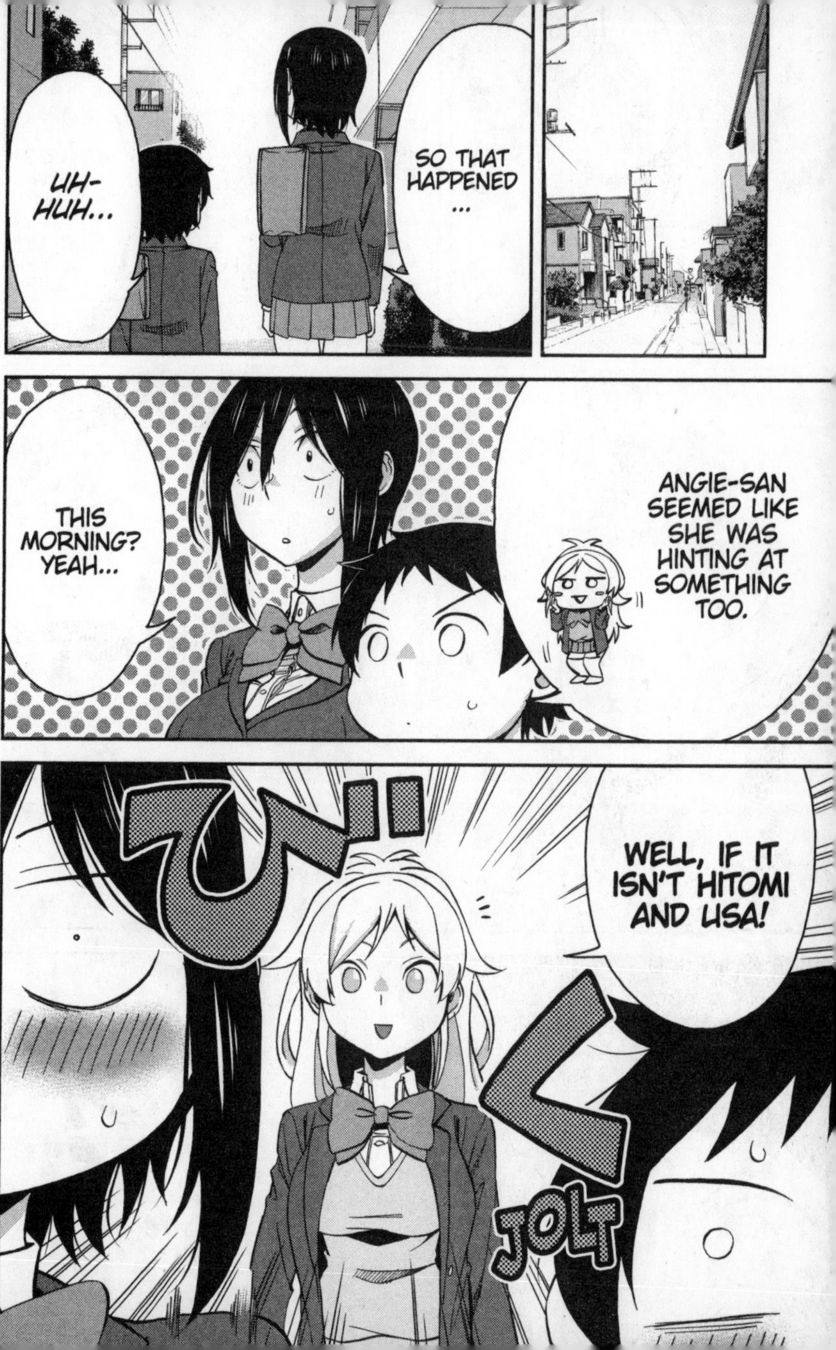
SO THAT HAPPENED ...
UH-HUH...
ANGIE-SAN SEEMED LIKE SHE WAS HINTING AT SOMETHING TOO.
THIS MORNING? YEAH...
WELL, IF IT ISN'T HITOMI AND USA!
JOLT

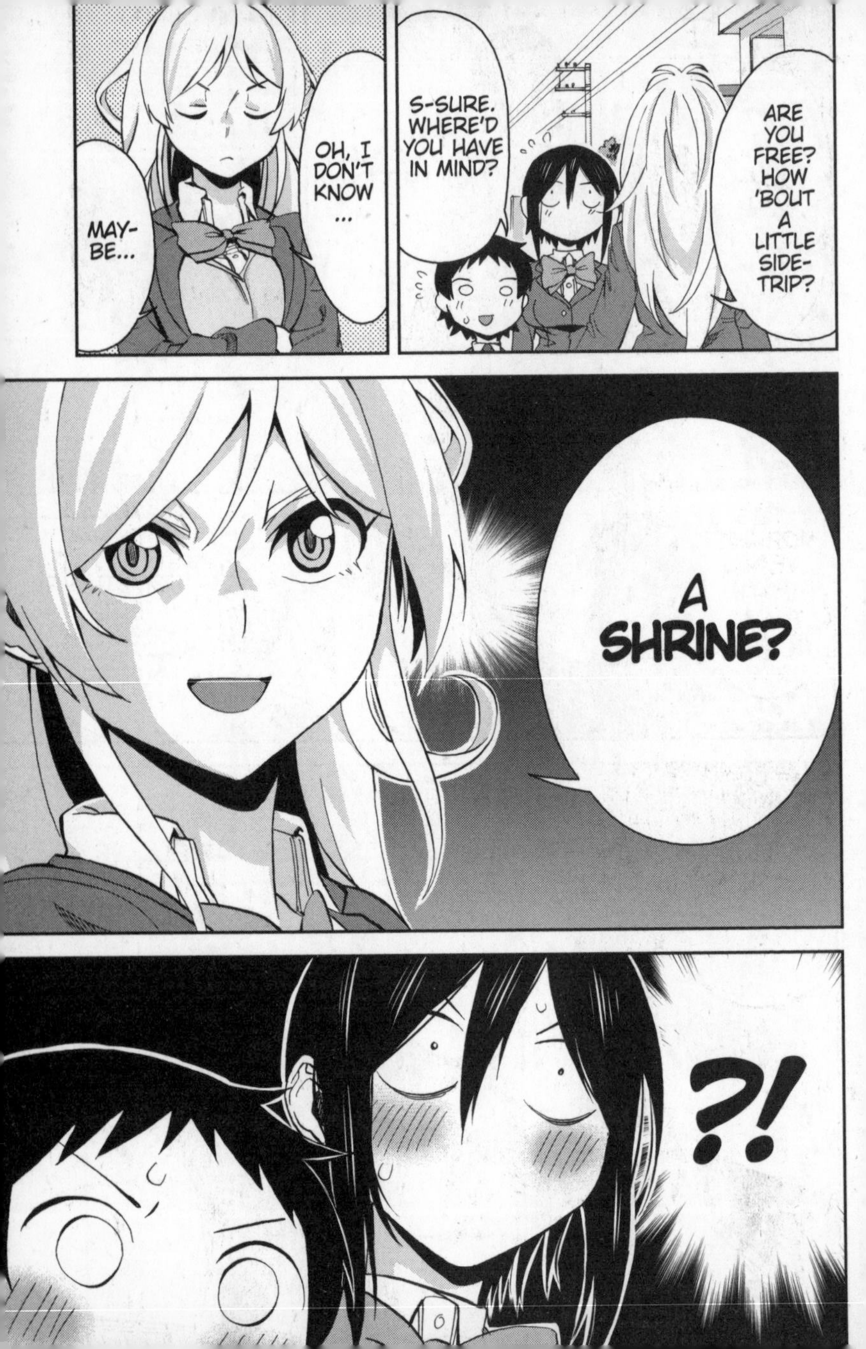
ARE YOU FREE? HOW 'BOUT A LITTLE SIDE-TRIP?
S-SURE. WHERE'D YOU HAVE IN MIND?
OH, I DON'T KNOW ...
MAY-BE...
A SHRINE?
?!

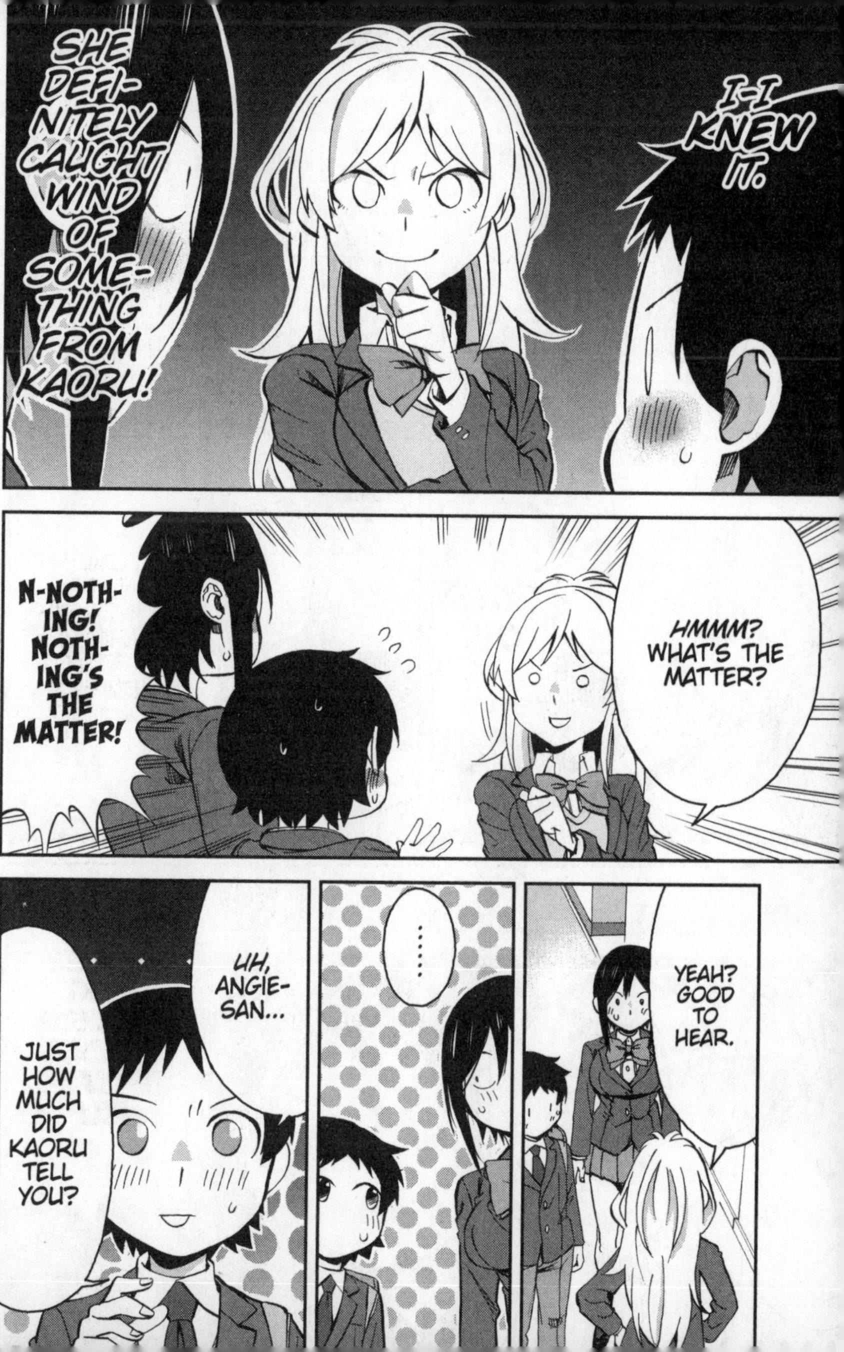
I-I KNEW IT.
SHE DEFI-NITELY CAUGHT WIND OF SOME-THING FROM KAORU!
HMMM? WHAT'S THE MATTER?
N-NOTHING! NOTHING'S THE MATTER!
YEAH? GOOD TO HEAR.
......
UH, ANGIE-SAN...
JUST HOW MUCH DID KAORU TELL YOU?

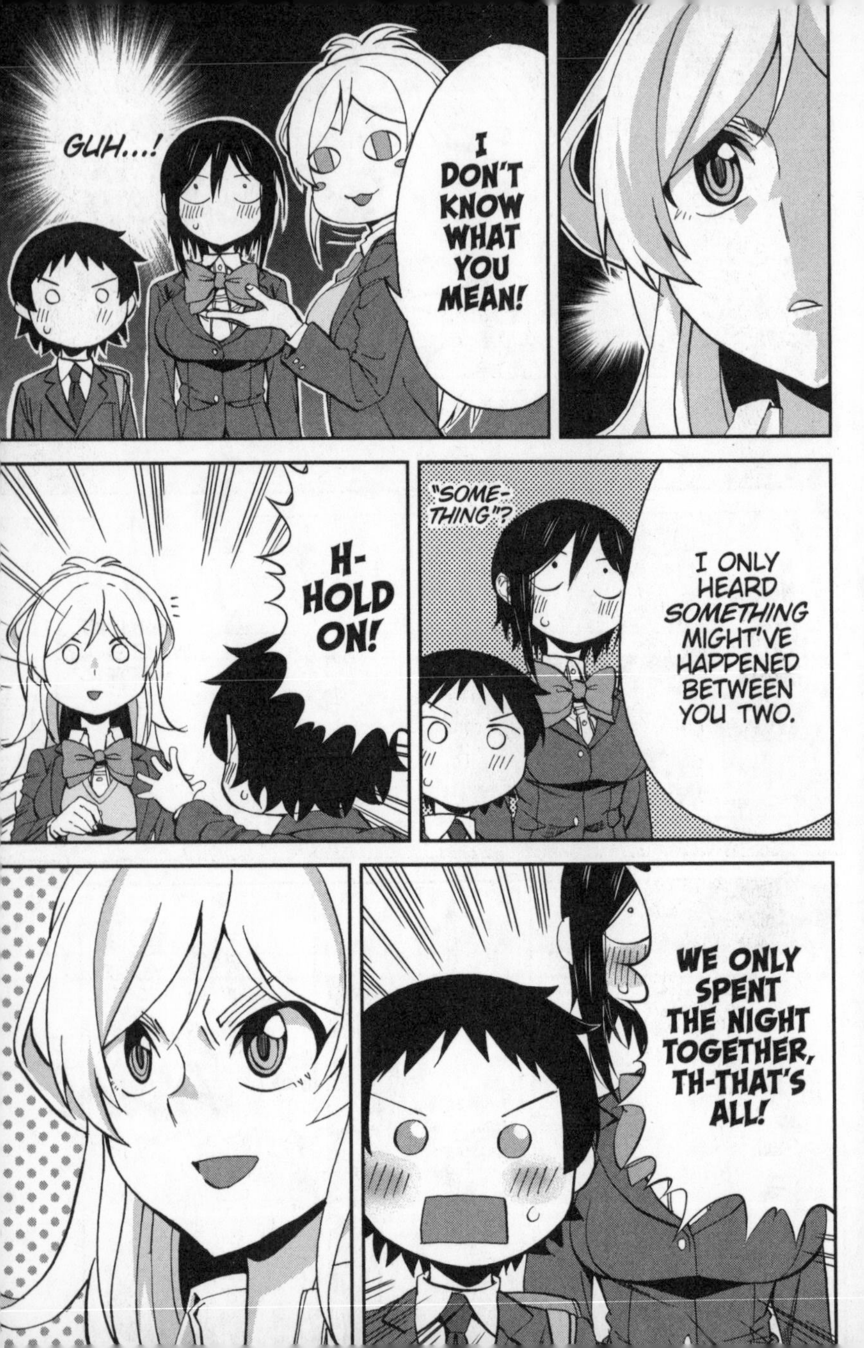
I DON'T KNOW WHAT YOU MEAN!
GUH...!
I ONLY HEARD SOMETHING MIGHT'VE HAPPENED BETWEEN YOU TWO.
"SOME-THING"?
H-HOLD ON!
WE ONLY SPENT THE NIGHT TOGETHER, TH-THAT'S ALL!

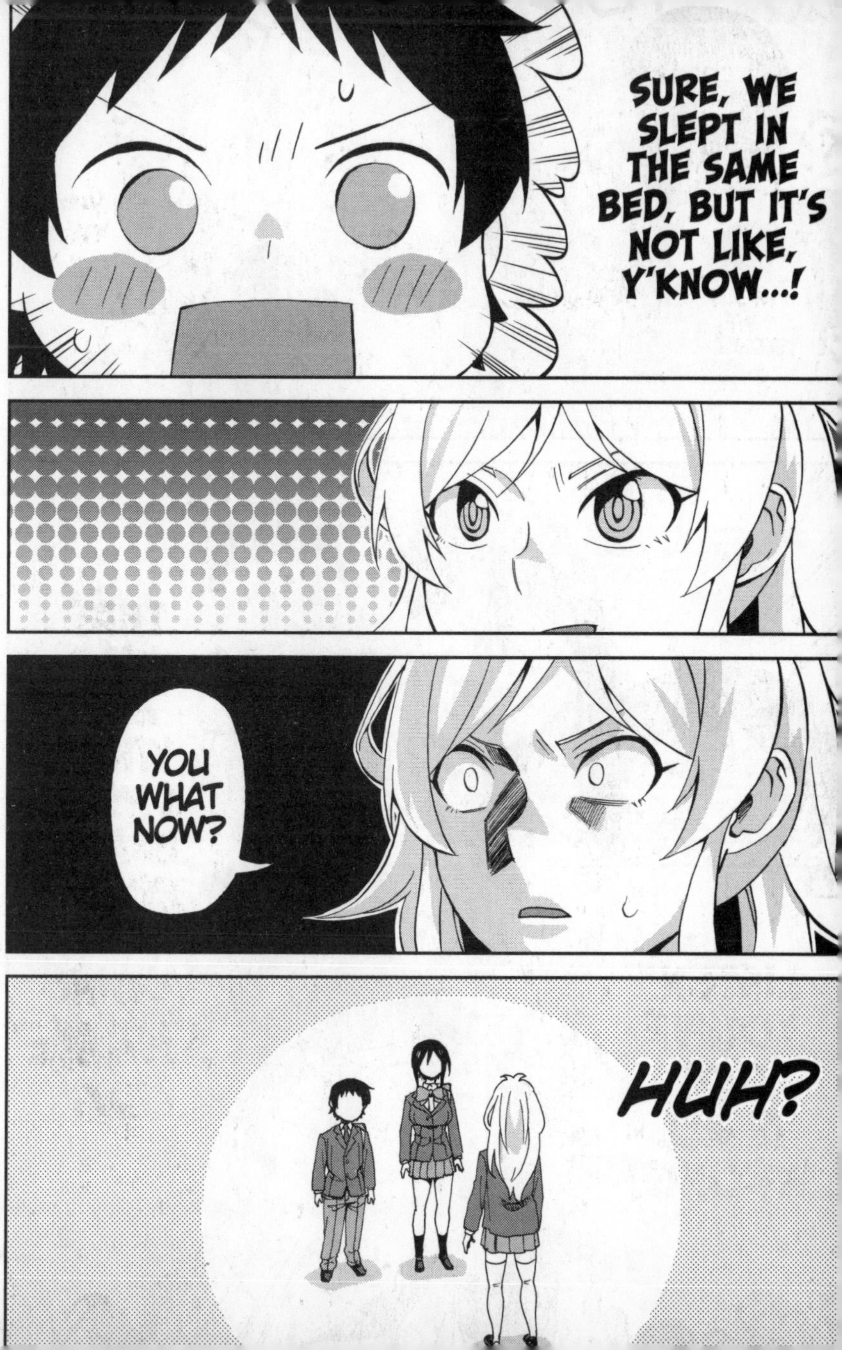
SURE, WE SLEPT IN THE SAME BED, BUT IT'S NOT LIKE, Y'KNOW...!
YOU WHAT NOW?
HUH?

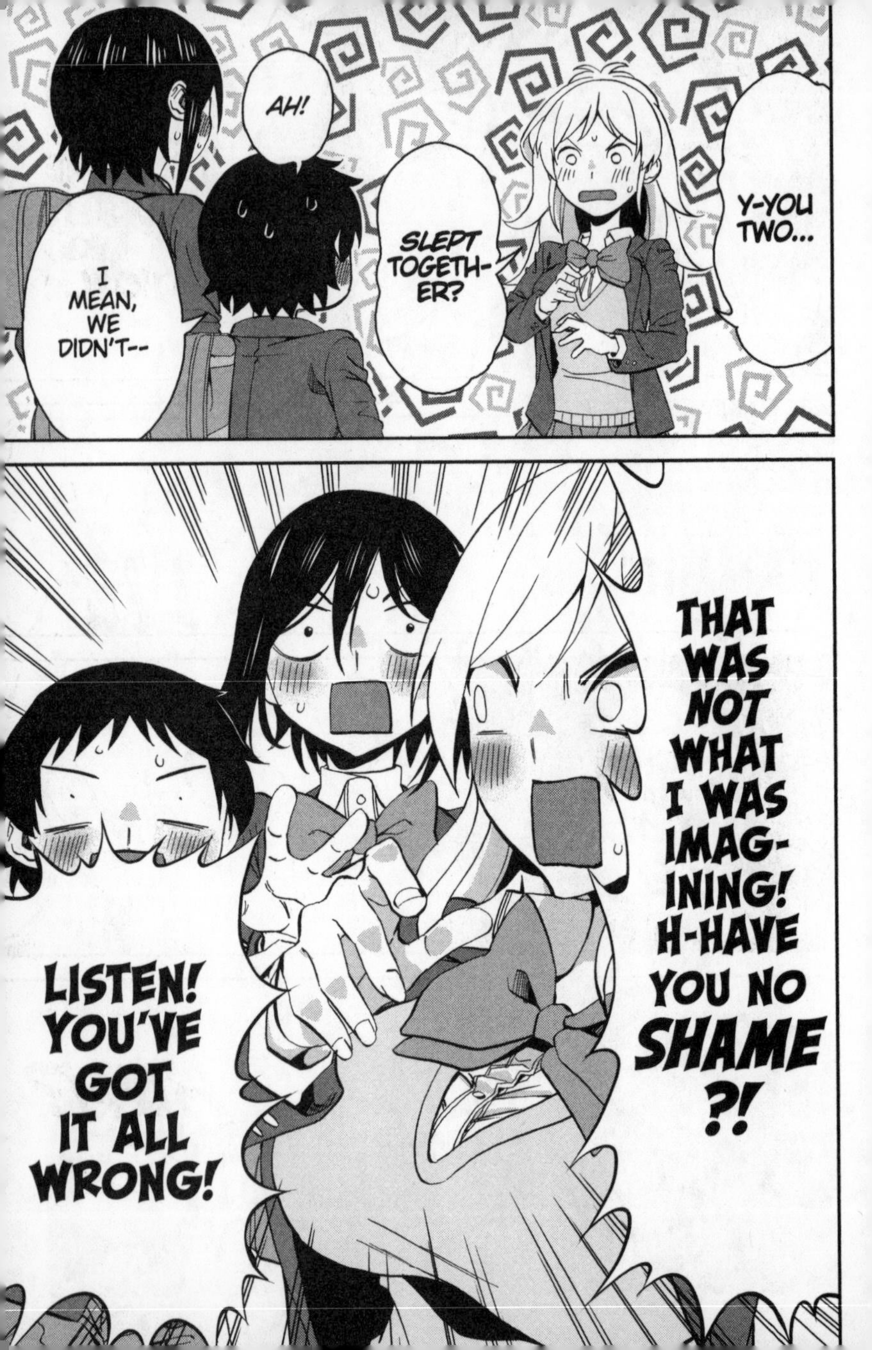
Y-YOU TWO...
SLEPT TOGETH-ER?
AH!
I MEAN, WE DIDN'T--
THAT WAS NOT WHAT I WAS IMAG-INING! H-HAVE YOU NO SHAME?!
LISTEN! YOU'VE GOT IT ALL WRONG!

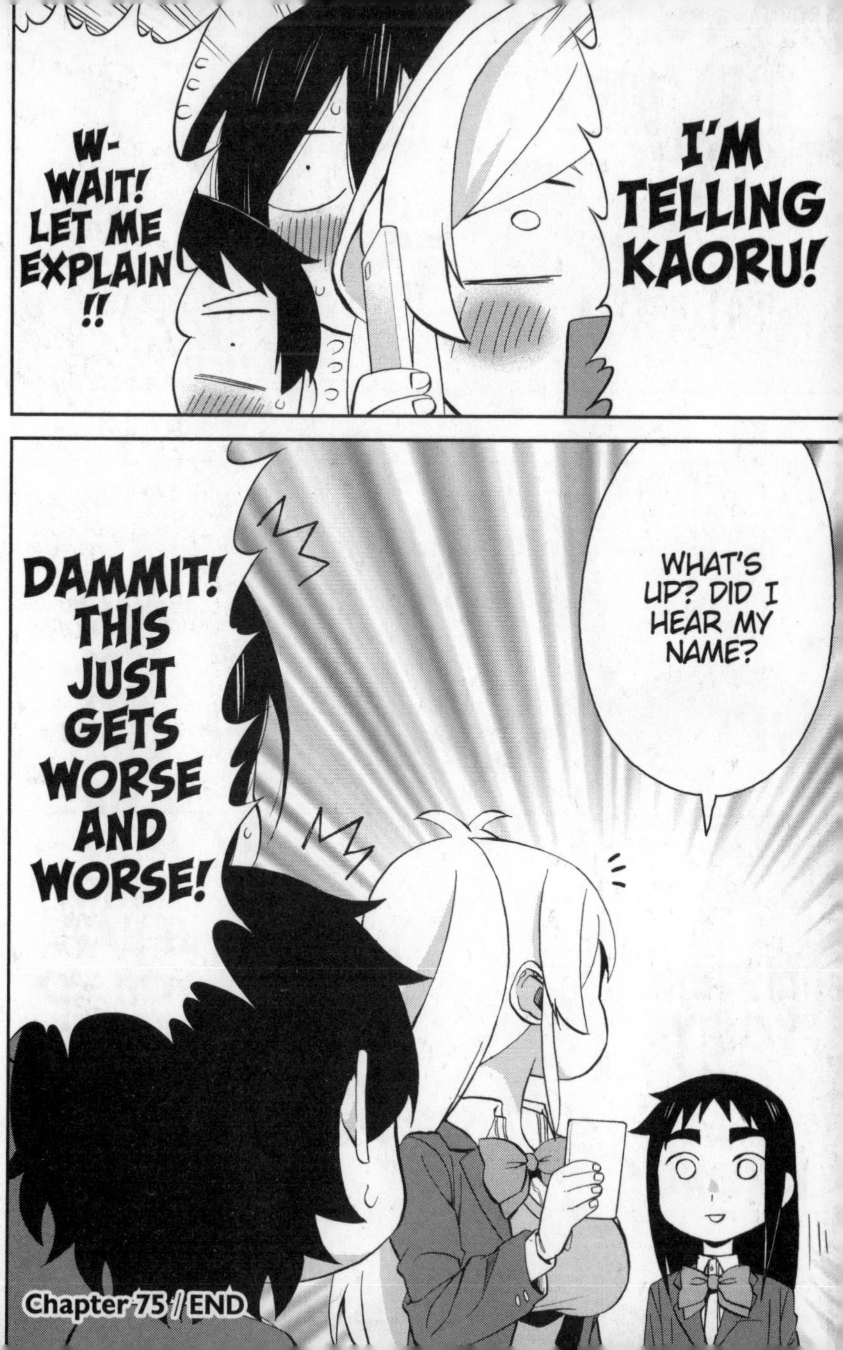
I'M TELLING KAORU!
W-WAIT! LET ME EXPLAIN!!
WHAT'S UP? DID I HEAR MY NAME?
DAMMIT! THIS JUST GETS WORSE AND WORSE!
Chapter 75 / END

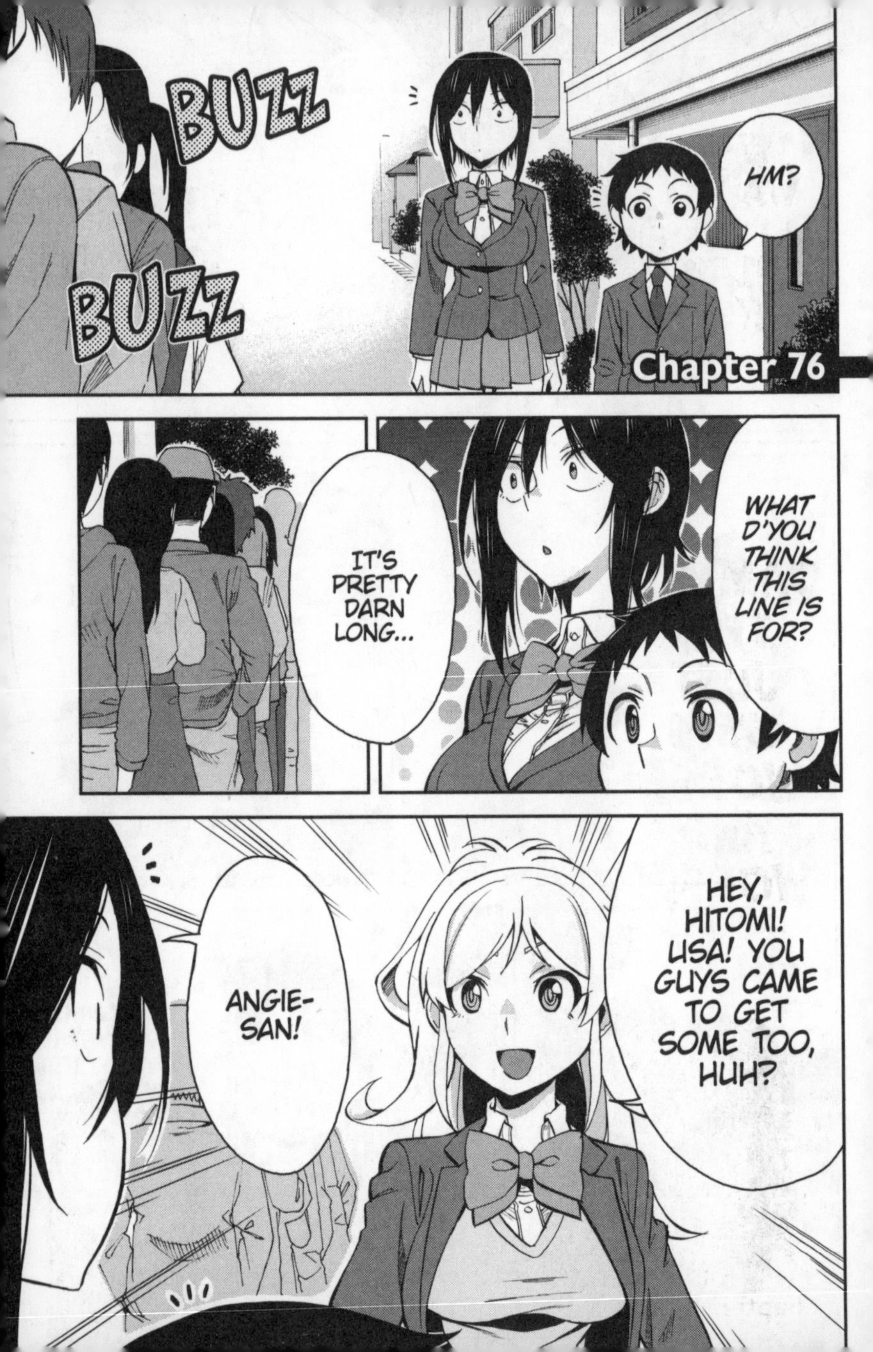
HM?
BUZZ
BUZZ
Chapter 76
WHAT D'YOU THINK THIS LINE IS FOR?
IT'S PRETTY DARN LONG...
HEY, HITOMI! USA! YOU GUYS CAME TO GET SOME TOO, HUH?
ANGIE-SAN!

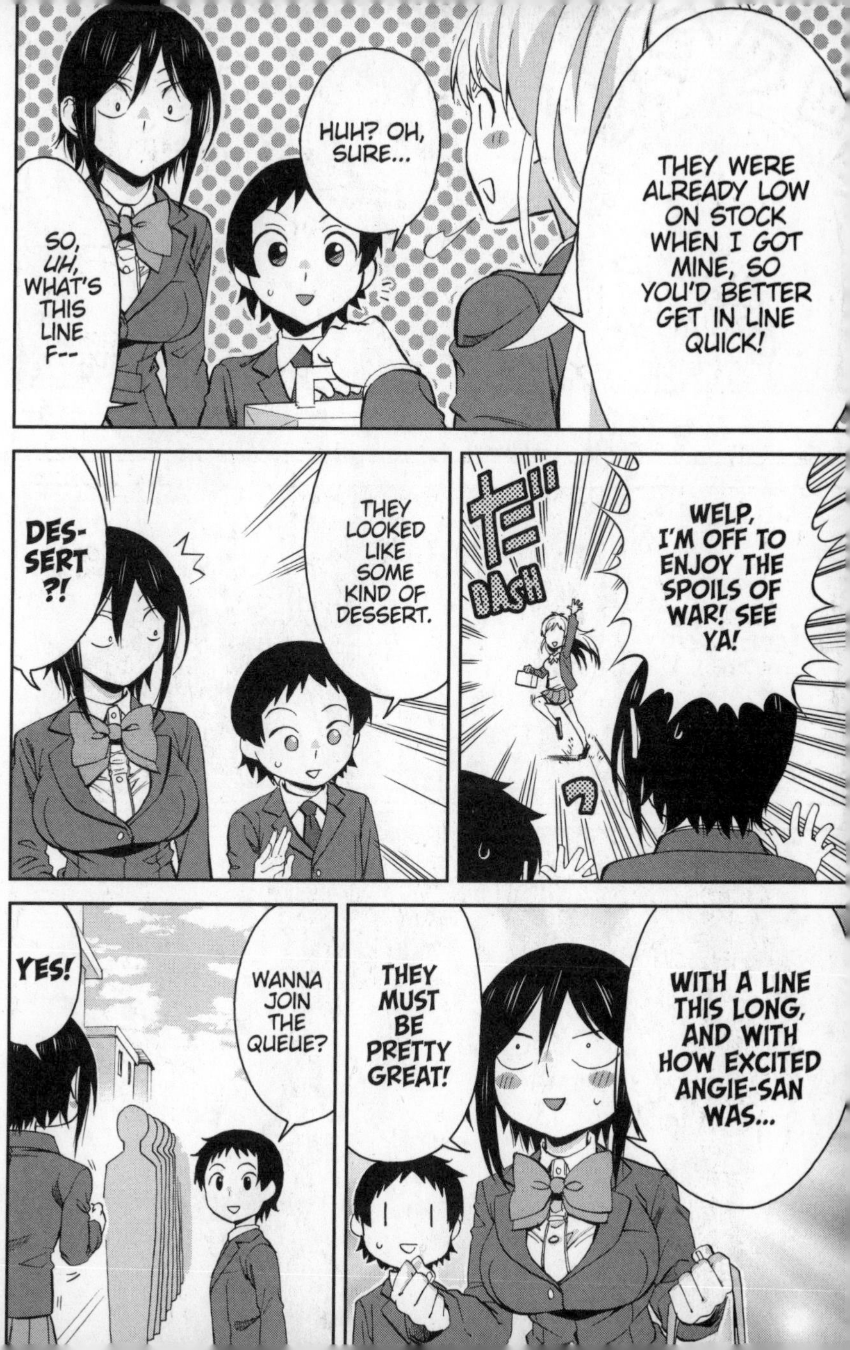
THEY WERE ALREADY LOW ON STOCK WHEN I GOT MINE, SO YOU'D BETTER GET IN LINE QUICK!
HUH? OH, SURE...
SO, UH, WHAT'S THIS LINE F--
WELP, I'M OFF TO ENJOY THE SPOILS OF WAR! SEE YA!
DASH
?
THEY LOOKED LIKE SOME KIND OF DESSERT.
DES-SERT?!
WITH A LINE THIS LONG, AND WITH HOW EXCITED ANGIE-SAN WAS...
THEY MUST BE PRETTY GREAT!
WANNA JOIN THE QUEUE?
YES!

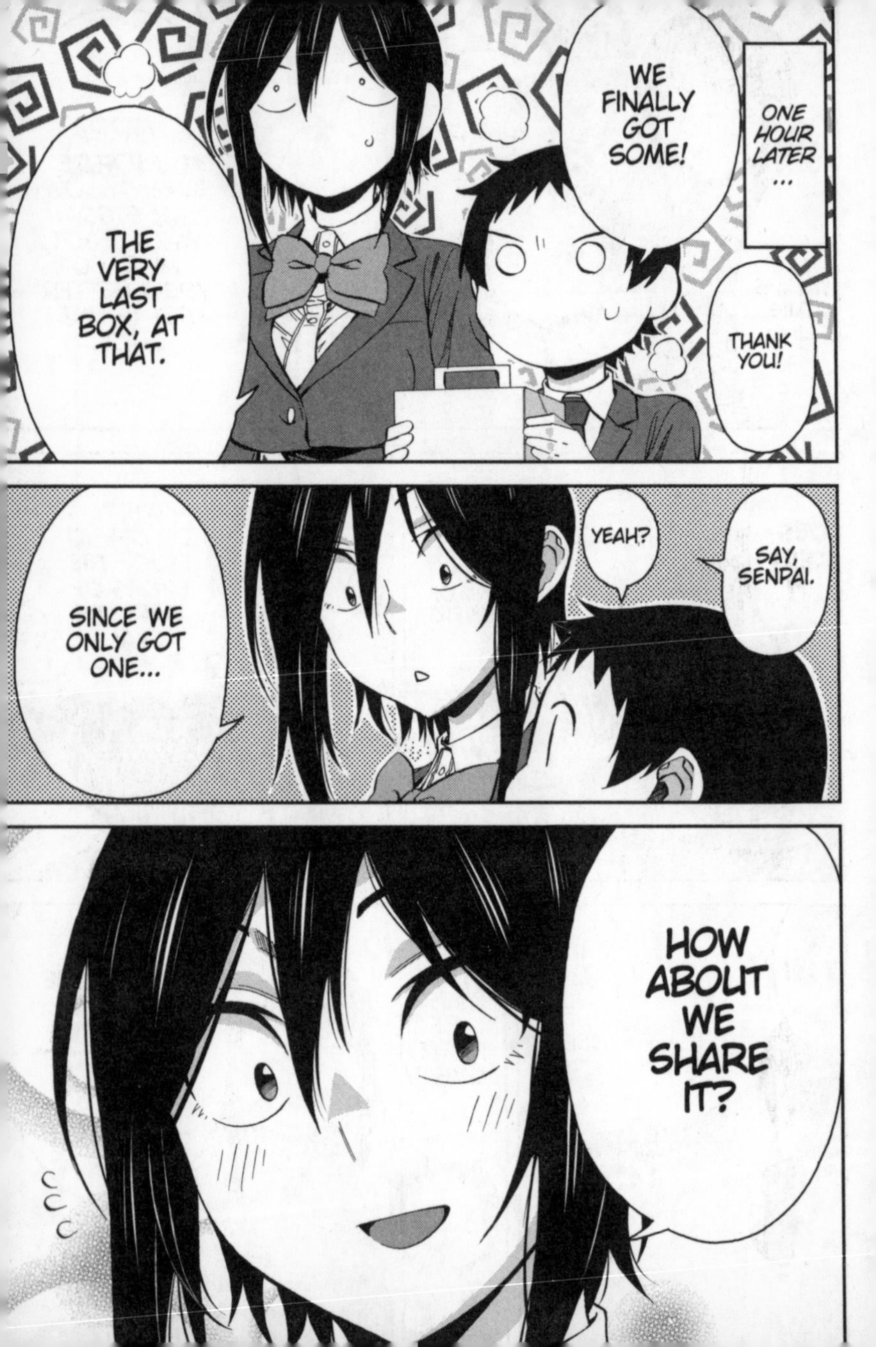
ONE HOUR LATER ...
WE FINALLY GOT SOME!
THANK YOU!
THE VERY LAST BOX, AT THAT.
SAY, SENPAI.
YEAH?
SINCE WE ONLY GOT ONE...
HOW ABOUT WE SHARE IT?

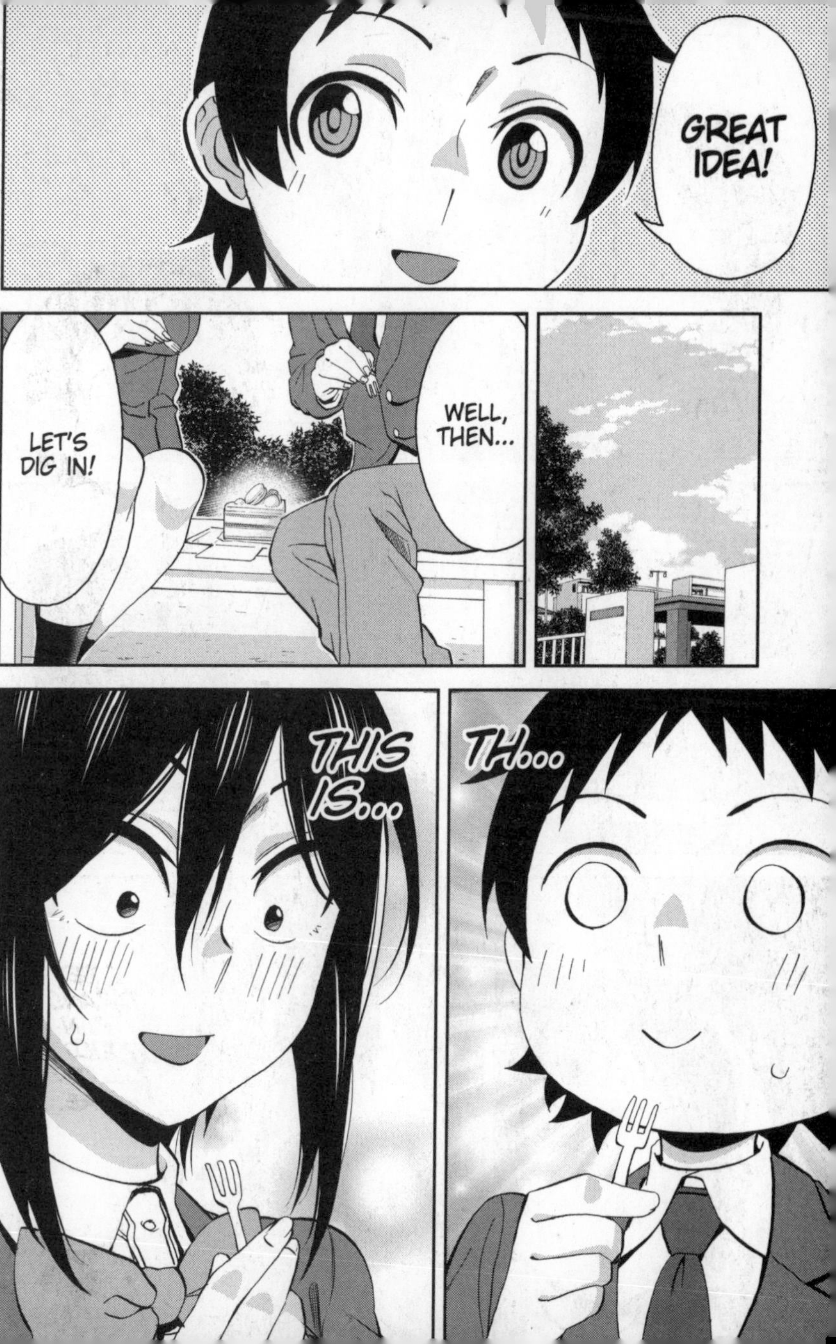
GREAT IDEA!
WELL, THEN...
LET'S DIG IN!
TH...
THIS IS...

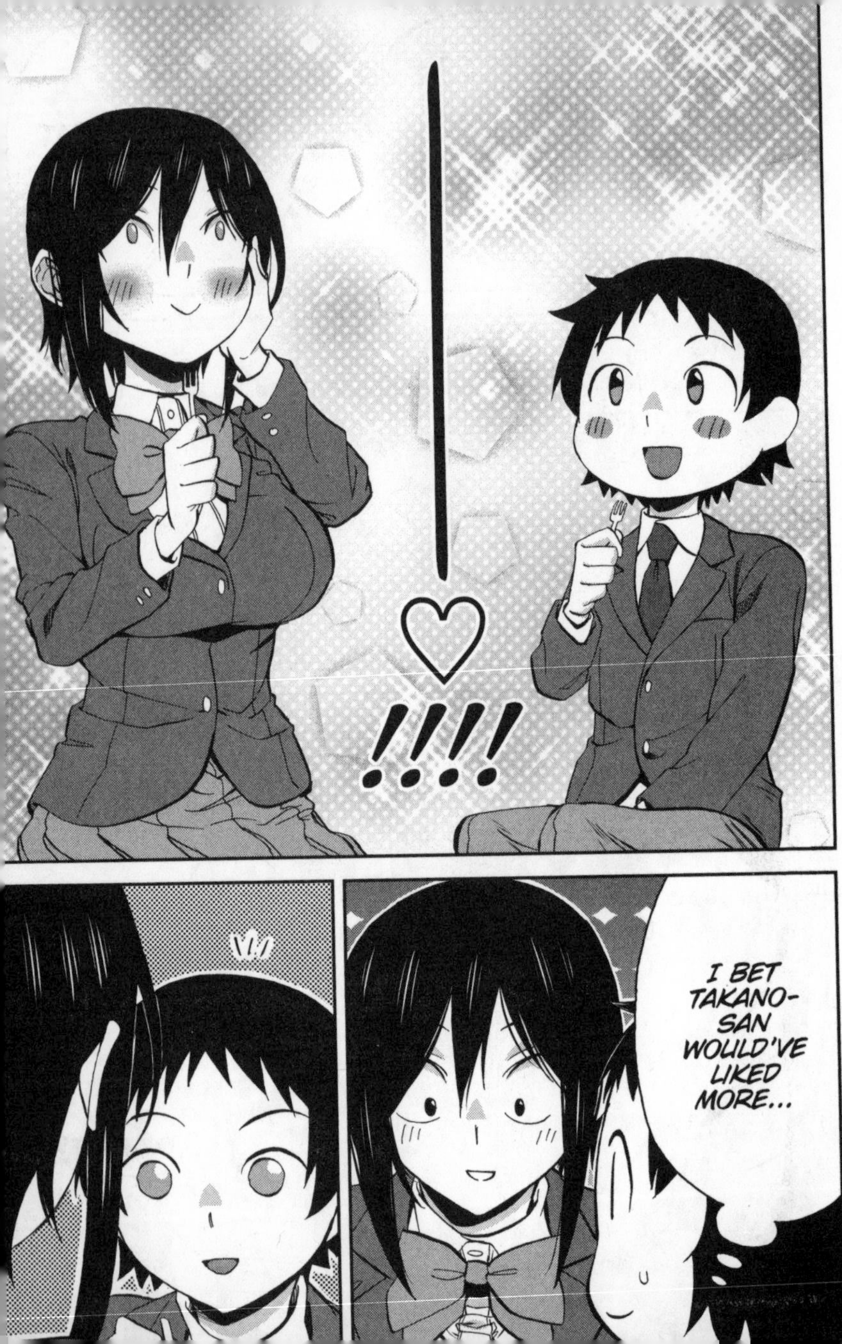
!!!!
I BET TAKANO-SAN WOULD'VE LIKED MORE...

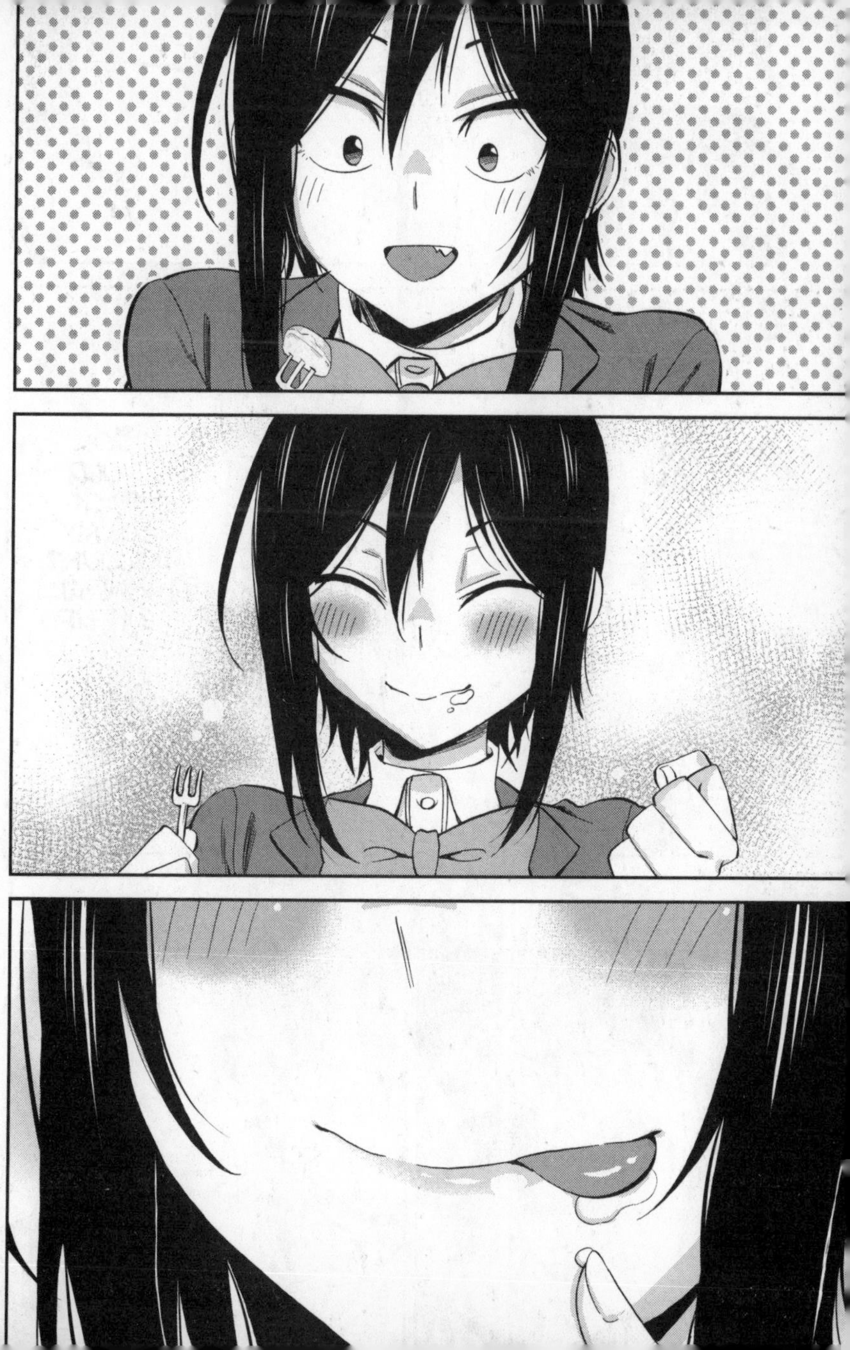

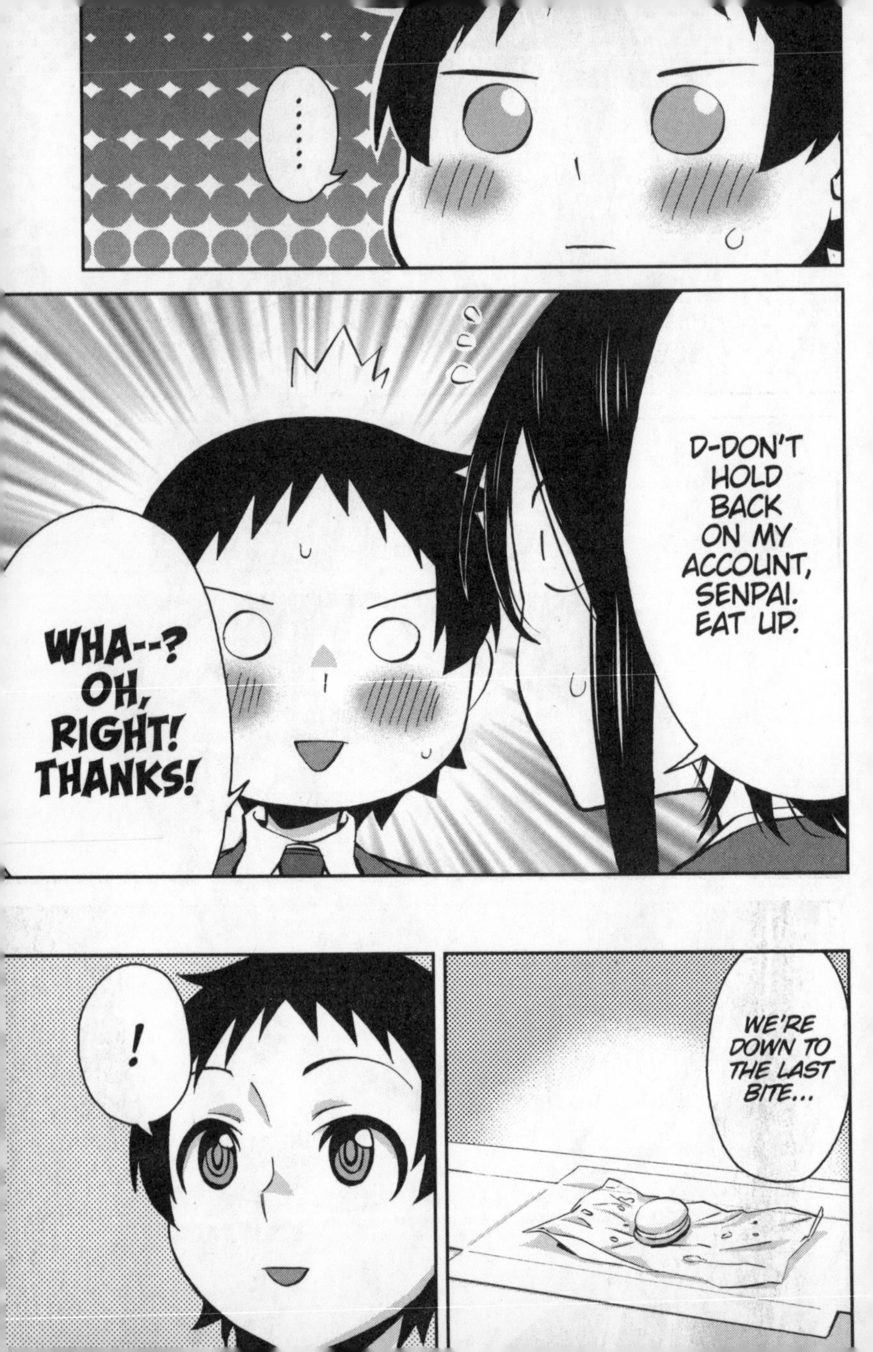
……
D-DON'T HOLD BACK ON MY ACCOUNT, SENPAI. EAT UP.
WHA--? OH, RIGHT! THANKS!
WE'RE DOWN TO THE LAST BITE...
!

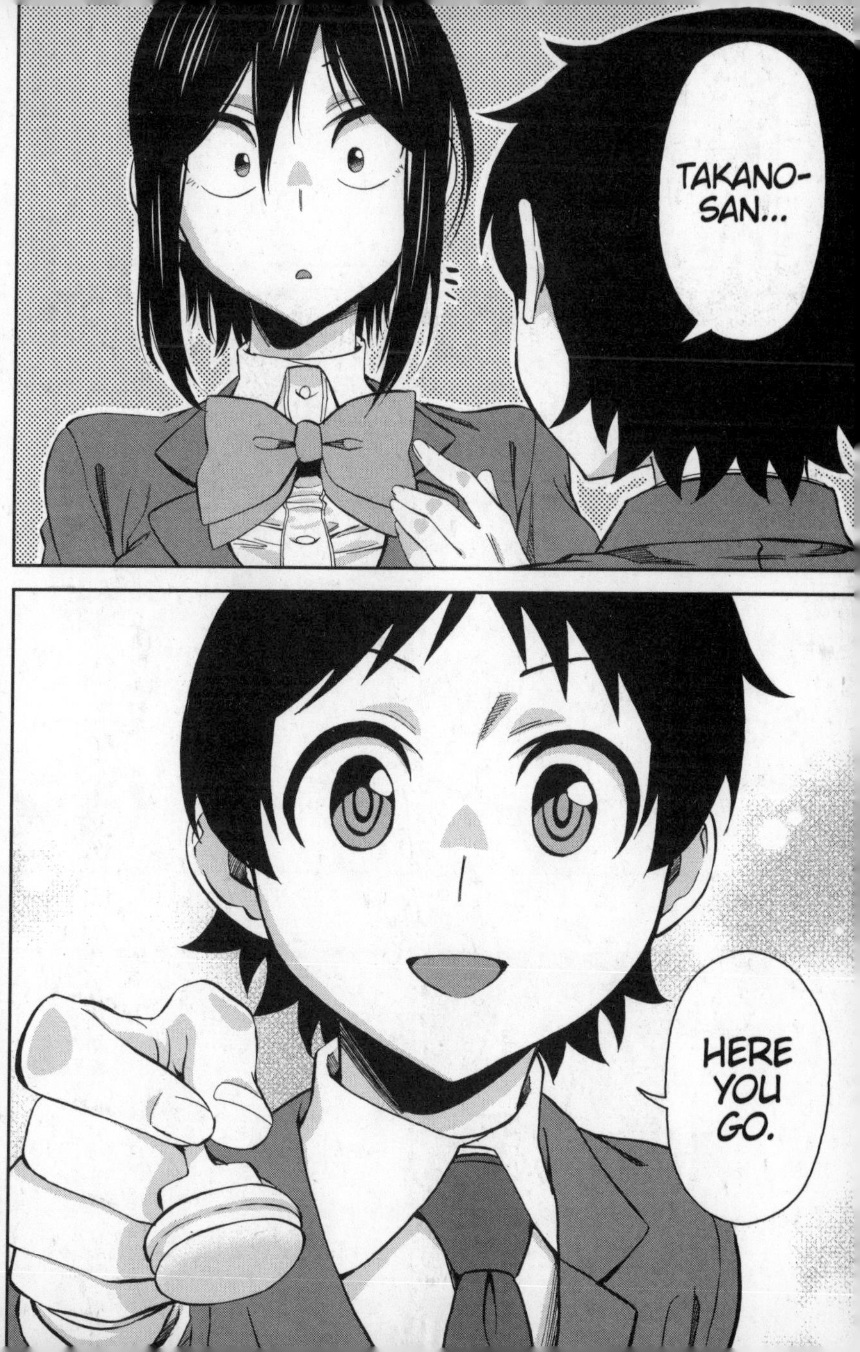
TAKANO-SAN...
HERE YOU GO.

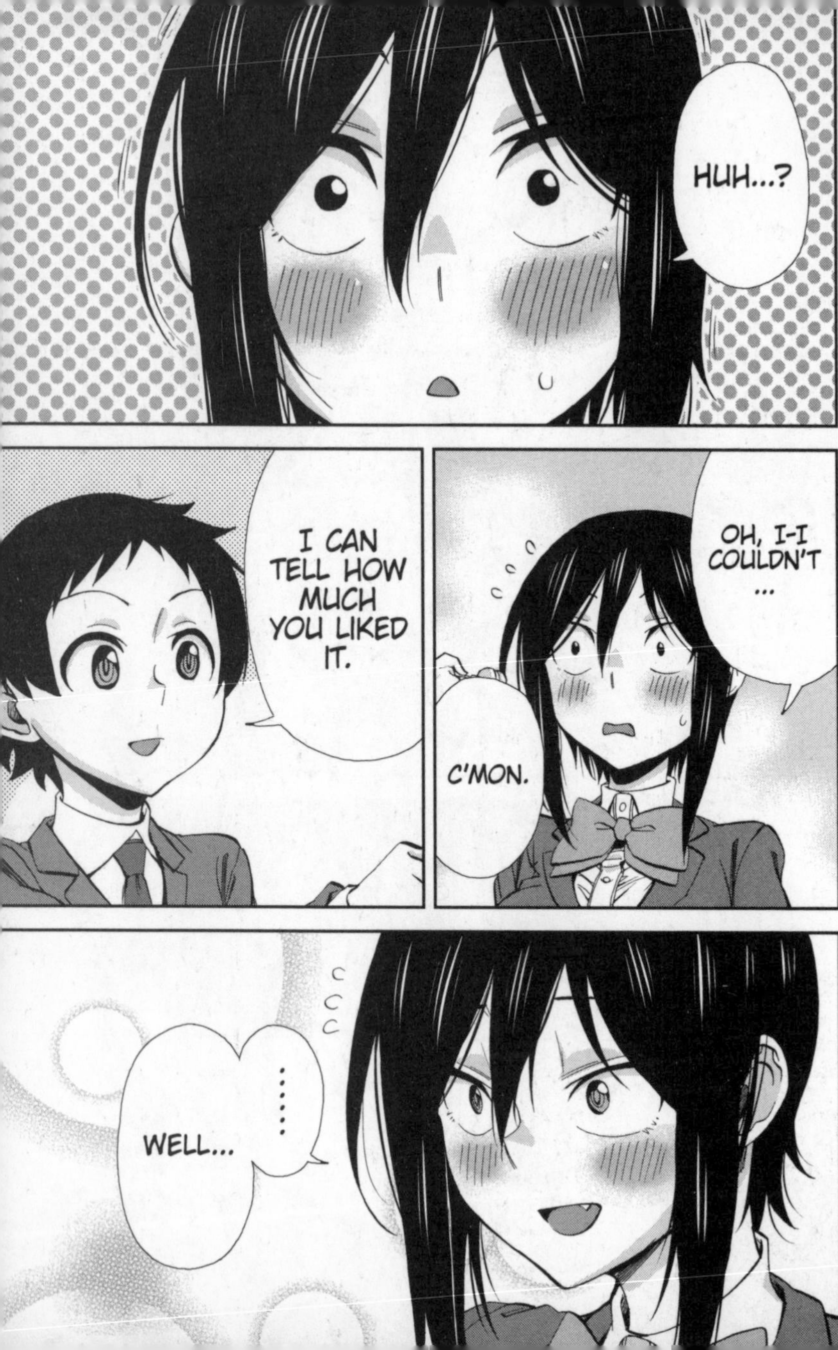
HUH...?
OH, I-I COULDN'T ...
C'MON.
I CAN TELL HOW MUCH YOU LIKED IT.
......
WELL...

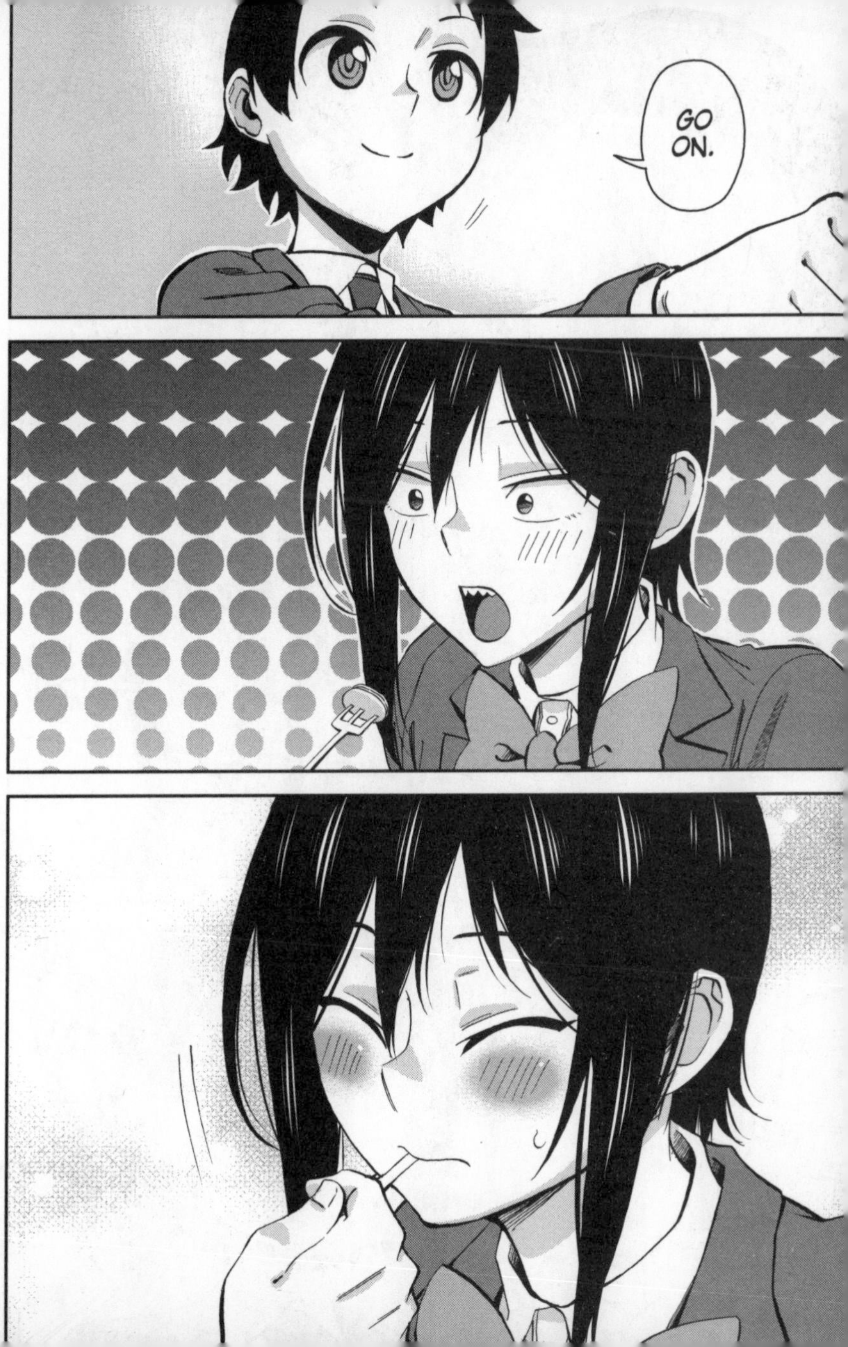
GO ON.

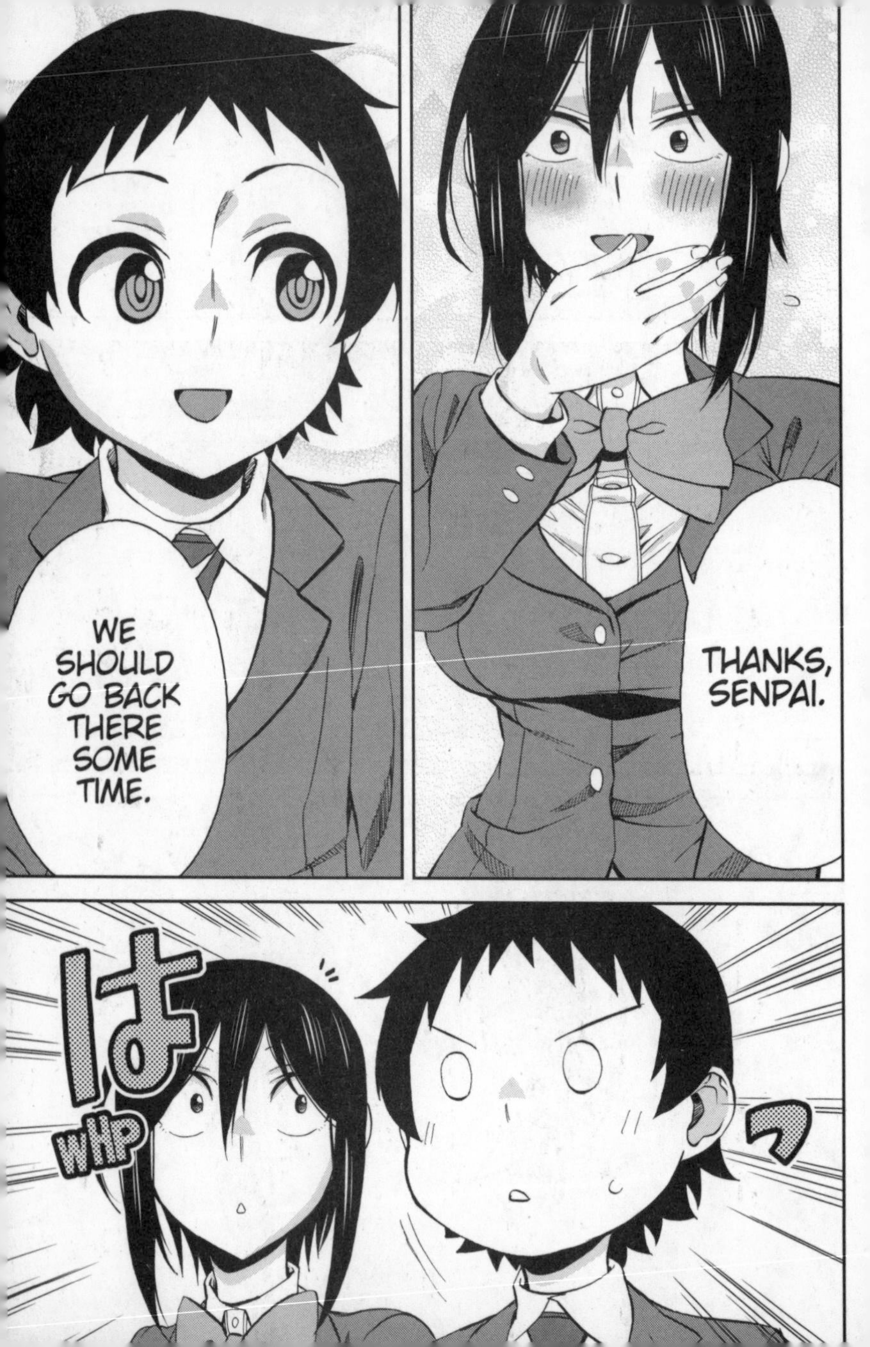
THANKS, SENPAI.
WE SHOULD GO BACK THERE SOME TIME.
つ
は
WHP

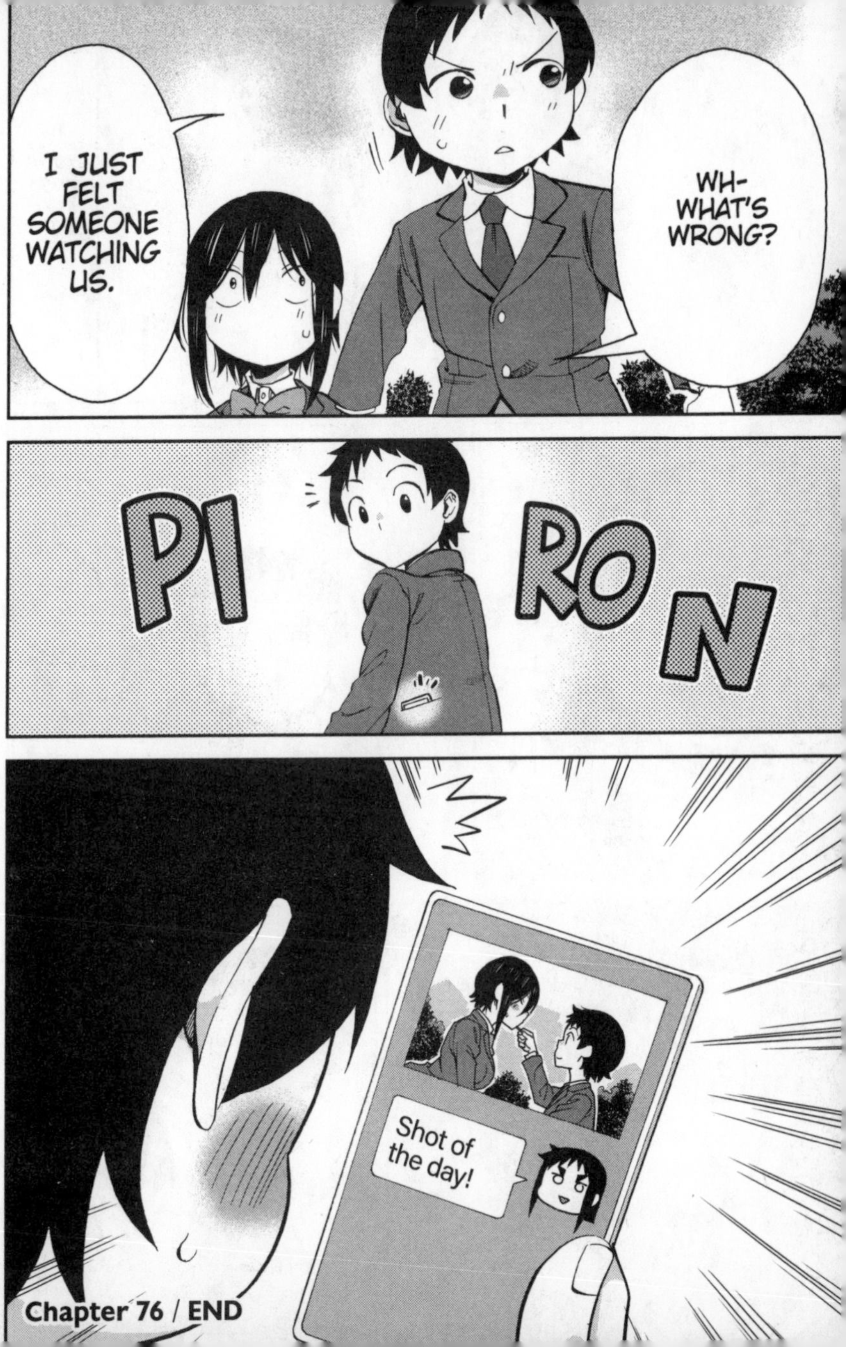
WH- WHAT'S WRONG?
I JUST FELT SOMEONE WATCHING US.
PI RO N
Shot of the day!
Chapter 76 / END

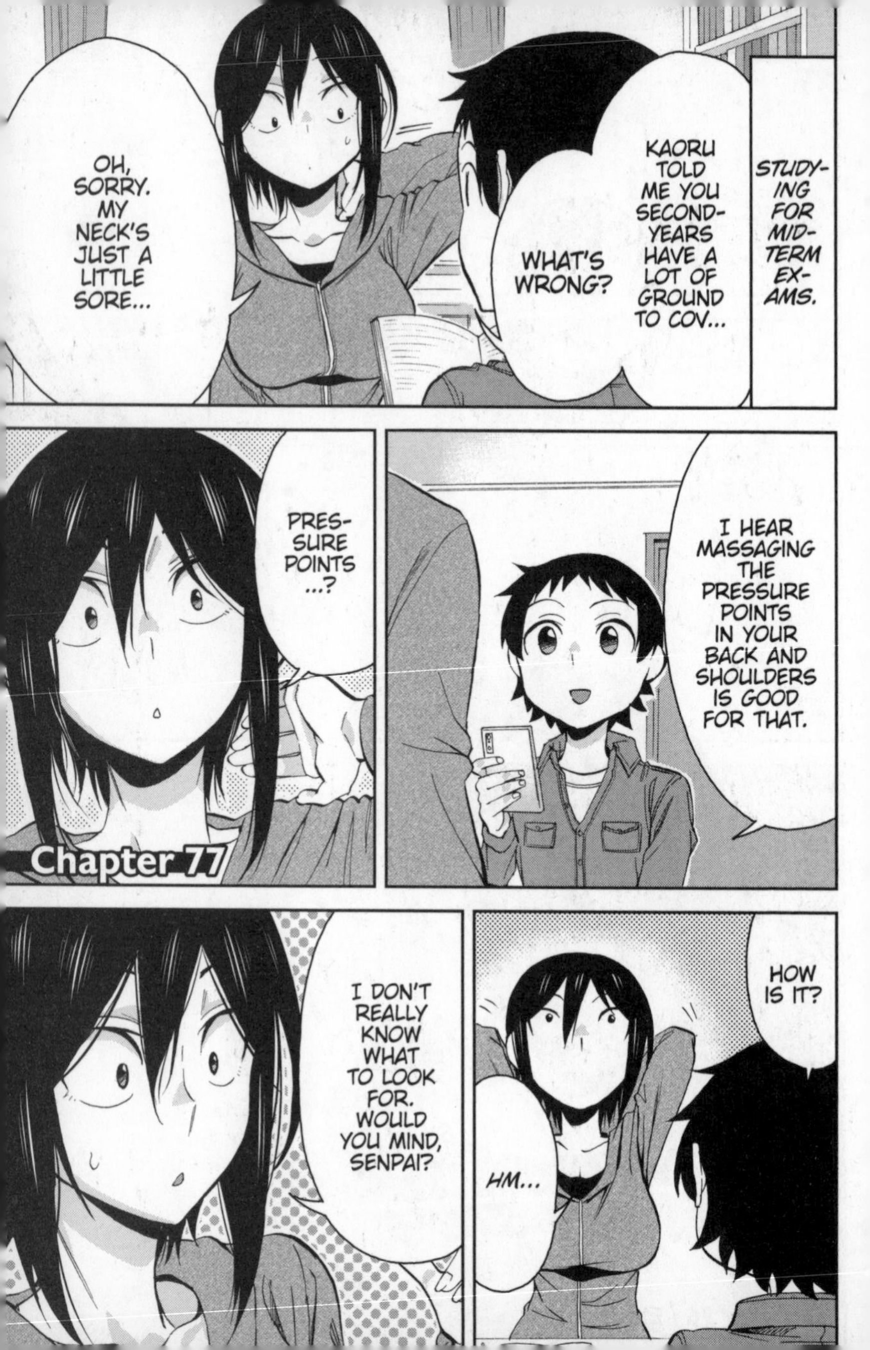
STUDYING FOR MIDTERM EXAMS.
KAORU TOLD ME YOU SECOND-YEARS HAVE A LOT OF GROUND TO COV...
WHAT'S WRONG?
OH, SORRY. MY NECK'S JUST A LITTLE SORE...
I HEAR MASSAGING THE PRESSURE POINTS IN YOUR BACK AND SHOULDERS IS GOOD FOR THAT.
PRESSURE POINTS ...?
Chapter 77
HOW IS IT?
HM...
I DON'T REALLY KNOW WHAT TO LOOK FOR. WOULD YOU MIND, SENPAI?

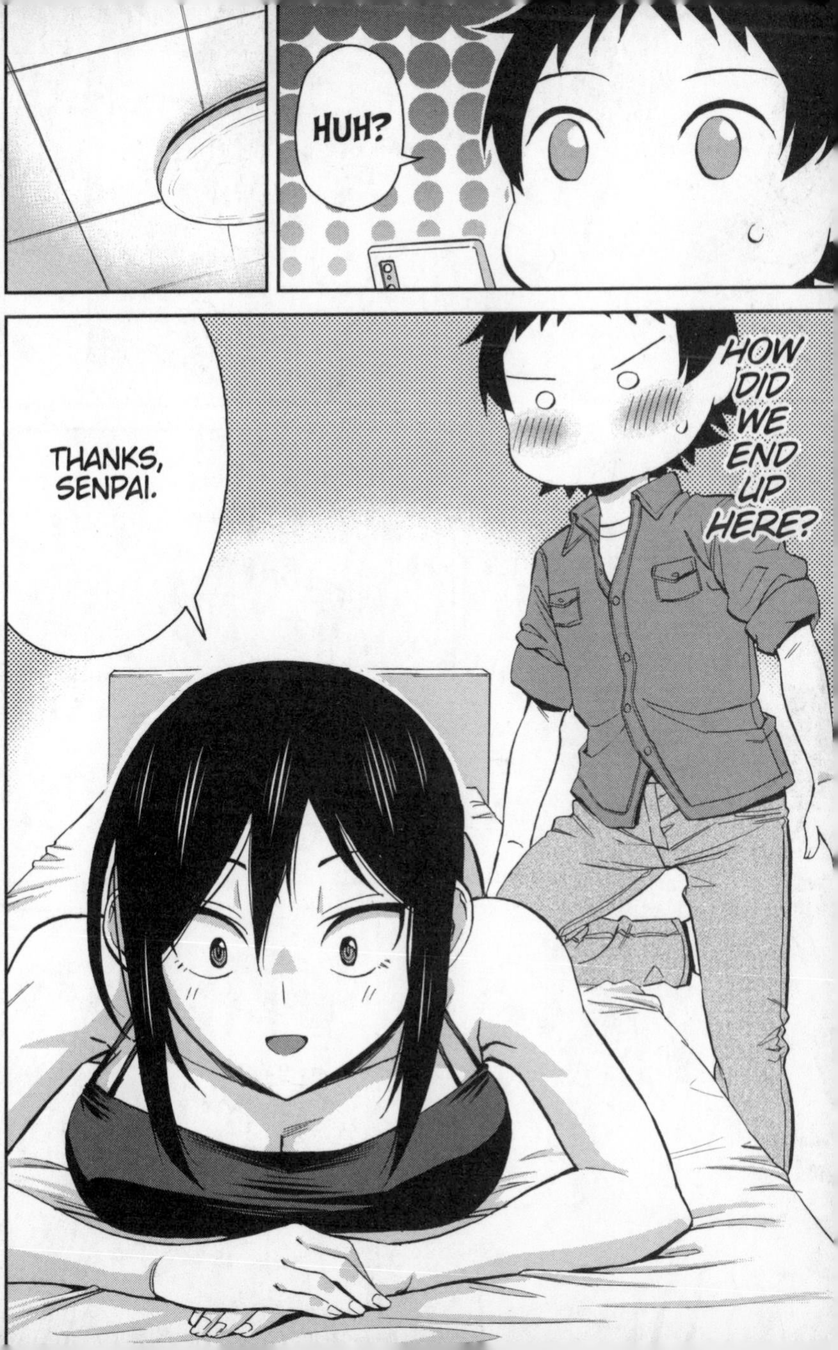
HUH?
HOW DID WE END UP HERE?
THANKS, SENPAI.

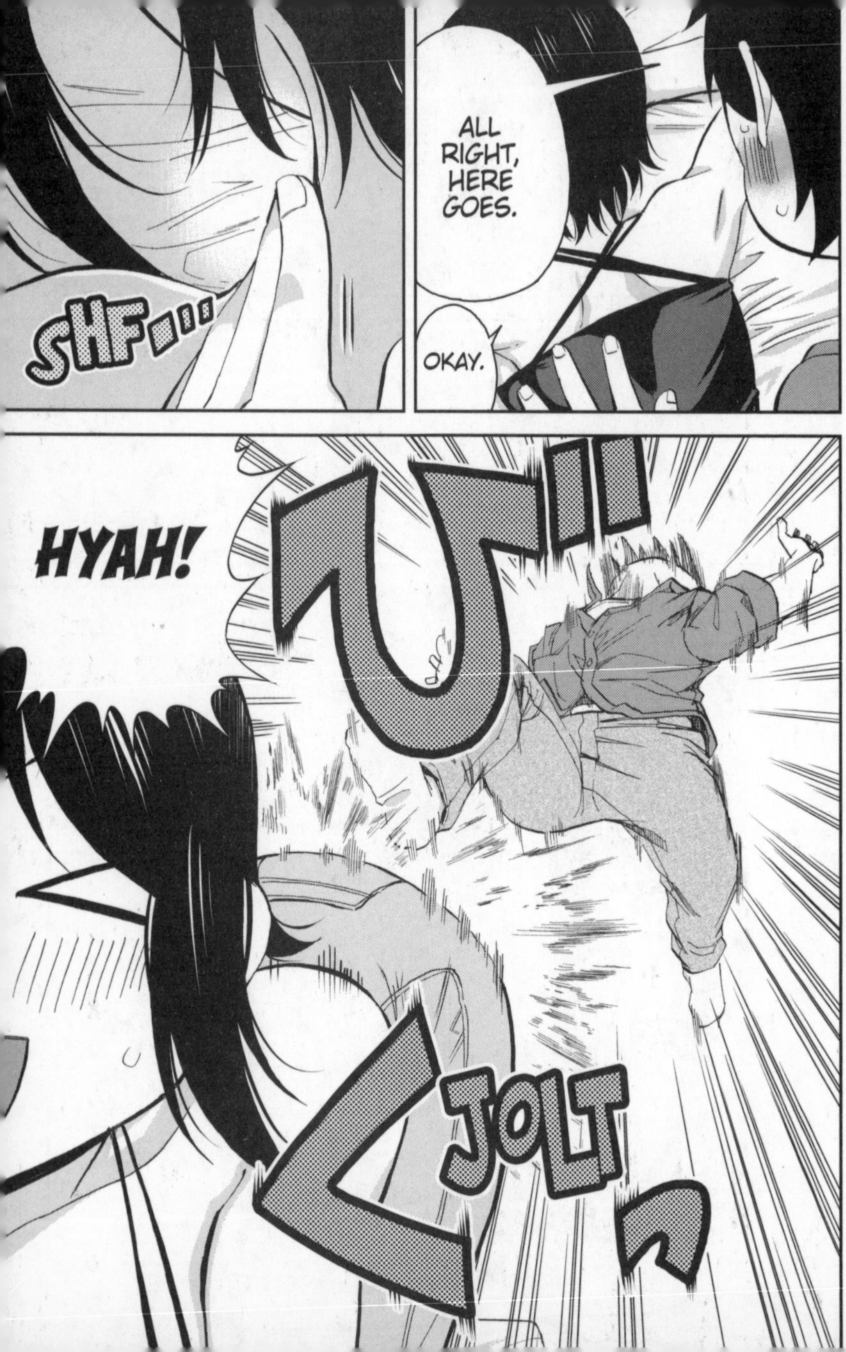
ALL RIGHT, HERE GOES.
OKAY.
SHF...
HYAH!
JOLT

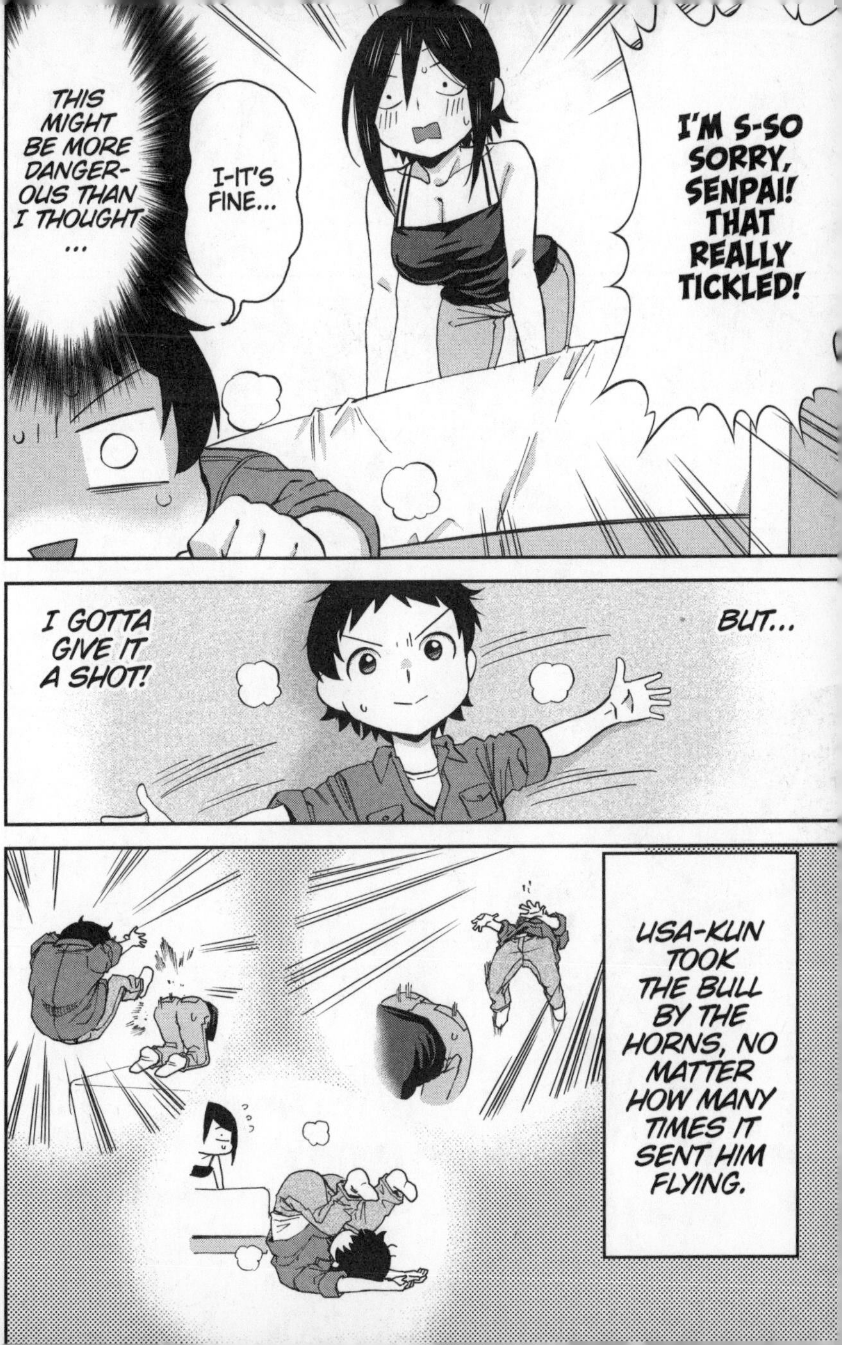
I'M S-SO SORRY, SENPAI! THAT REALLY TICKLED!
I-IT'S FINE...
THIS MIGHT BE MORE DANGER-OUS THAN I THOUGHT ...
BUT...
I GOTTA GIVE IT A SHOT!
USA-KUN TOOK THE BULL BY THE HORNS, NO MATTER HOW MANY TIMES IT SENT HIM FLYING.

THAT'S OKAY.

HOW'S THIS?

HUH?

AH HA HA! PEACHY.

SORRY ABOUT ALL THAT, SENPAI. ARE YOU ALL RIGHT?

RAGGED

IT SHOULD BE SMOOTH SAILING FROM HERE ON OUT.

I THINK I'VE FOUND ALL HER TICKLISH POINTS.

NN...!

UM, SEN-PAI...

N-NO...

S-SORRY!! DID THAT HURT?

S-SURE...

I THINK THAT'S THE SPOT. PLEASE, KEEP GOING.

NN...!

AH...!

RIGHT THERE! THAT FEELS AMAZING!

S-SENPAI...

HN...!!

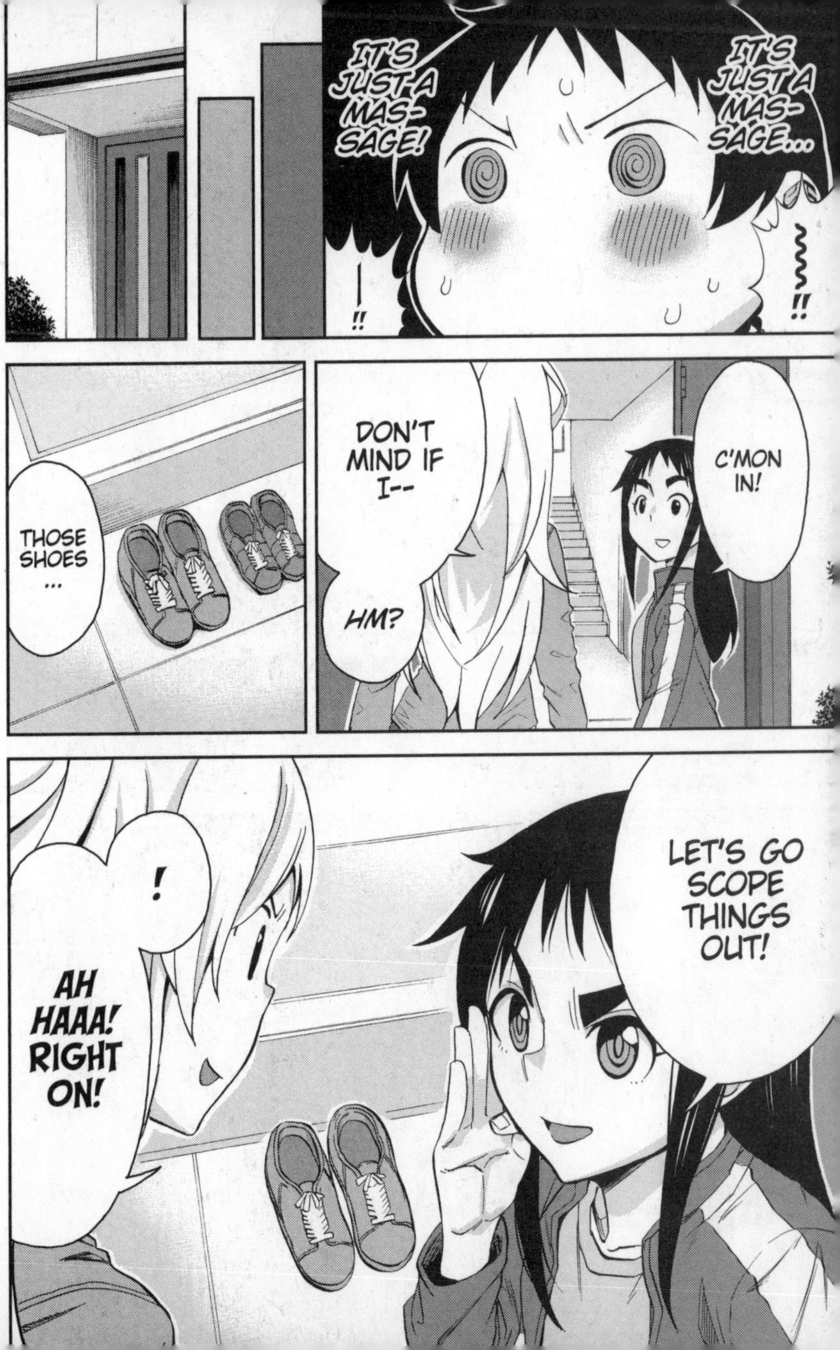
IT'S JUST A MAS-SAGE...
IT'S JUST A MAS-SAGE!
!!
!!
C'MON IN!
DON'T MIND IF I--
HM?
THOSE SHOES ...
LET'S GO SCOPE THINGS OUT!
!
AH HAAA! RIGHT ON!

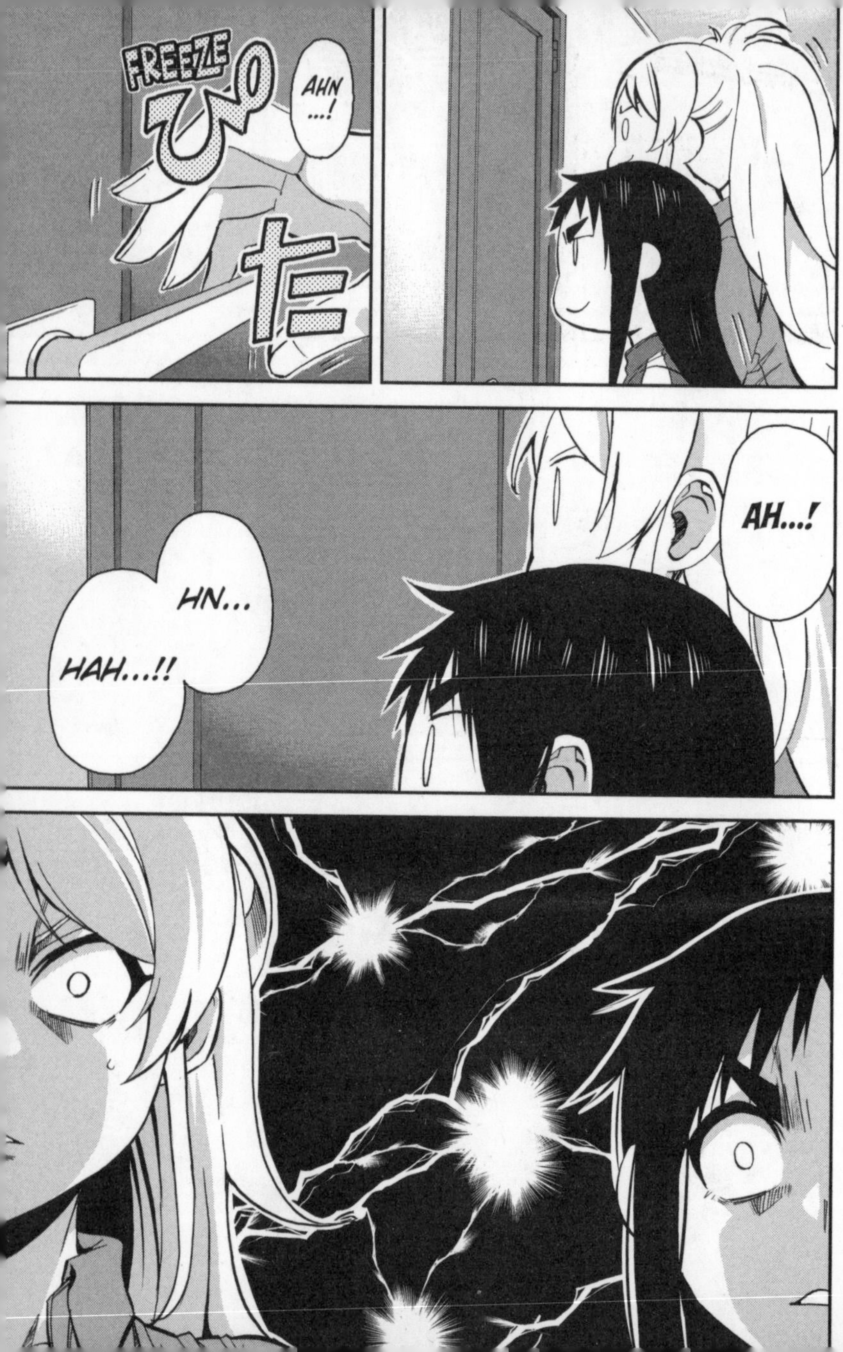
FREEZE
ぴた
AHN ...!
AH...!
HN... HAH...!!

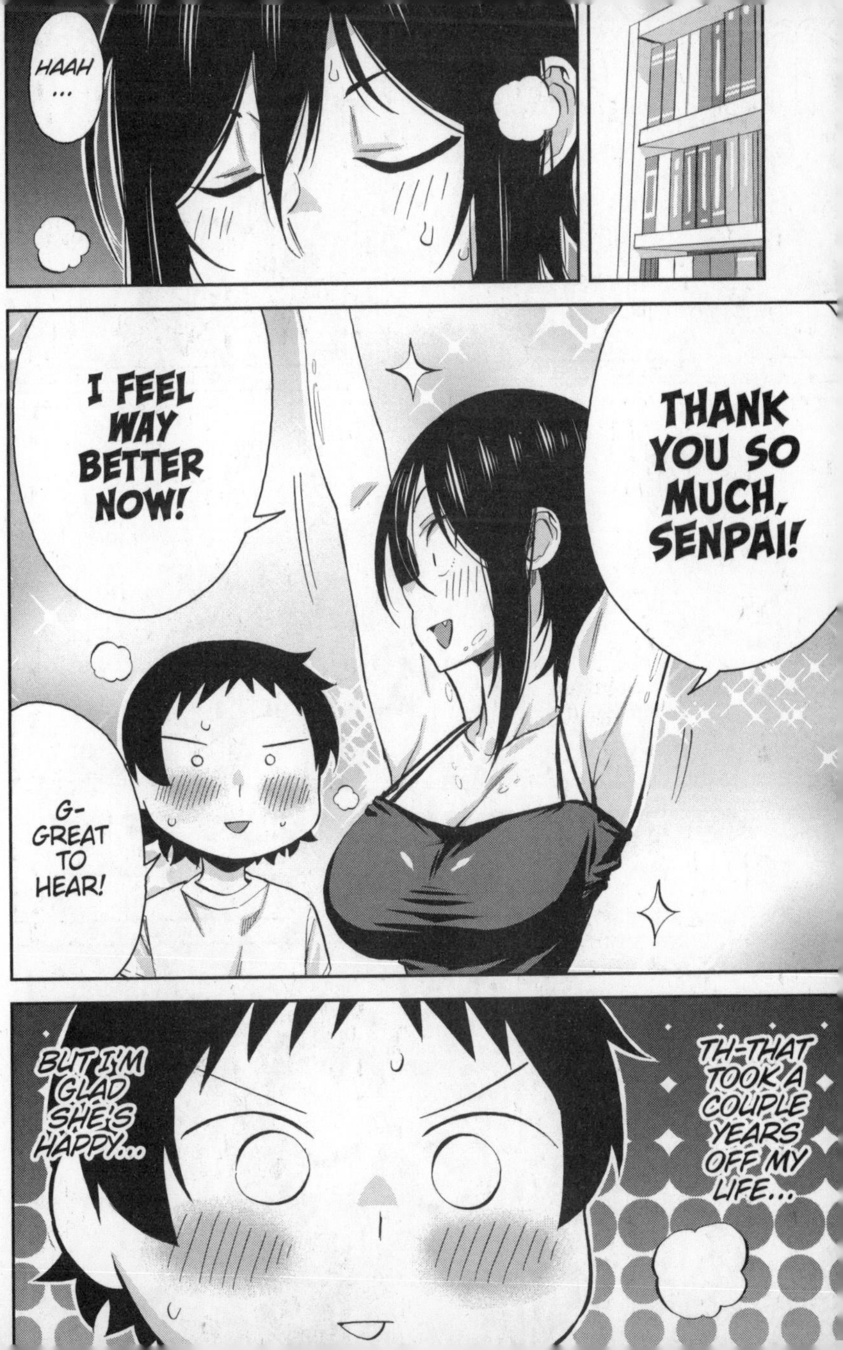
HAAH ...
THANK YOU SO MUCH, SENPAI!
I FEEL WAY BETTER NOW!
G-GREAT TO HEAR!
TH-THAT TOOK A COUPLE YEARS OFF MY LIFE...
BUT I'M GLAD SHE'S HAPPY...

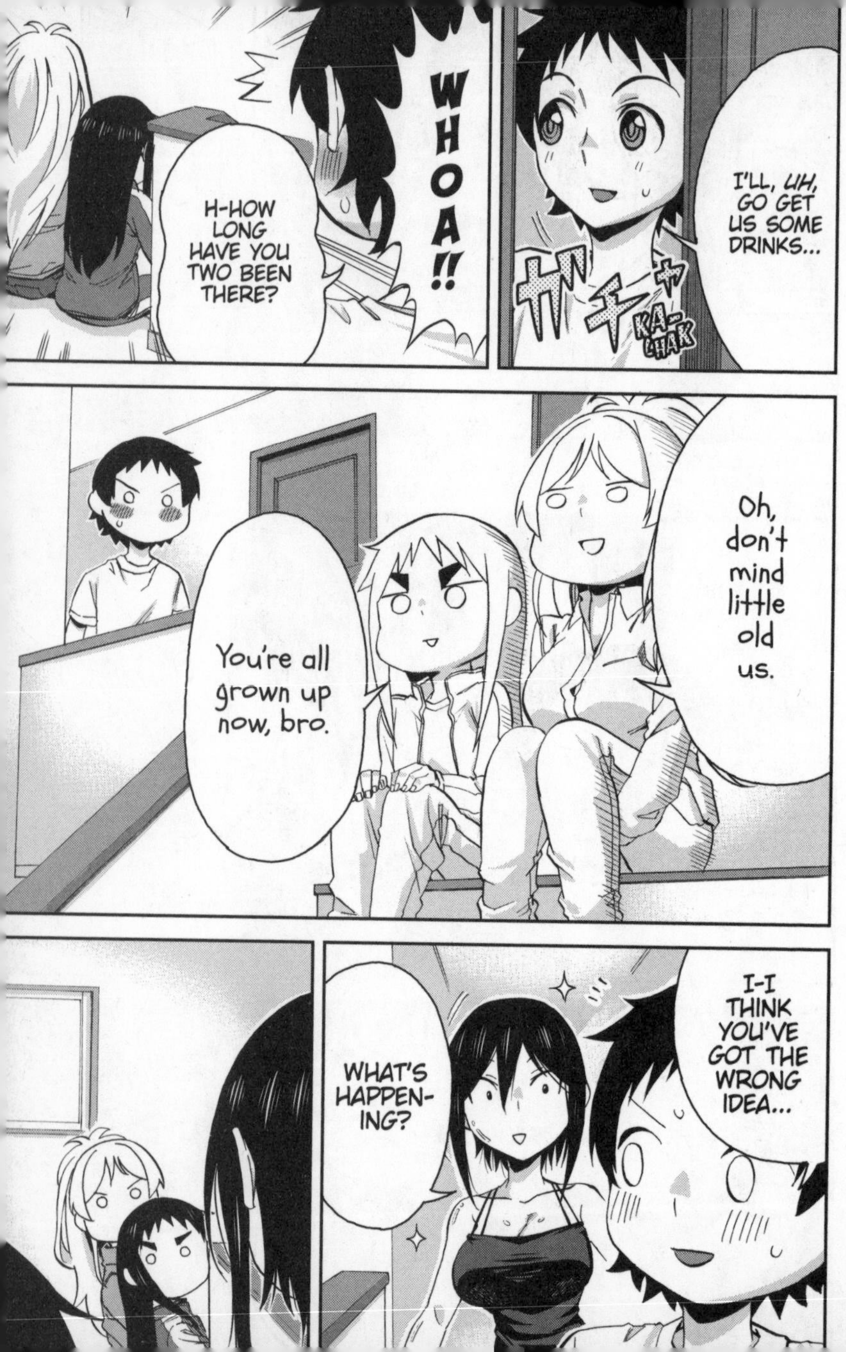
I'LL, UH, GO GET US SOME DRINKS...
KA-CHAK
WHOA!!
H-HOW LONG HAVE YOU TWO BEEN THERE?
Oh, don't mind little old us.
You're all grown up now, bro.
I-I THINK YOU'VE GOT THE WRONG IDEA...
WHAT'S HAPPEN-ING?

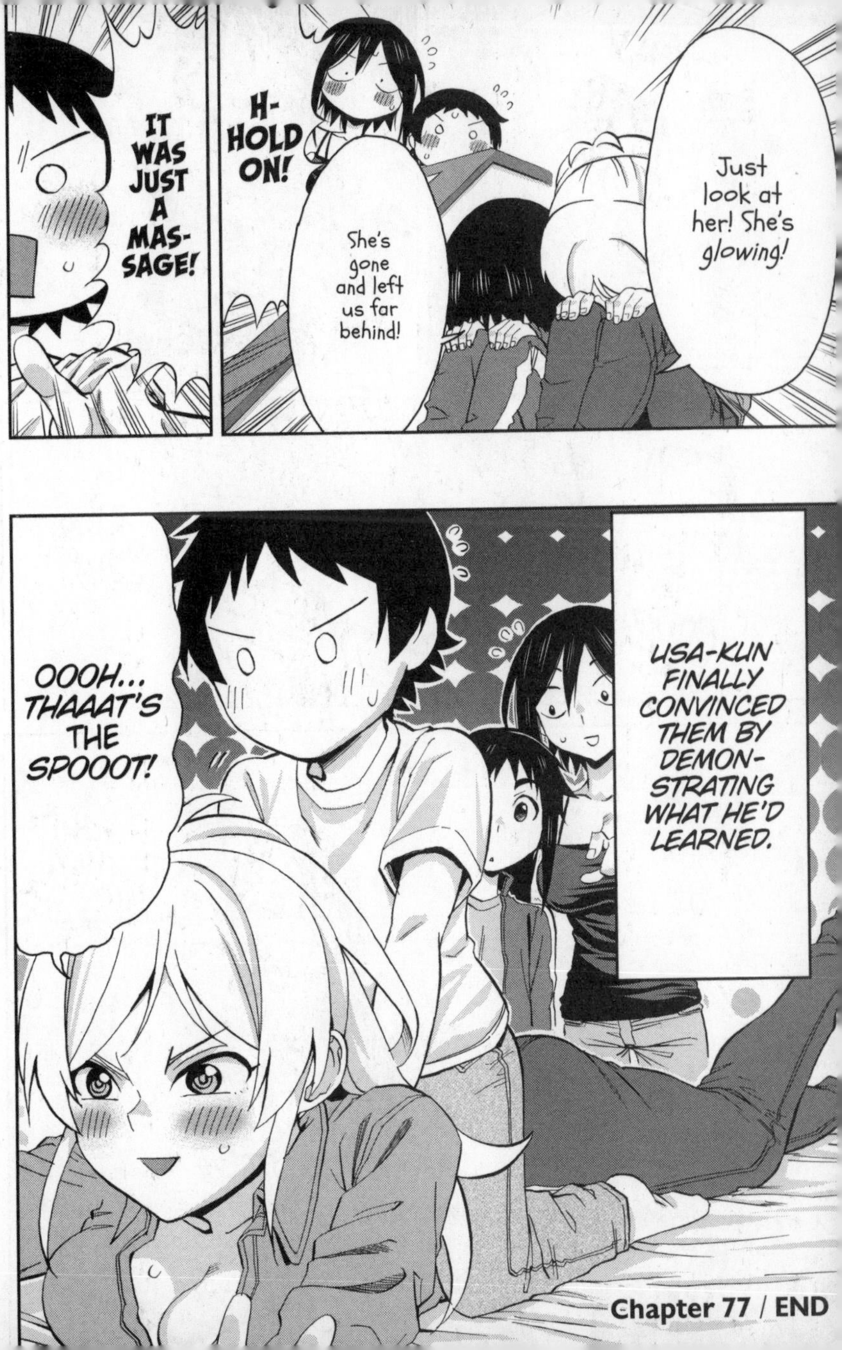
Just look at her! She's glowing!
She's gone and left us far behind!
H-HOLD ON!
IT WAS JUST A MAS-SAGE!
USA-KUN FINALLY CONVINCED THEM BY DEMON-STRATING WHAT HE'D LEARNED.
OOOH... THAAAT'S THE SPOOOT!
Chapter 77 / END

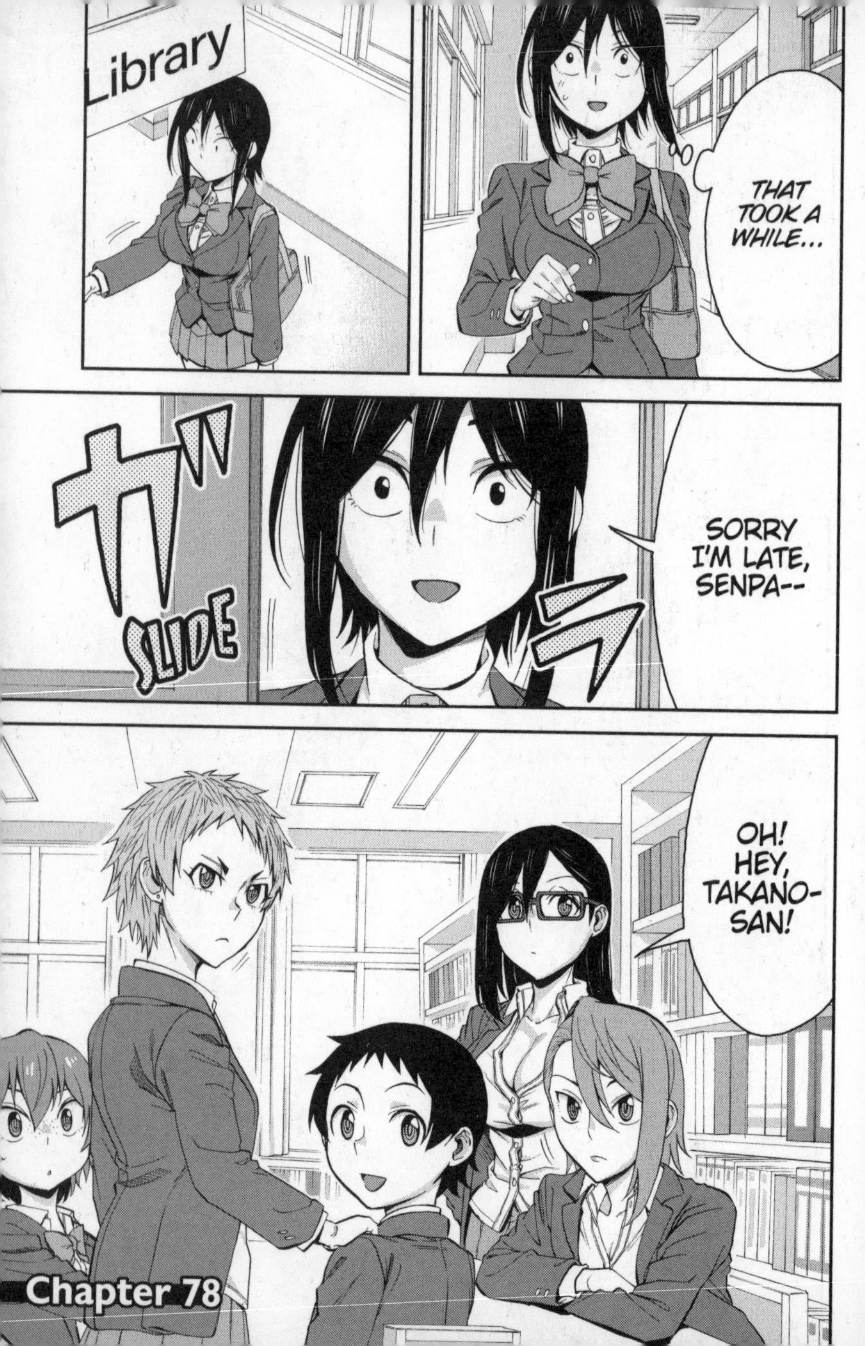
THAT TOOK A WHILE...
Library
ガラ
SLIDE
SORRY I'M LATE, SENPA--
OH! HEY, TAKANO-SAN!
Chapter 78

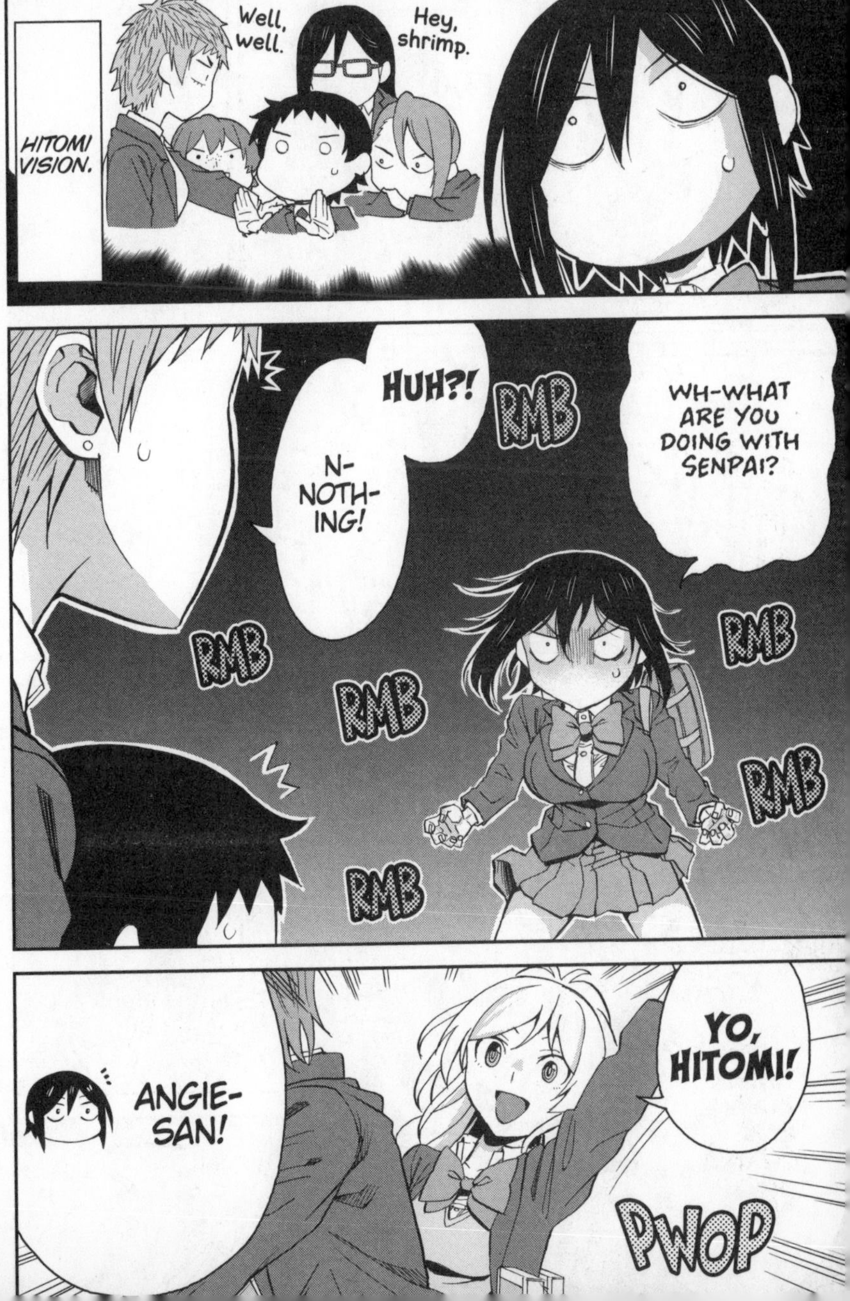
Hey, shrimp.
Well, well.
HITOMI VISION.
WH-WHAT ARE YOU DOING WITH SENPAI?
RMB
HUH?!
N-NOTH-ING!
RMB
RMB
RMB
RMB
RMB
YO, HITOMI!
PWOP
ANGIE-SAN!

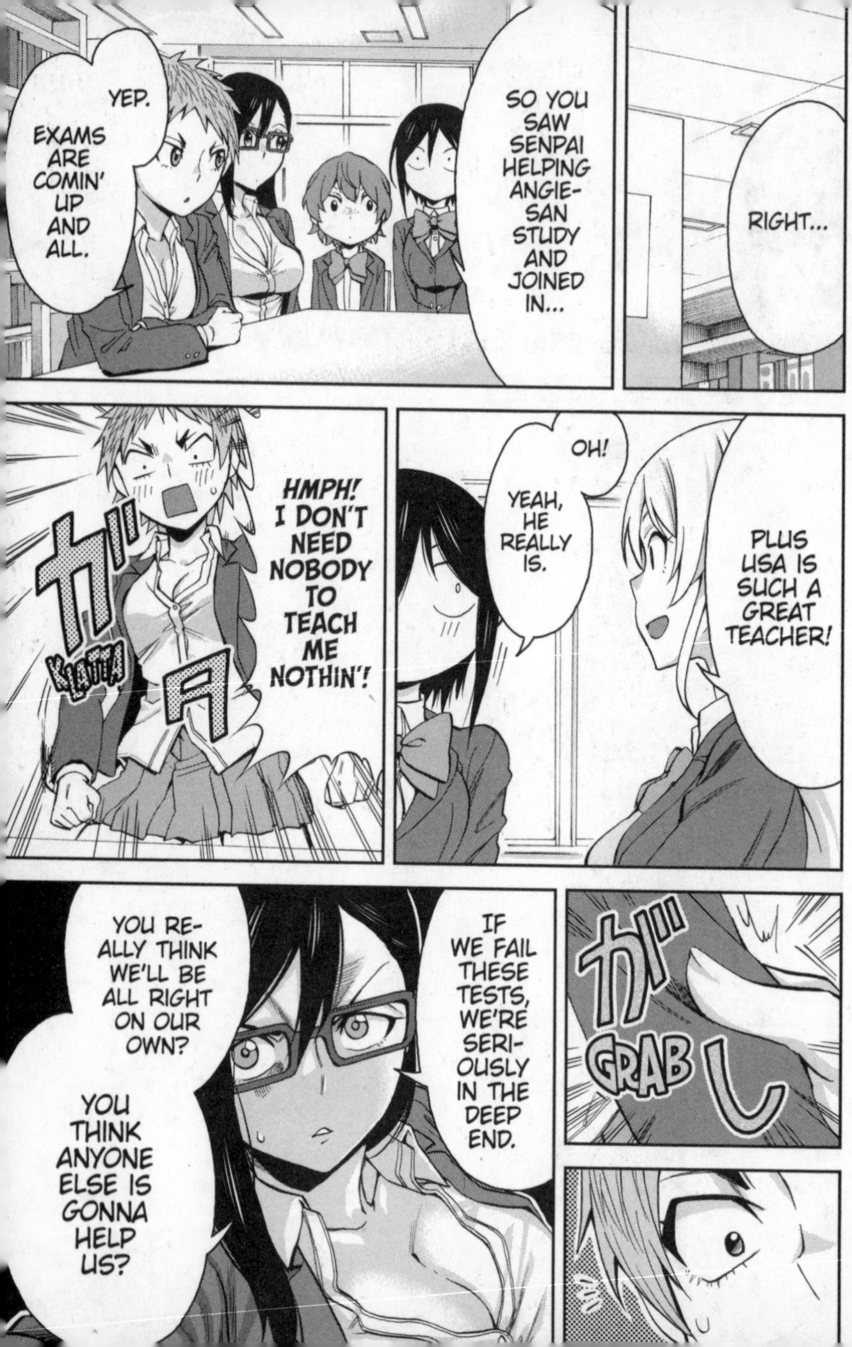
RIGHT...
SO YOU SAW SENPAI HELPING ANGIE-SAN STUDY AND JOINED IN...
YEP. EXAMS ARE COMIN' UP AND ALL.
PLUS USA IS SUCH A GREAT TEACHER!
OH! YEAH, HE REALLY IS.
HMPH! I DON'T NEED NOBODY TO TEACH ME NOTHIN'!
KLATTA
GRAB
IF WE FAIL THESE TESTS, WE'RE SERIOUSLY IN THE DEEP END.
YOU REALLY THINK WE'LL BE ALL RIGHT ON OUR OWN?
YOU THINK ANYONE ELSE IS GONNA HELP US?

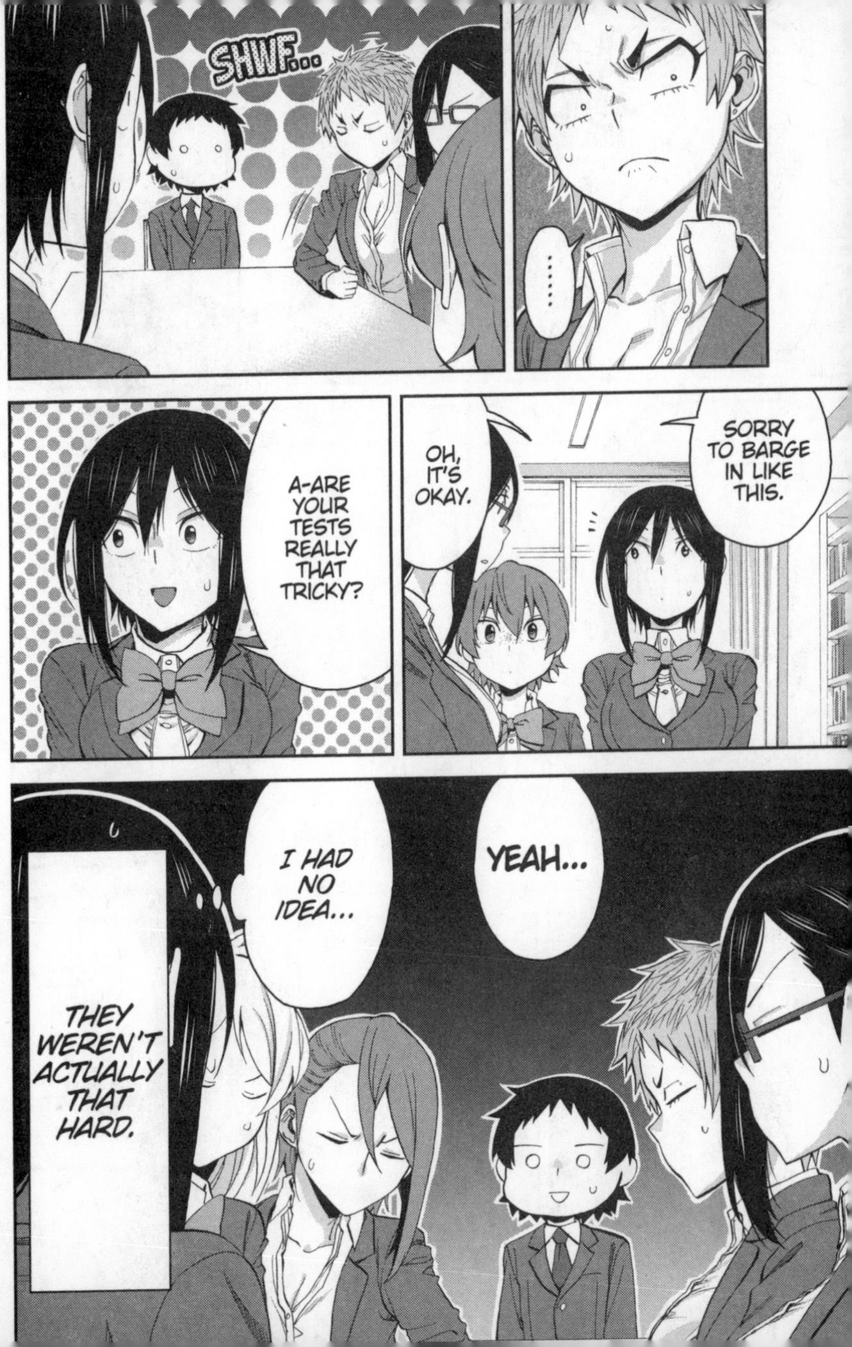
......
SHWF...
SORRY TO BARGE IN LIKE THIS.
OH, IT'S OKAY.
A-ARE YOUR TESTS REALLY THAT TRICKY?
YEAH...
I HAD NO IDEA...
THEY WEREN'T ACTUALLY THAT HARD.

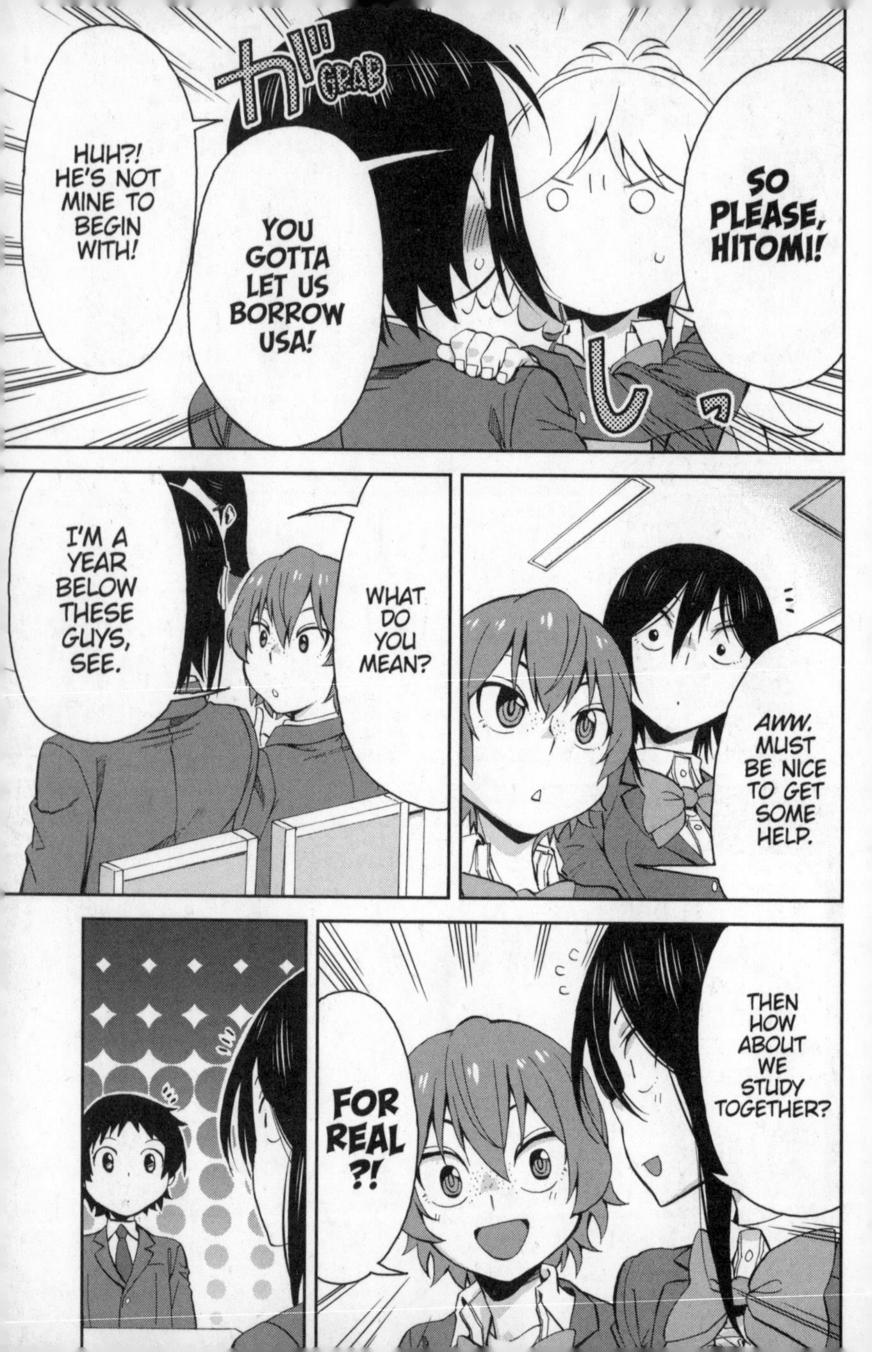
GRAB
SO PLEASE, HITOMI!
YOU GOTTA LET US BORROW USA!
HUH?! HE'S NOT MINE TO BEGIN WITH!
AWW. MUST BE NICE TO GET SOME HELP.
WHAT DO YOU MEAN?
I'M A YEAR BELOW THESE GUYS, SEE.
THEN HOW ABOUT WE STUDY TOGETHER?
FOR REAL?!

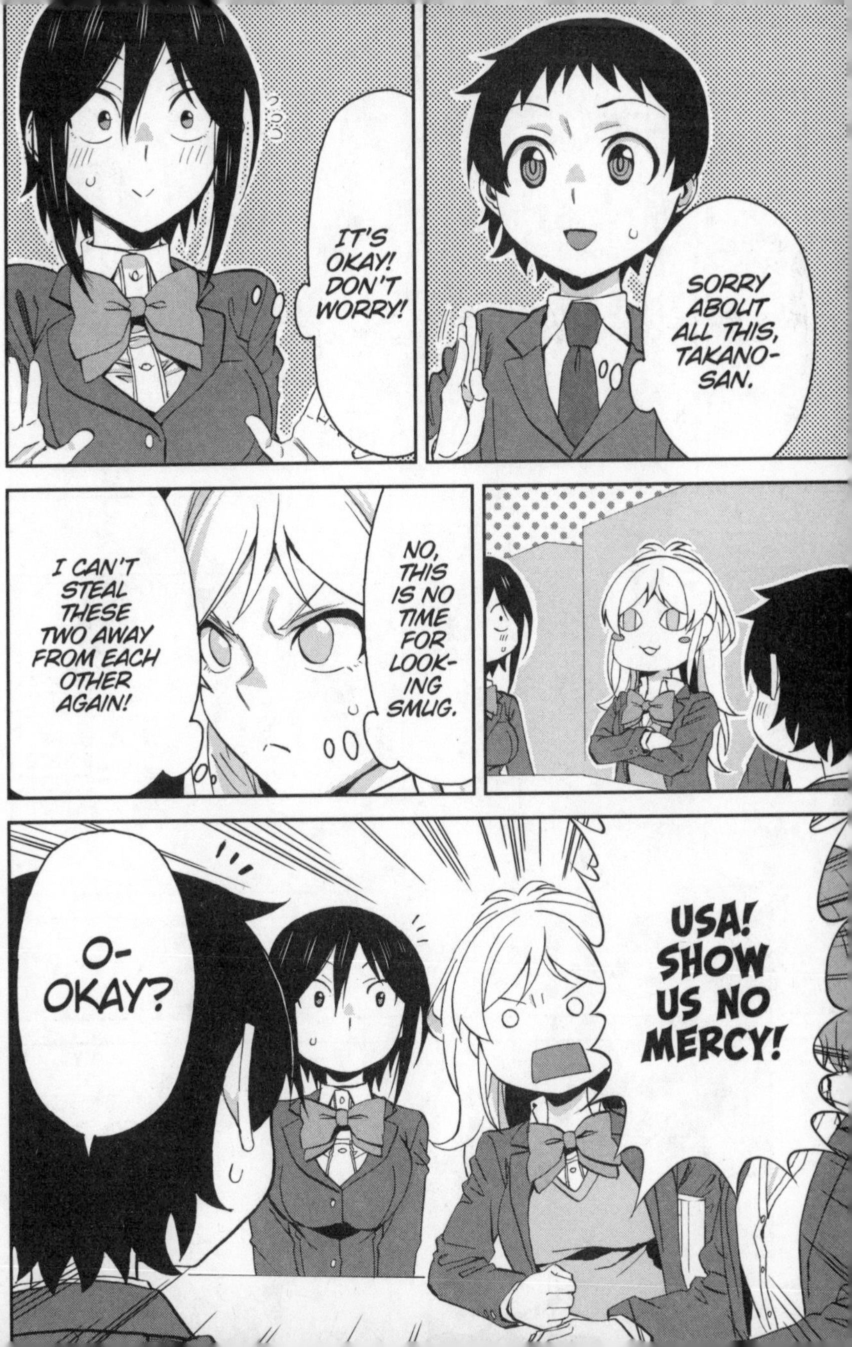
SORRY ABOUT ALL THIS, TAKANO-SAN.
IT'S OKAY! DON'T WORRY!
NO, THIS IS NO TIME FOR LOOKING SMUG.
I CAN'T STEAL THESE TWO AWAY FROM EACH OTHER AGAIN!
USA! SHOW US NO MERCY!
O-OKAY?

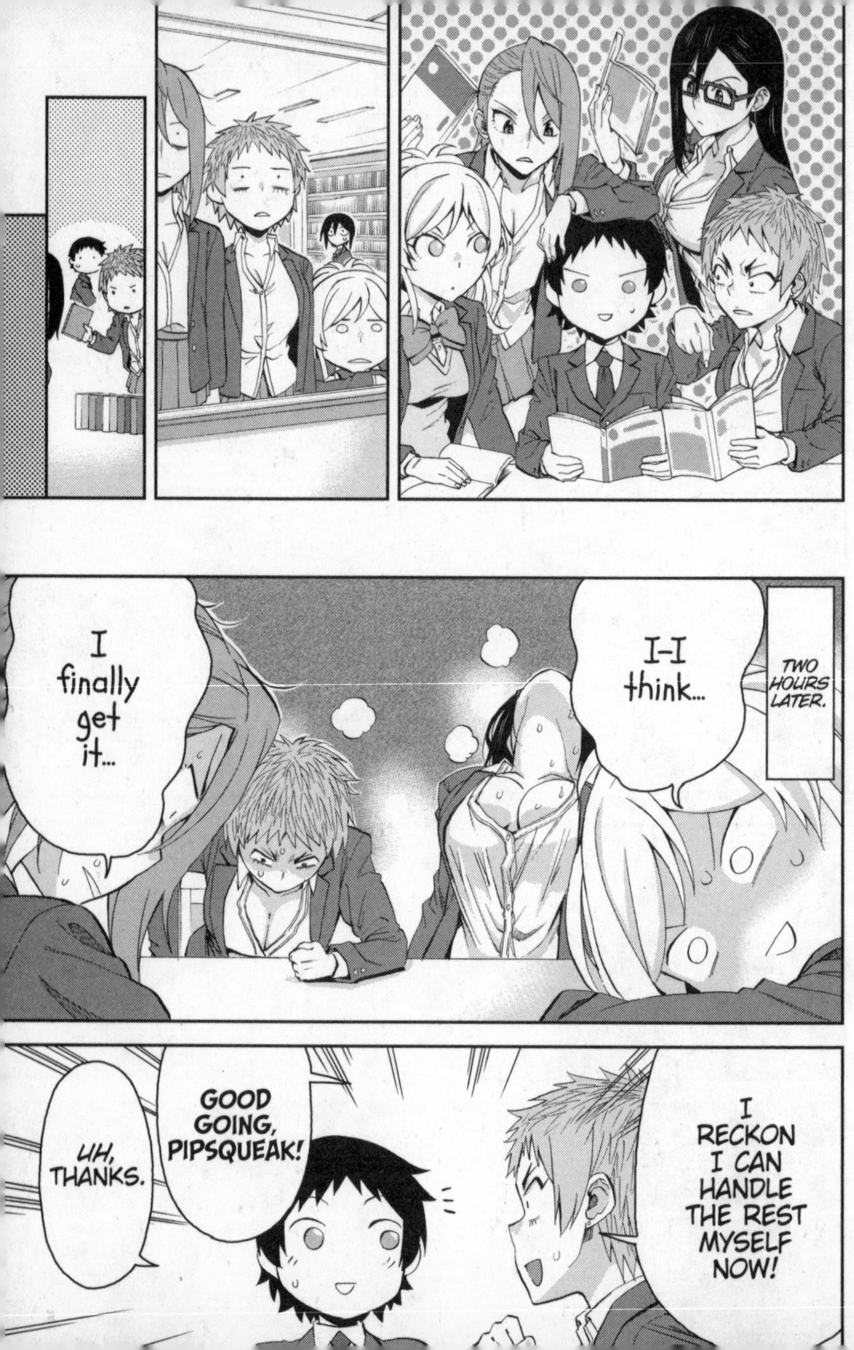
TWO HOURS LATER.
I-I think...
I finally get it...
I RECKON I CAN HANDLE THE REST MYSELF NOW!
GOOD GOING, PIPSQUEAK!
UH, THANKS.

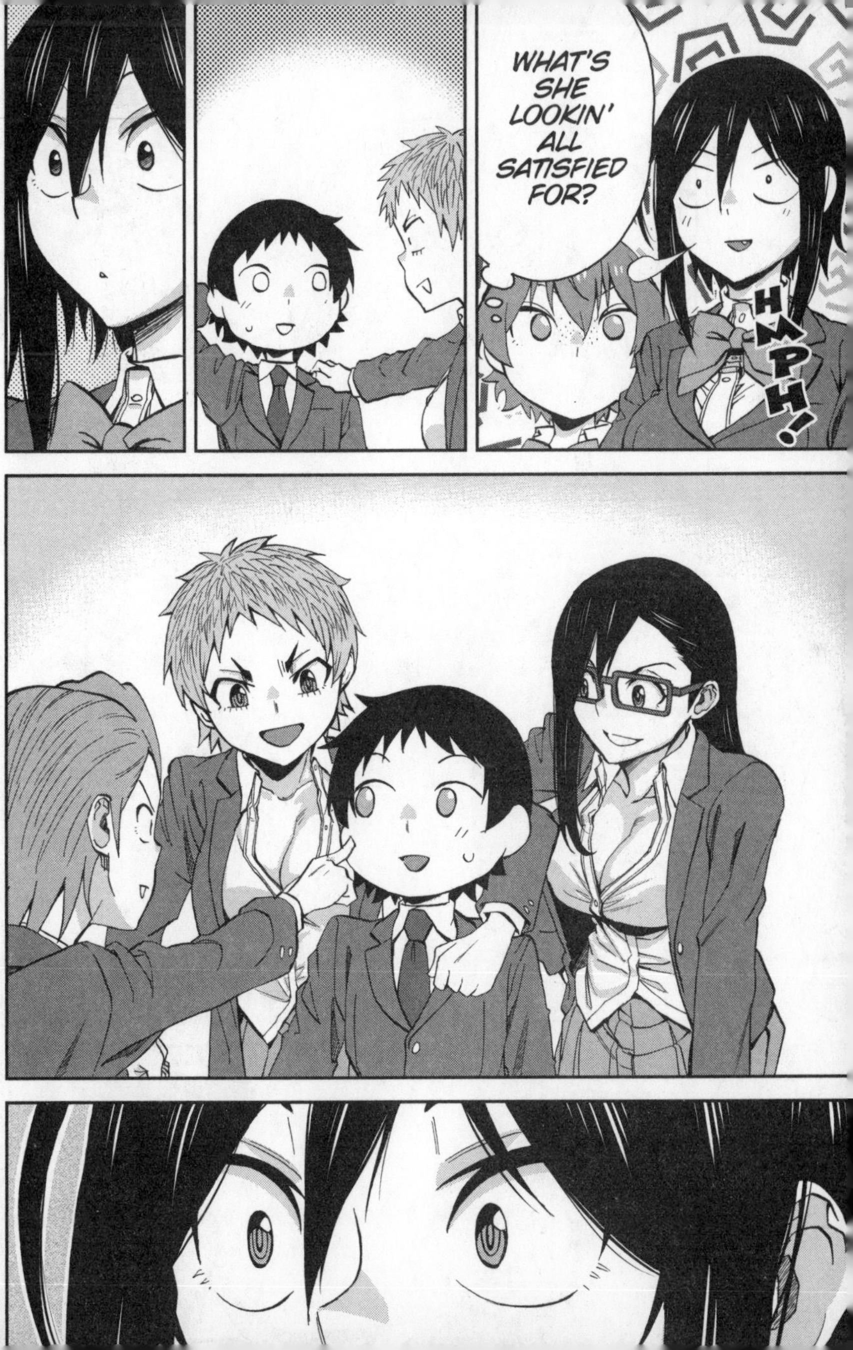
WHAT'S SHE LOOKIN' ALL SATISFIED FOR?
HMPH!

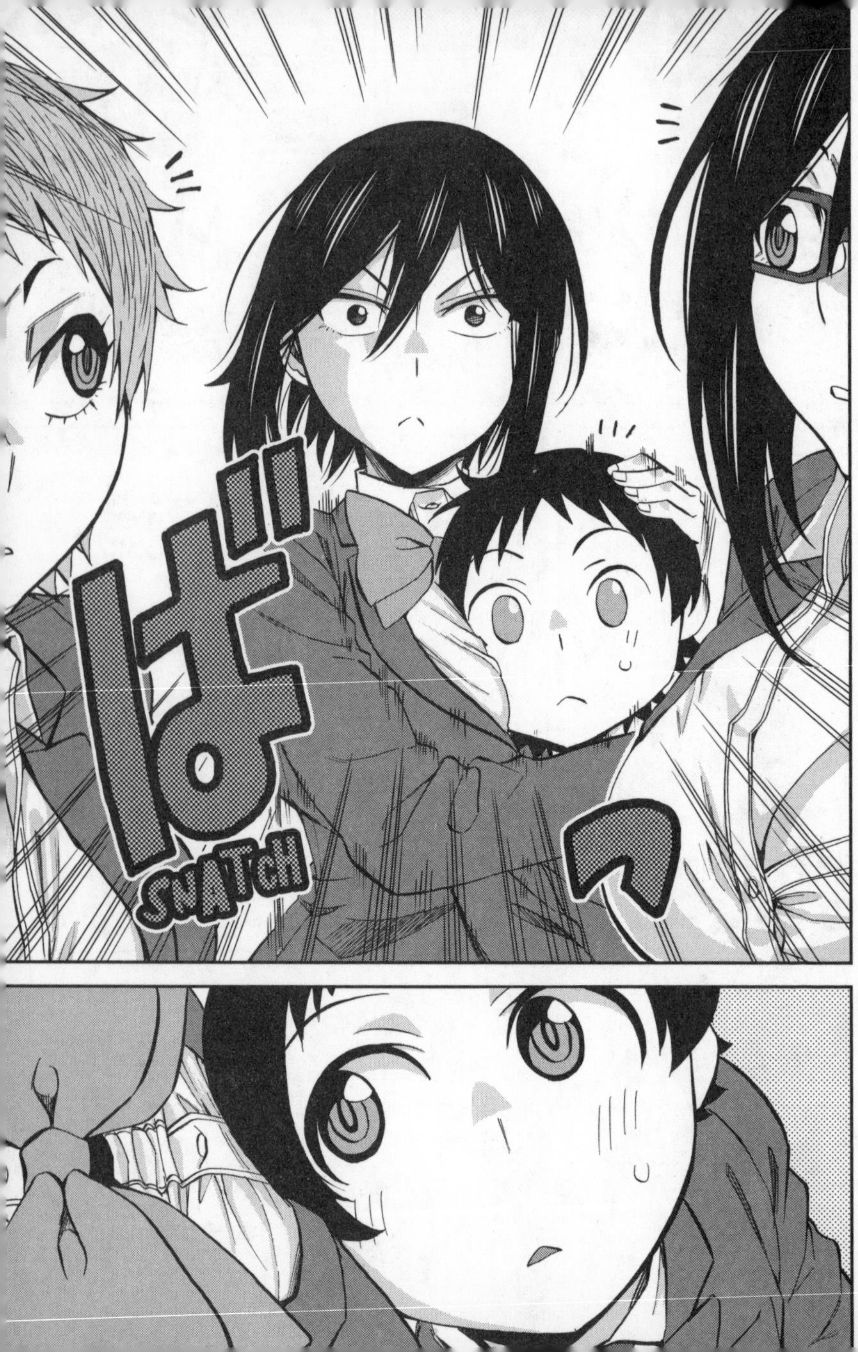
ばっ
SNATCH

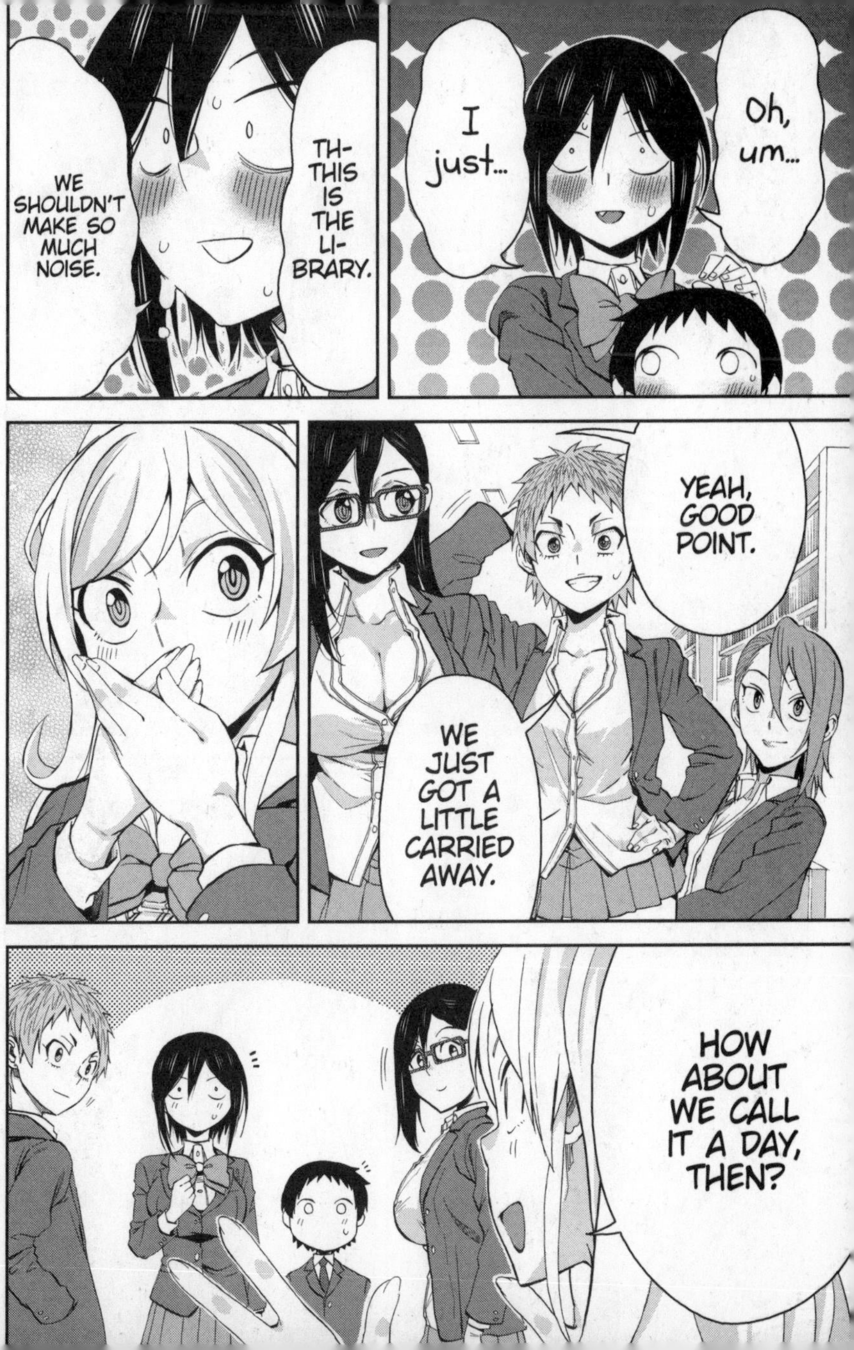
Oh, um...
I just...
TH-THIS IS THE LI-BRARY.
WE SHOULDN'T MAKE SO MUCH NOISE.
YEAH, GOOD POINT.
WE JUST GOT A LITTLE CARRIED AWAY.
HOW ABOUT WE CALL IT A DAY, THEN?

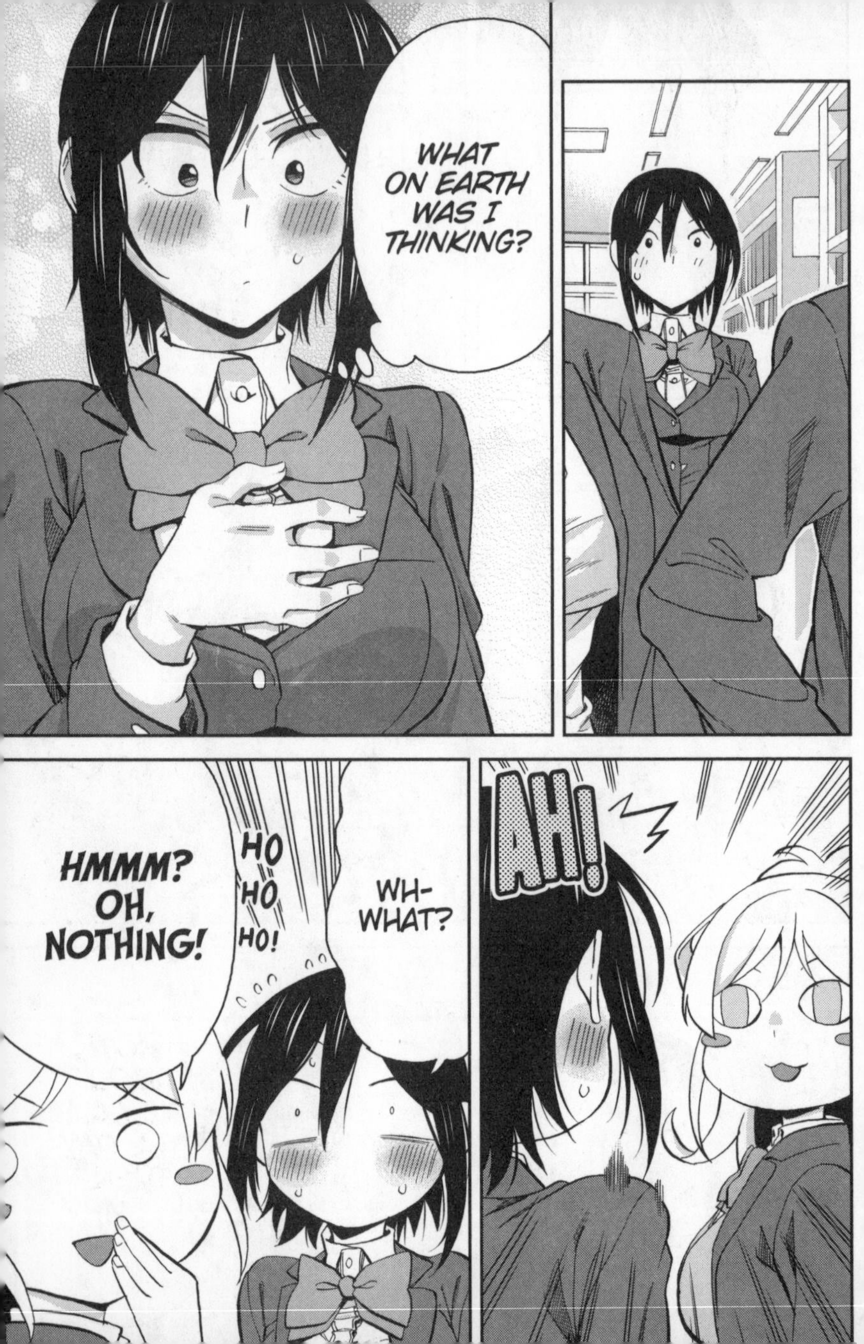
WHAT ON EARTH WAS I THINKING?
AH!
WH- WHAT?
HO HO HO!
HMMM? OH, NOTHING!

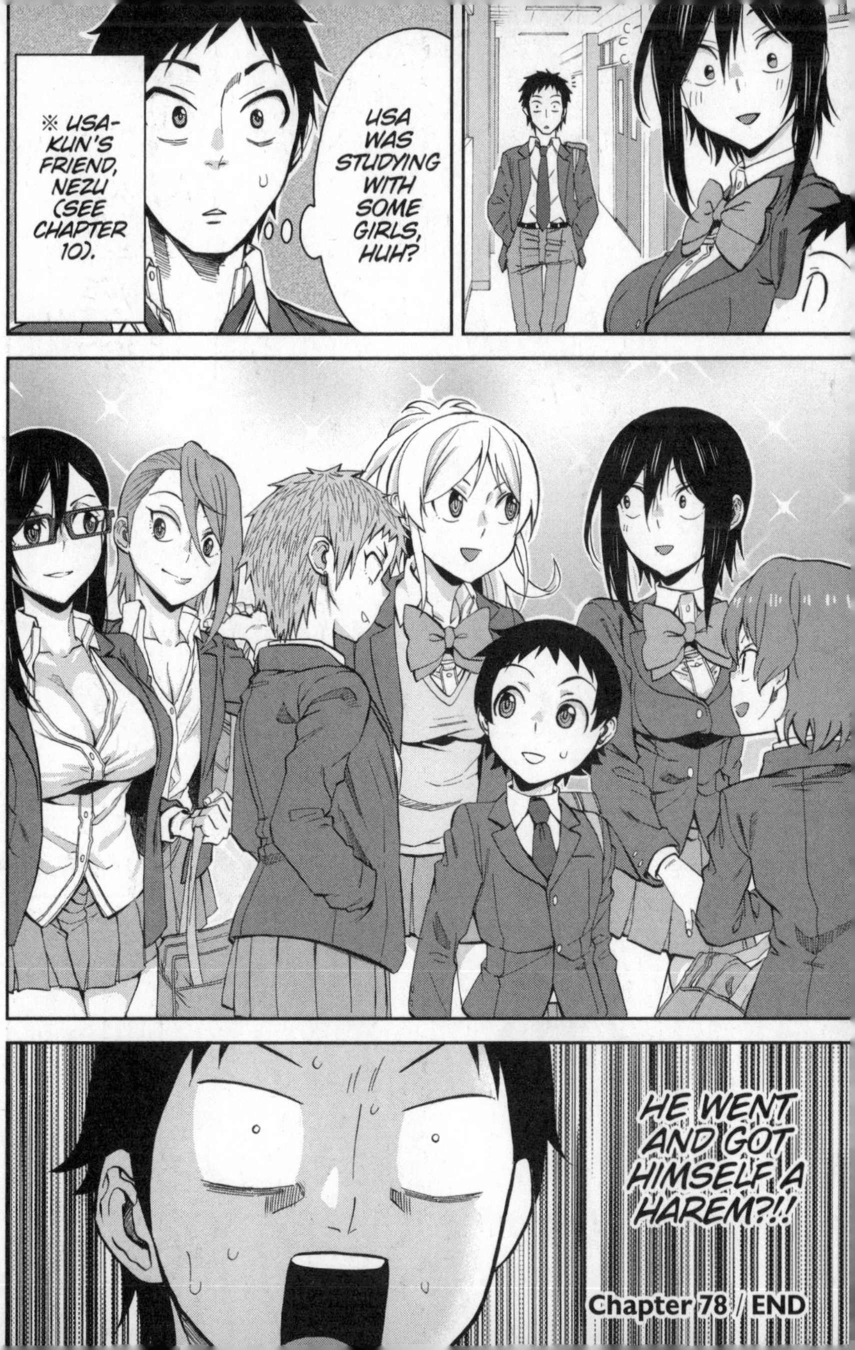
USA WAS STUDYING WITH SOME GIRLS, HUH?
※ USA-KUN'S FRIEND, NEZU (SEE CHAPTER 10).
HE WENT AND GOT HIMSELF A HAREM?!!
Chapter 78 / END

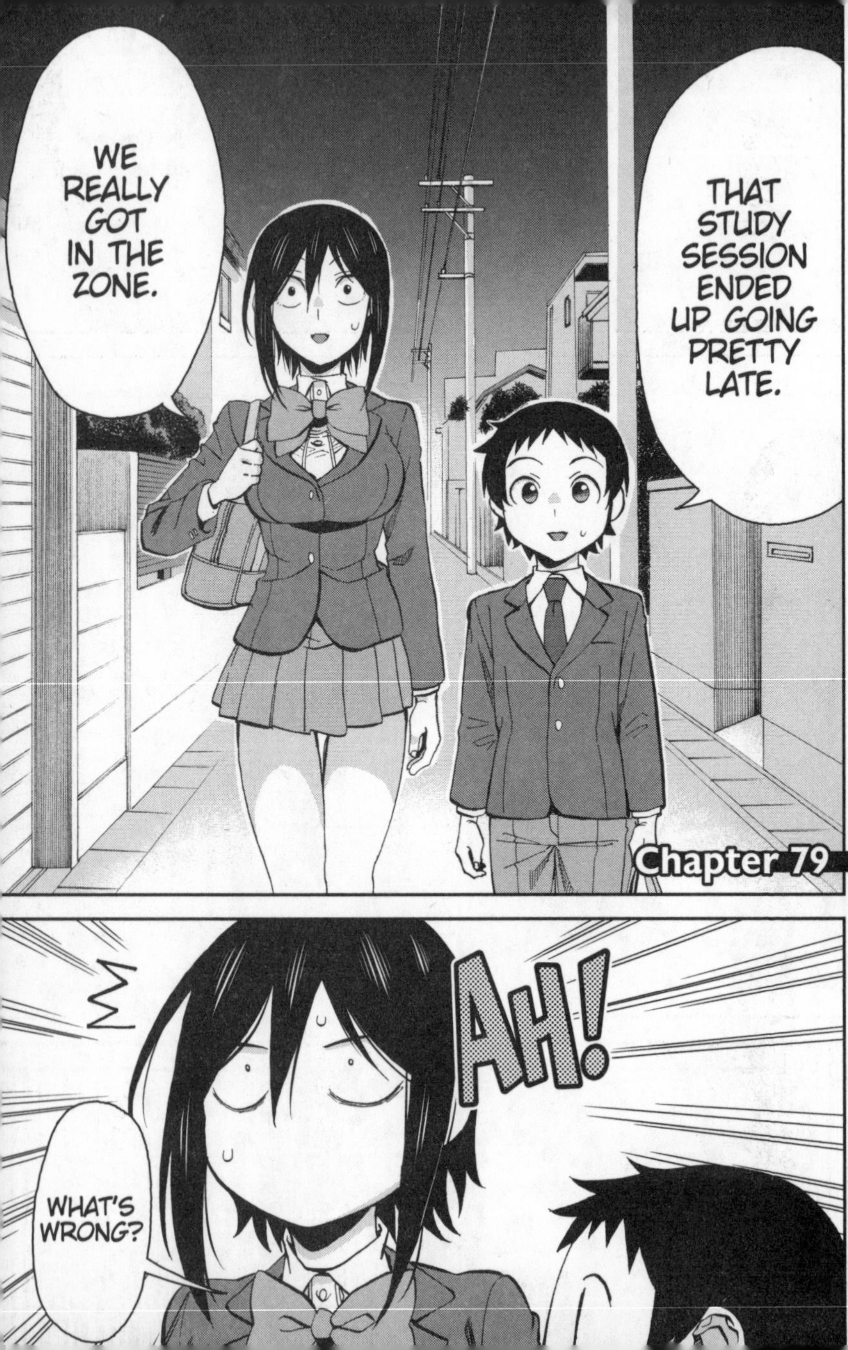
THAT STUDY SESSION ENDED UP GOING PRETTY LATE.
WE REALLY GOT IN THE ZONE.
Chapter 79
AH!
WHAT'S WRONG?

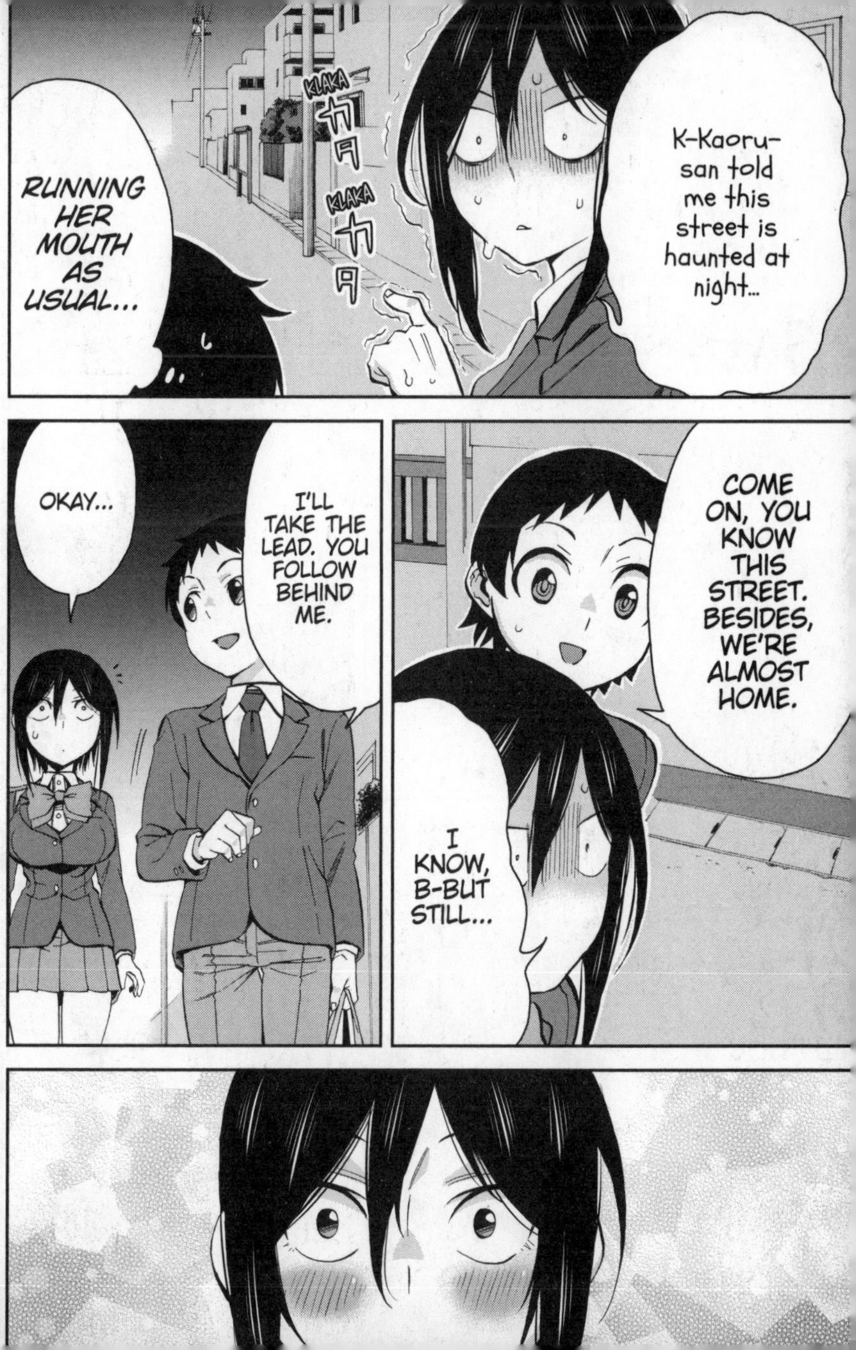
K-Kaoru-san told me this street is haunted at night...
KLAKA
KLAKA
RUNNING HER MOUTH AS USUAL...
COME ON, YOU KNOW THIS STREET. BESIDES, WE'RE ALMOST HOME.
I KNOW, B-BUT STILL...
I'LL TAKE THE LEAD. YOU FOLLOW BEHIND ME.
OKAY...

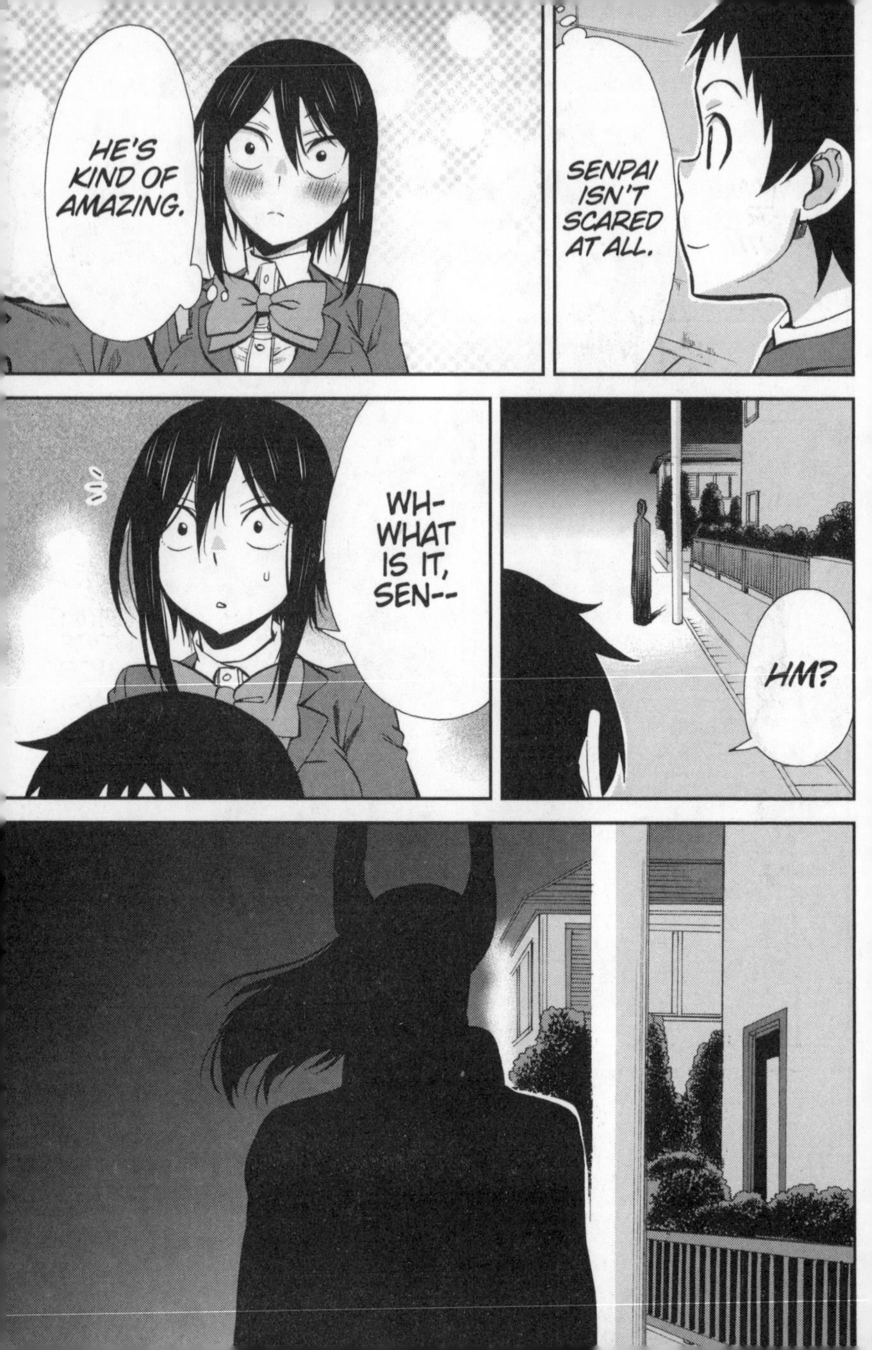
SENPAI ISN'T SCARED AT ALL.
HE'S KIND OF AMAZING.
HM?
WH- WHAT IS IT, SEN--

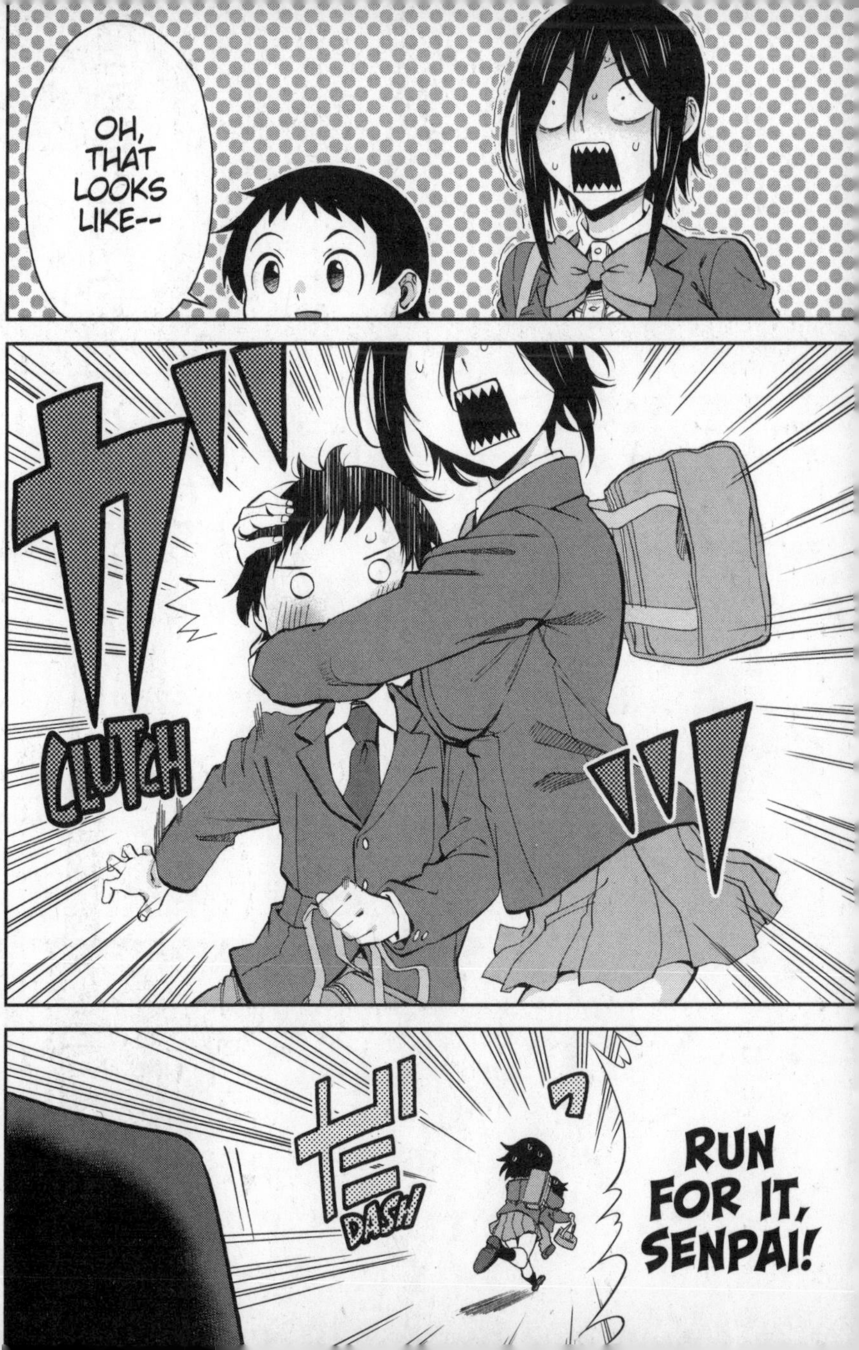
OH, THAT LOOKS LIKE--
CLUTCH
DASH
RUN FOR IT, SENPAI!

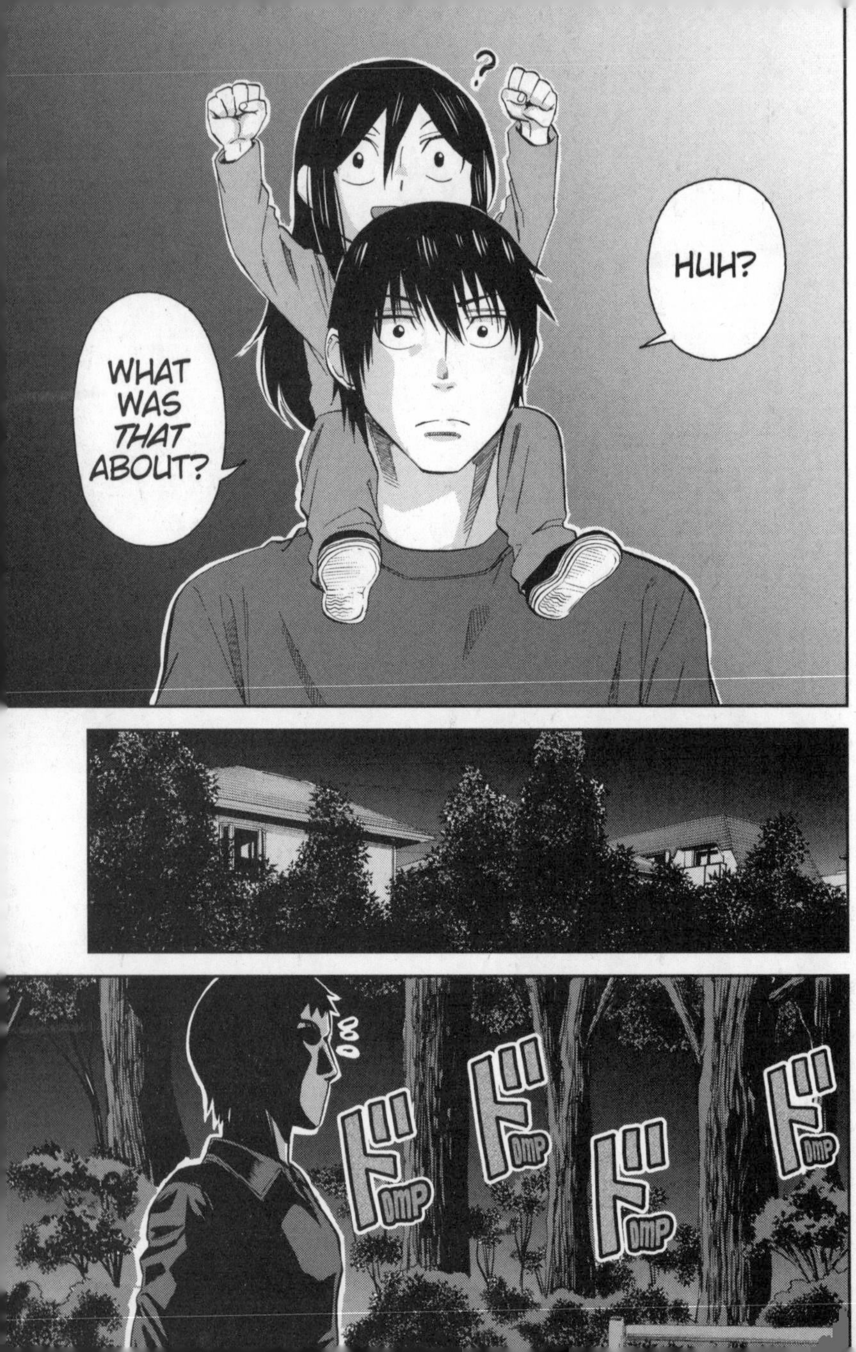
HUH?
WHAT WAS THAT ABOUT?
?
ドOMP
ドOMP
ドOMP
ドOMP

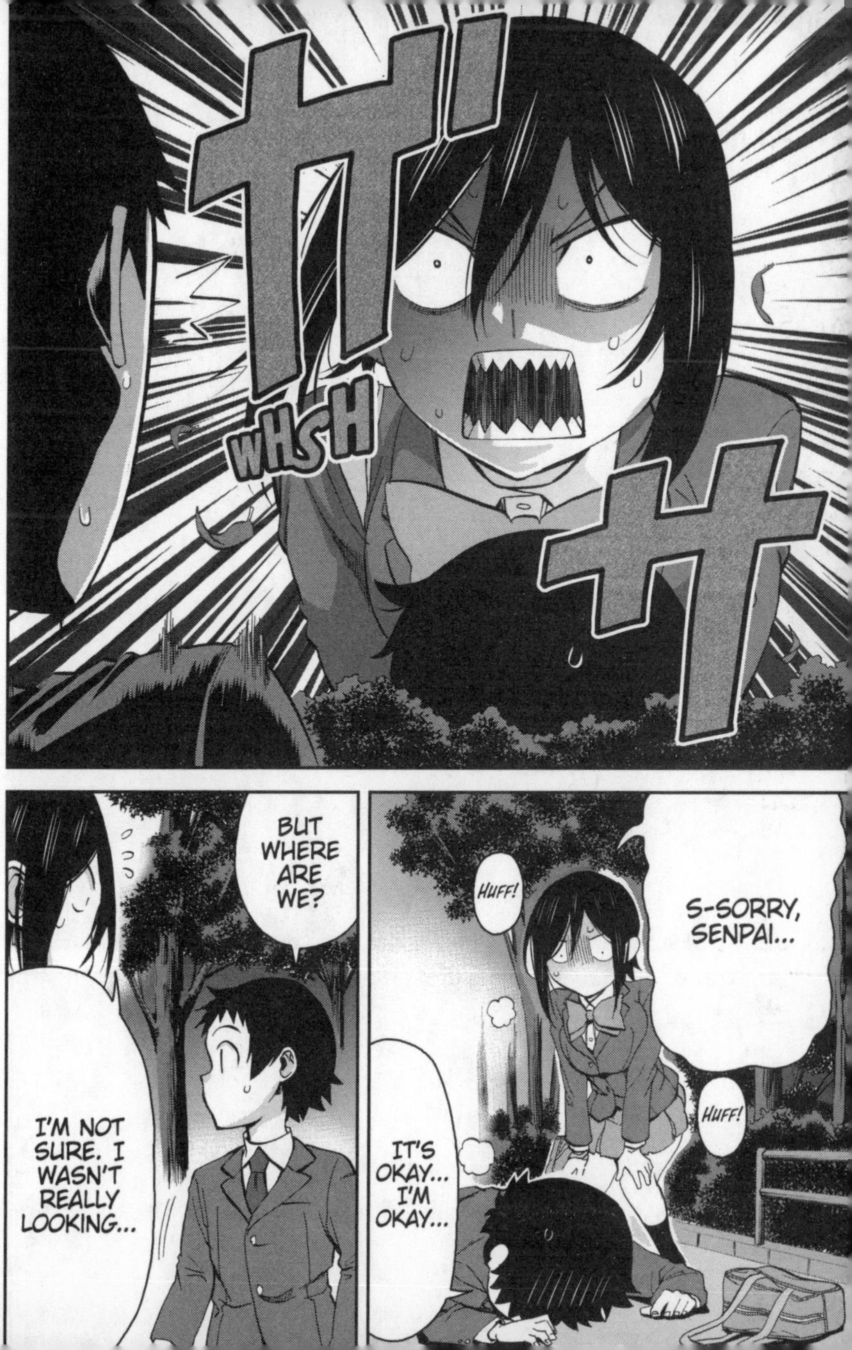
ザ
WHSH
サ
S-SORRY, SENPAI...
HUFF!
HUFF!
IT'S OKAY... I'M OKAY...
BUT WHERE ARE WE?
I'M NOT SURE. I WASN'T REALLY LOOKING...

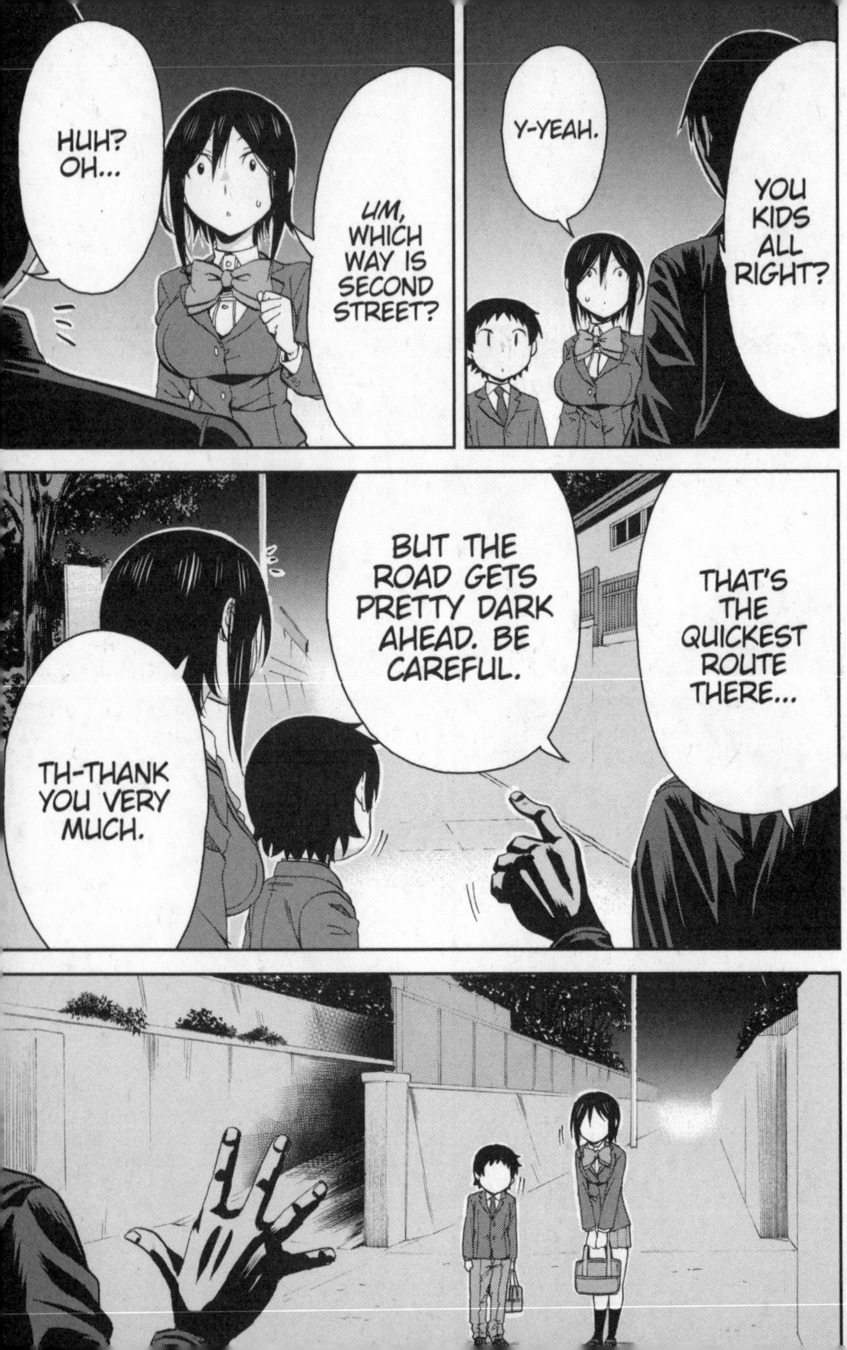
YOU KIDS ALL RIGHT?
Y-YEAH.
UM, WHICH WAY IS SECOND STREET?
HUH? OH...
THAT'S THE QUICKEST ROUTE THERE...
BUT THE ROAD GETS PRETTY DARK AHEAD. BE CAREFUL.
TH-THANK YOU VERY MUCH.

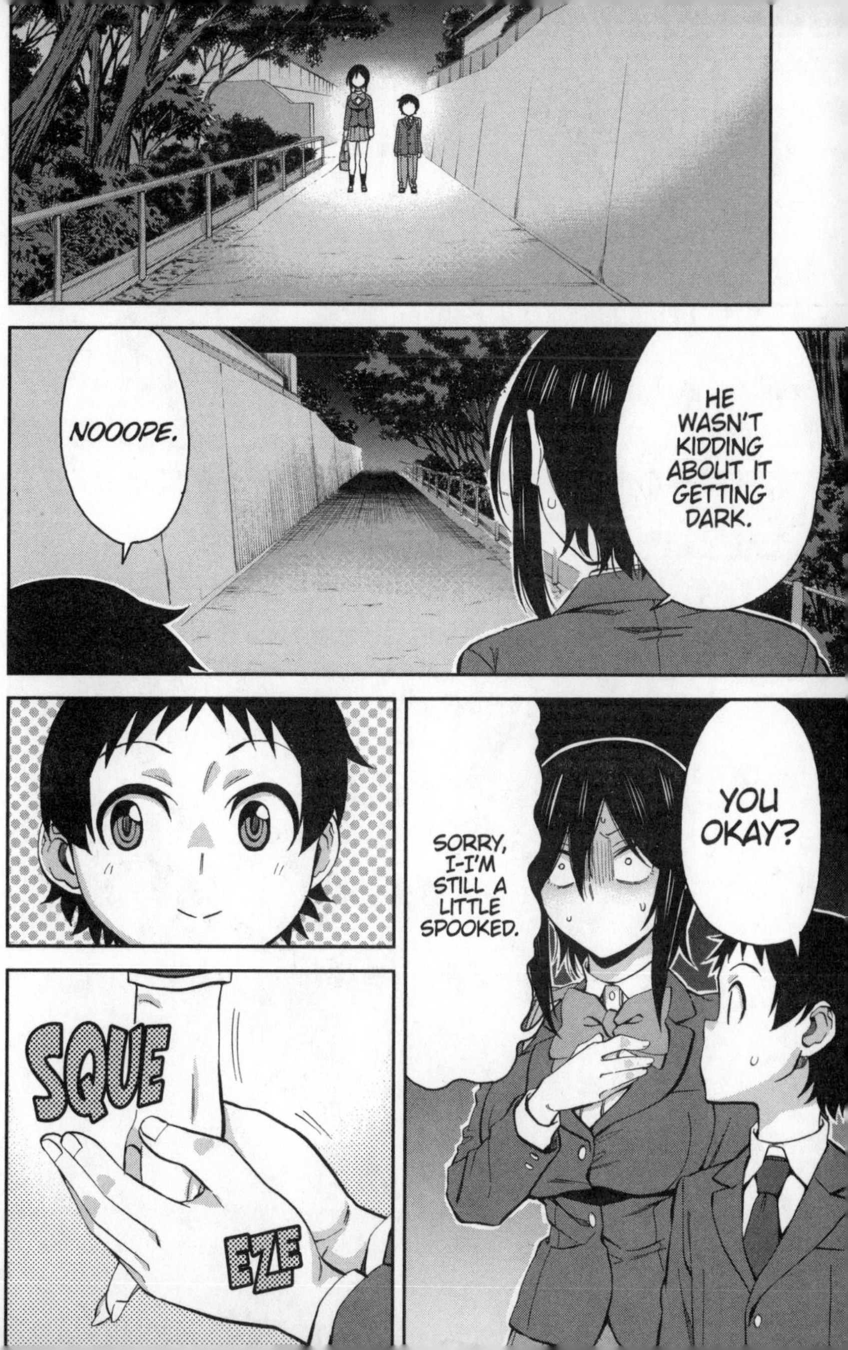
HE WASN'T KIDDING ABOUT IT GETTING DARK.
NOOOPE.
YOU OKAY?
SORRY, I-I'M STILL A LITTLE SPOOKED.
SQUEEZE

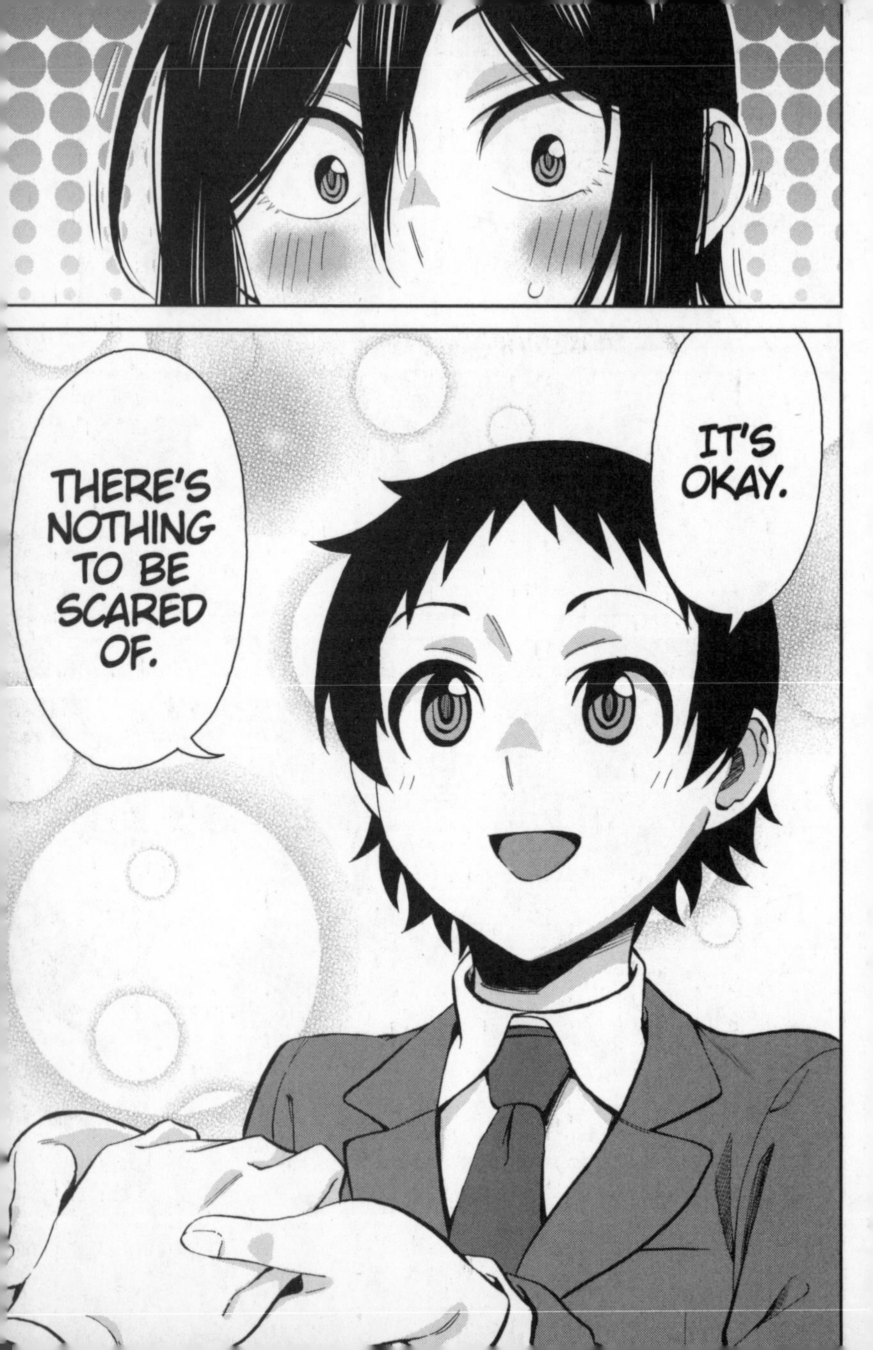
IT'S OKAY.
THERE'S NOTHING TO BE SCARED OF.

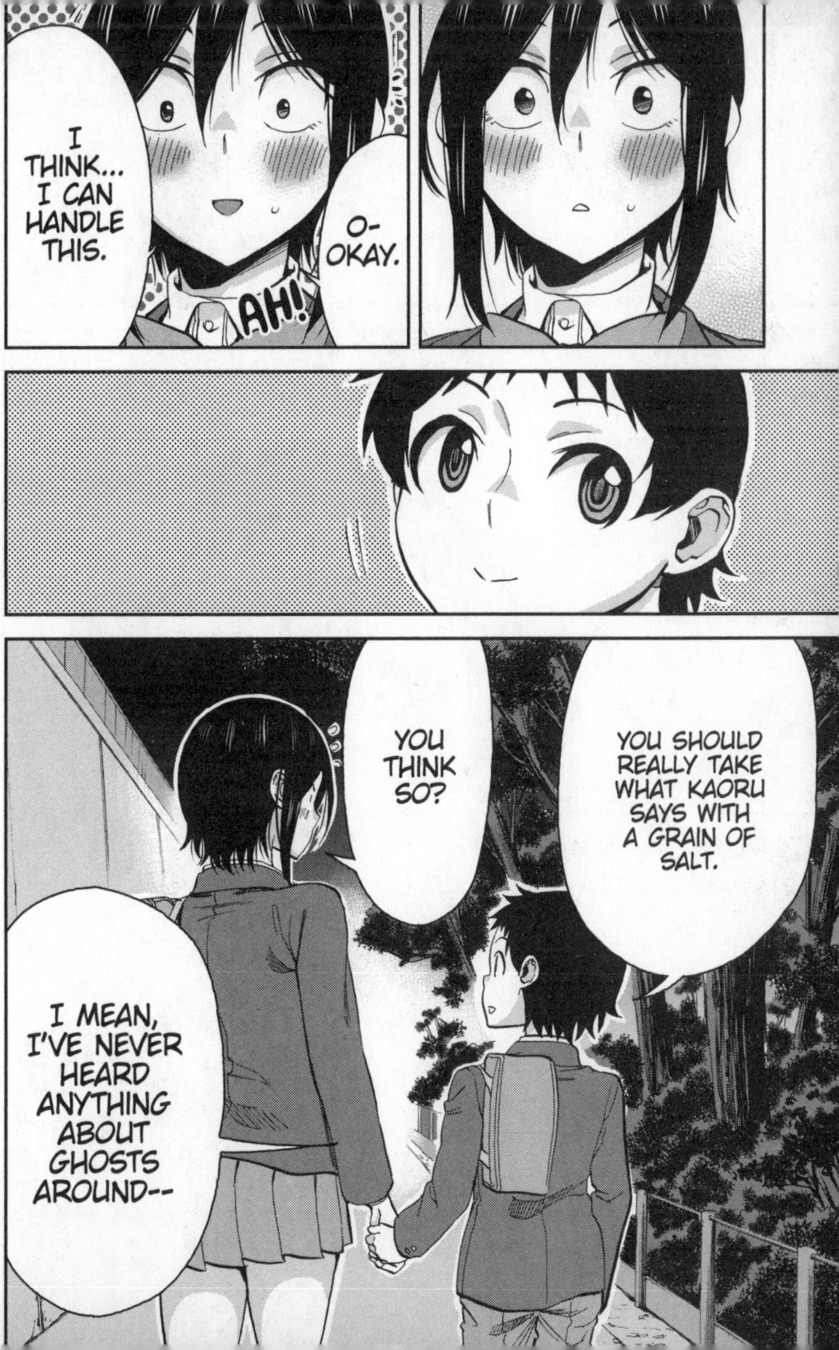
O-OKAY.
I THINK... I CAN HANDLE THIS.
AH!
YOU SHOULD REALLY TAKE WHAT KAORU SAYS WITH A GRAIN OF SALT.
YOU THINK SO?
I MEAN, I'VE NEVER HEARD ANYTHING ABOUT GHOSTS AROUND--

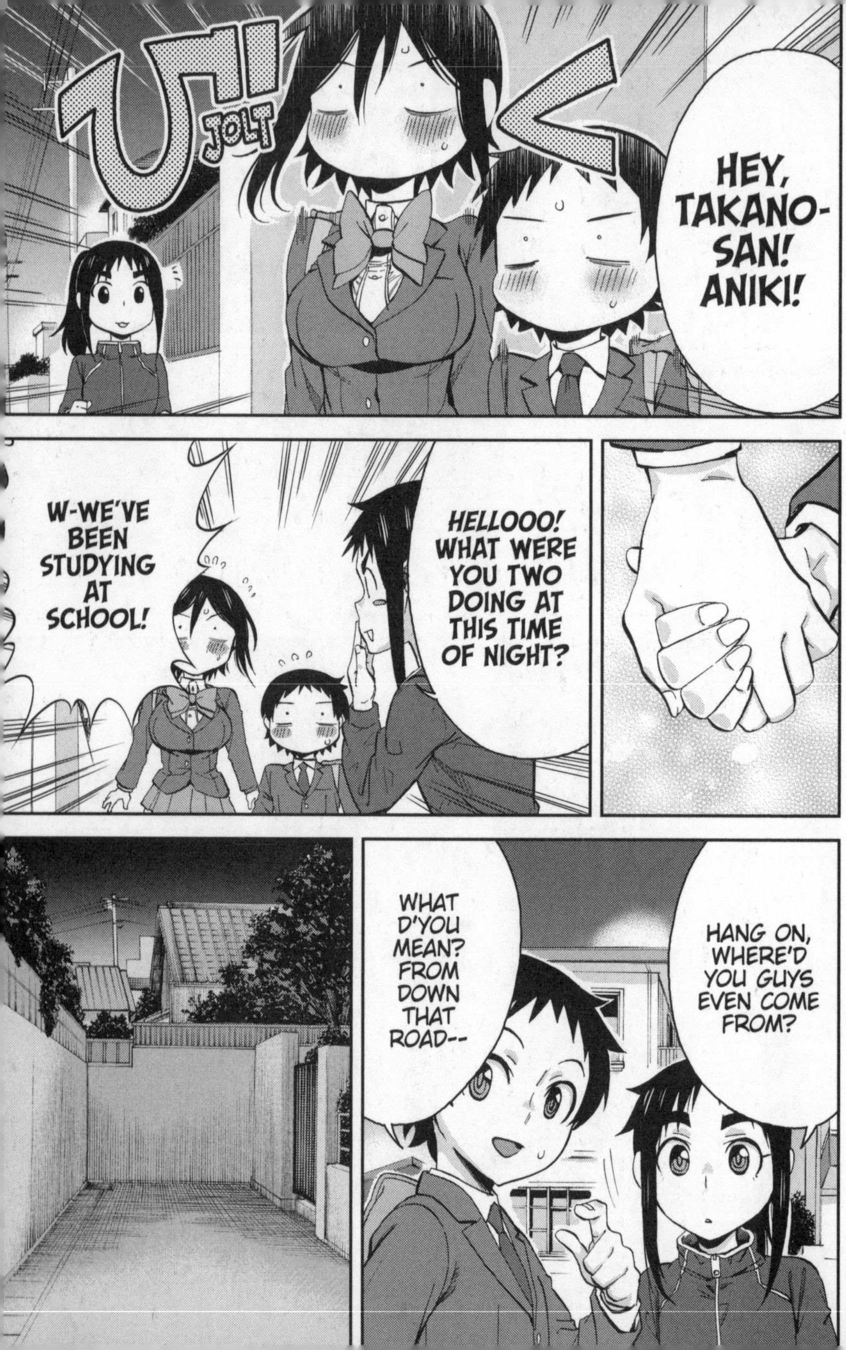
HEY, TAKANO-SAN! ANIKI!
JOLT
HELLOOO! WHAT WERE YOU TWO DOING AT THIS TIME OF NIGHT?
W-WE'VE BEEN STUDYING AT SCHOOL!
HANG ON, WHERE'D YOU GUYS EVEN COME FROM?
WHAT D'YOU MEAN? FROM DOWN THAT ROAD--

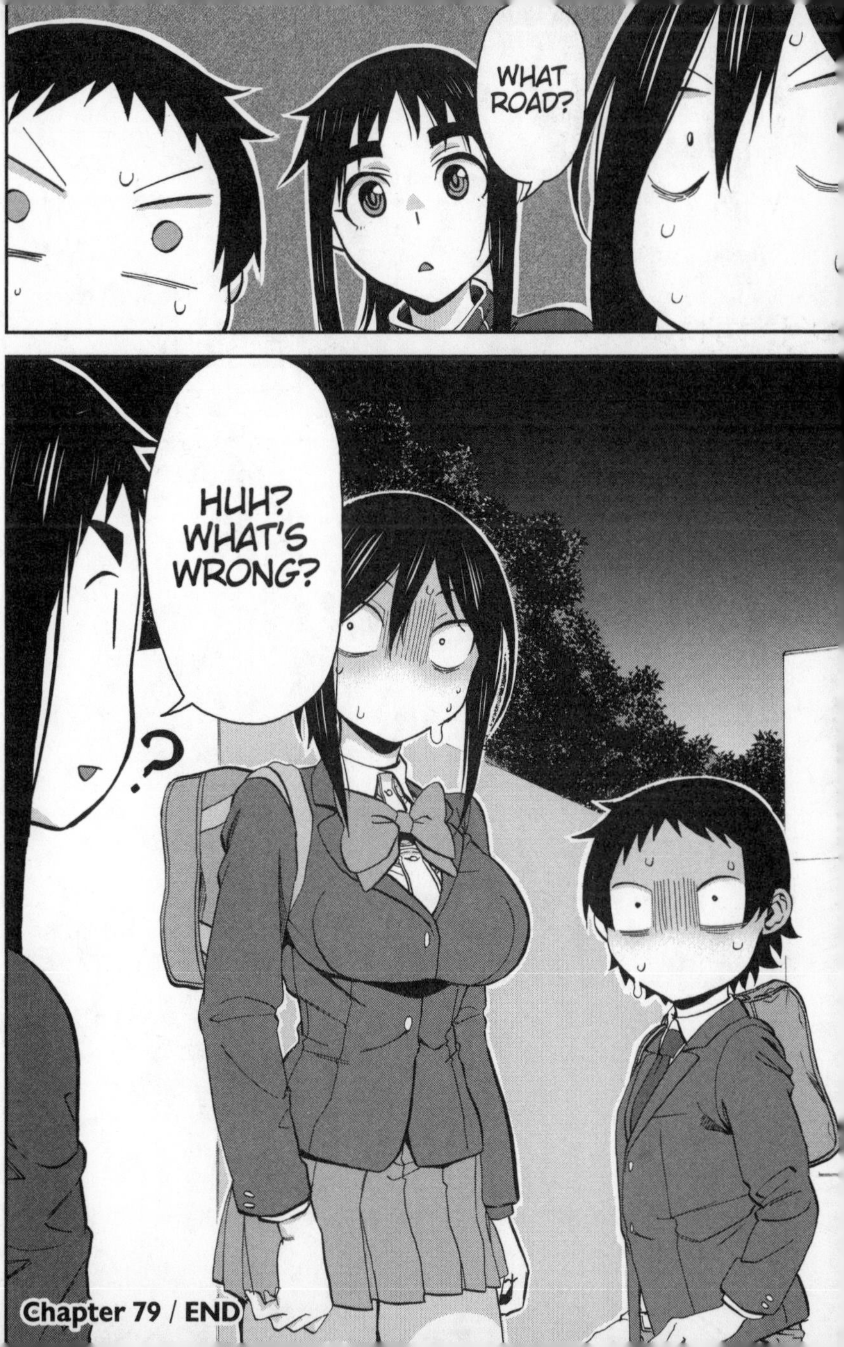
WHAT ROAD?
HUH? WHAT'S WRONG?
Chapter 79 / END

Chapter 80

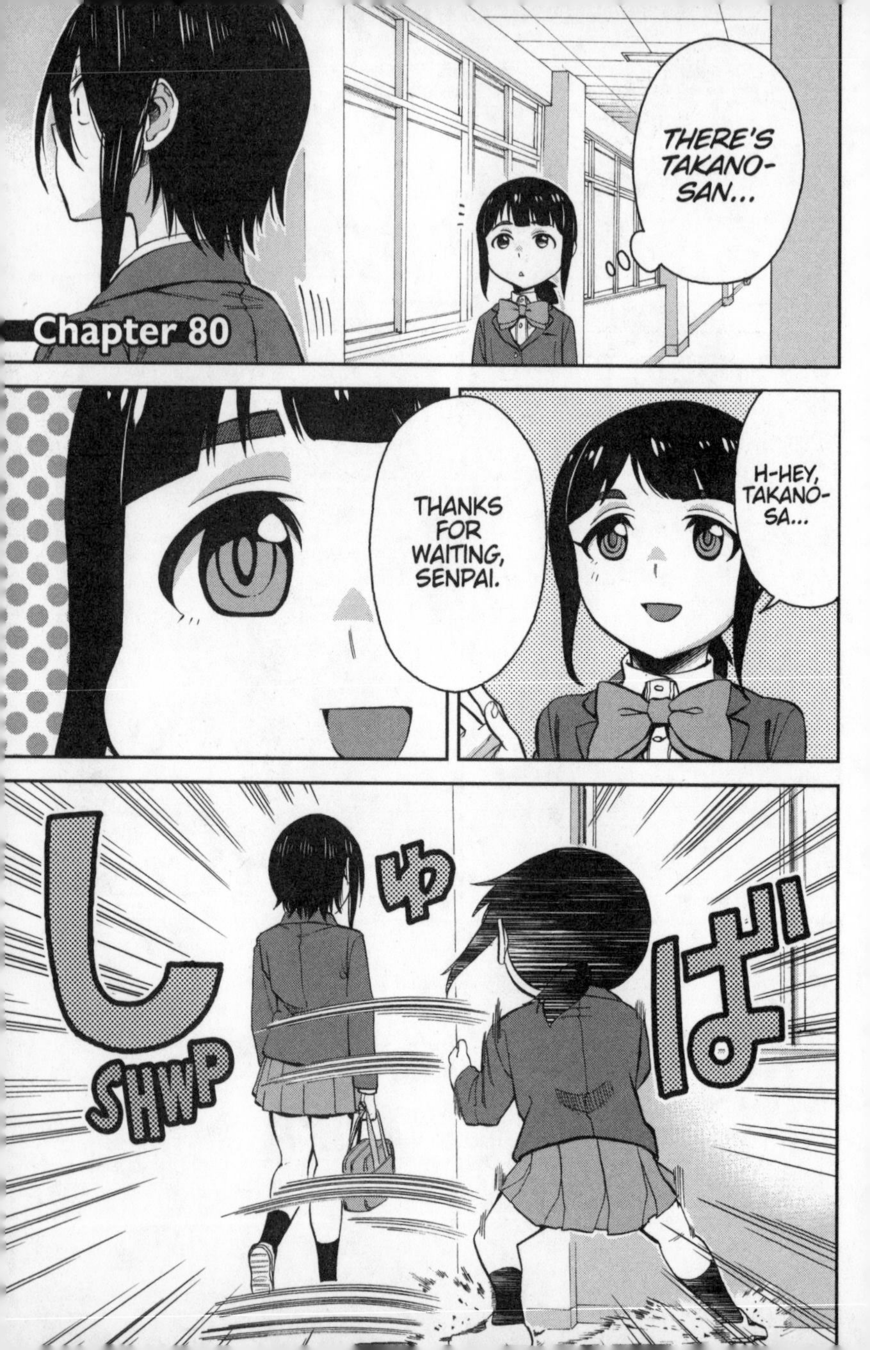
THERE'S TAKANO-SAN...
H-HEY, TAKANO-SA...
THANKS FOR WAITING, SENPAI.
しゅぱ
SHWP

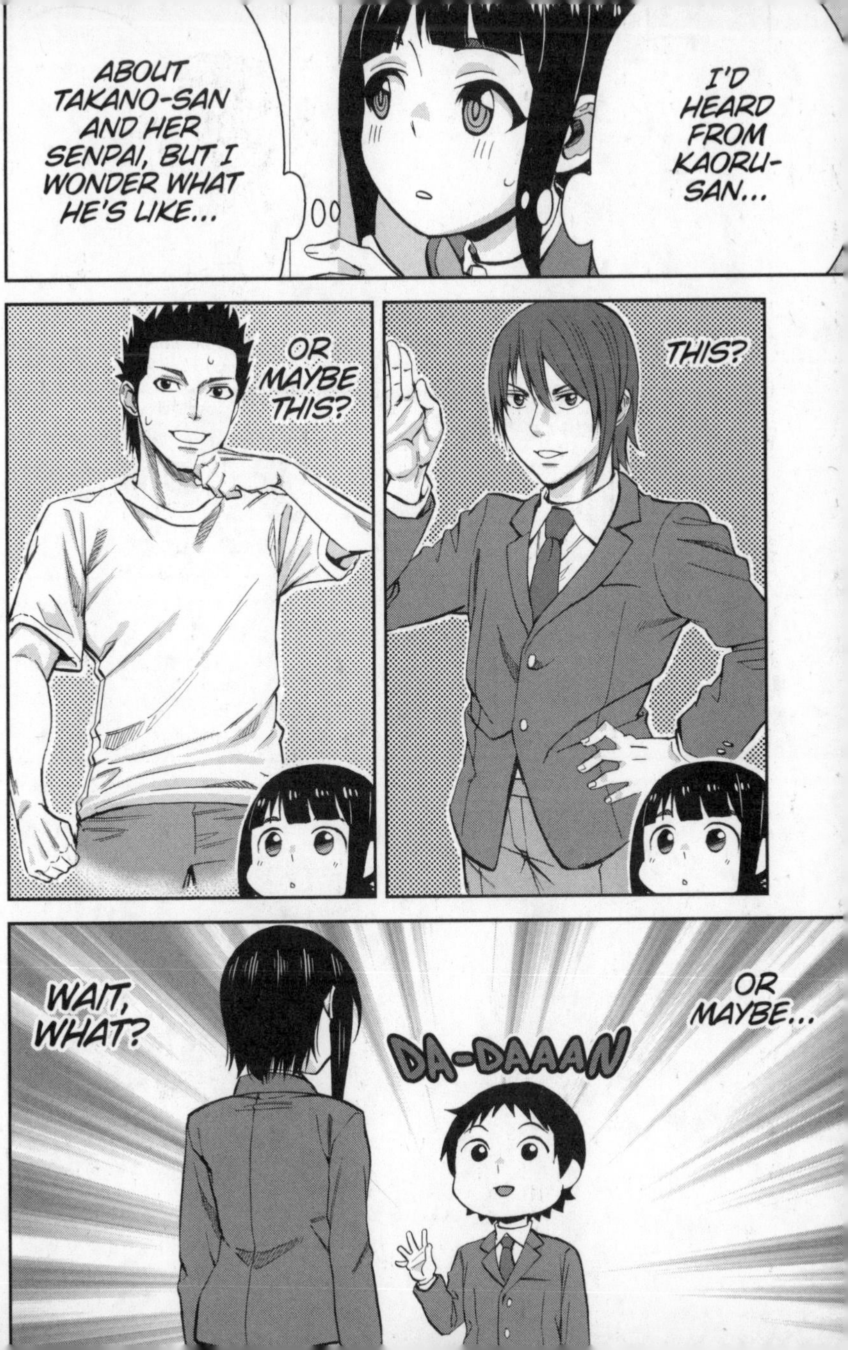
I'D HEARD FROM KAORU-SAN...
ABOUT TAKANO-SAN AND HER SENPAI, BUT I WONDER WHAT HE'S LIKE...
THIS?
OR MAYBE THIS?
OR MAYBE...
DA-DAAAN
WAIT, WHAT?

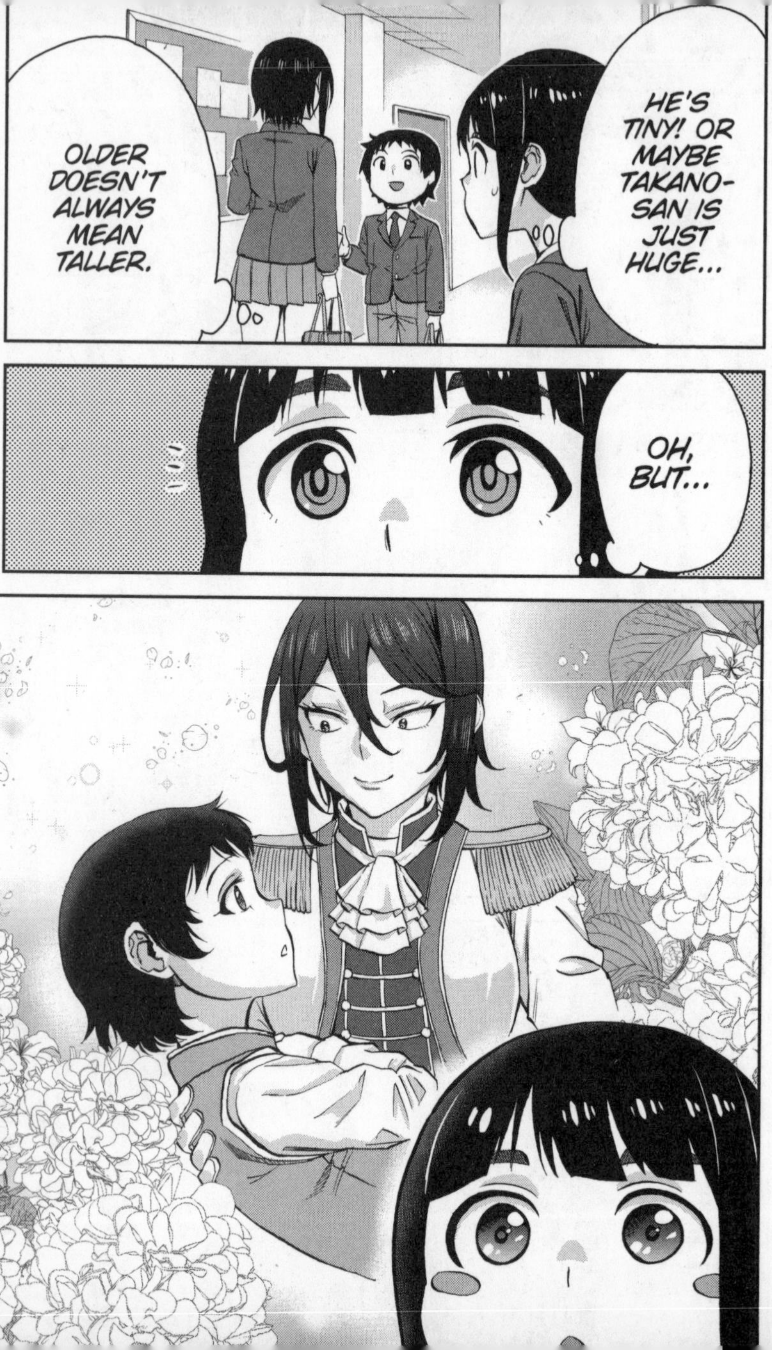
HE'S TINY! OR MAYBE TAKANO-SAN IS JUST HUGE...
OLDER DOESN'T ALWAYS MEAN TALLER.
OH, BUT...

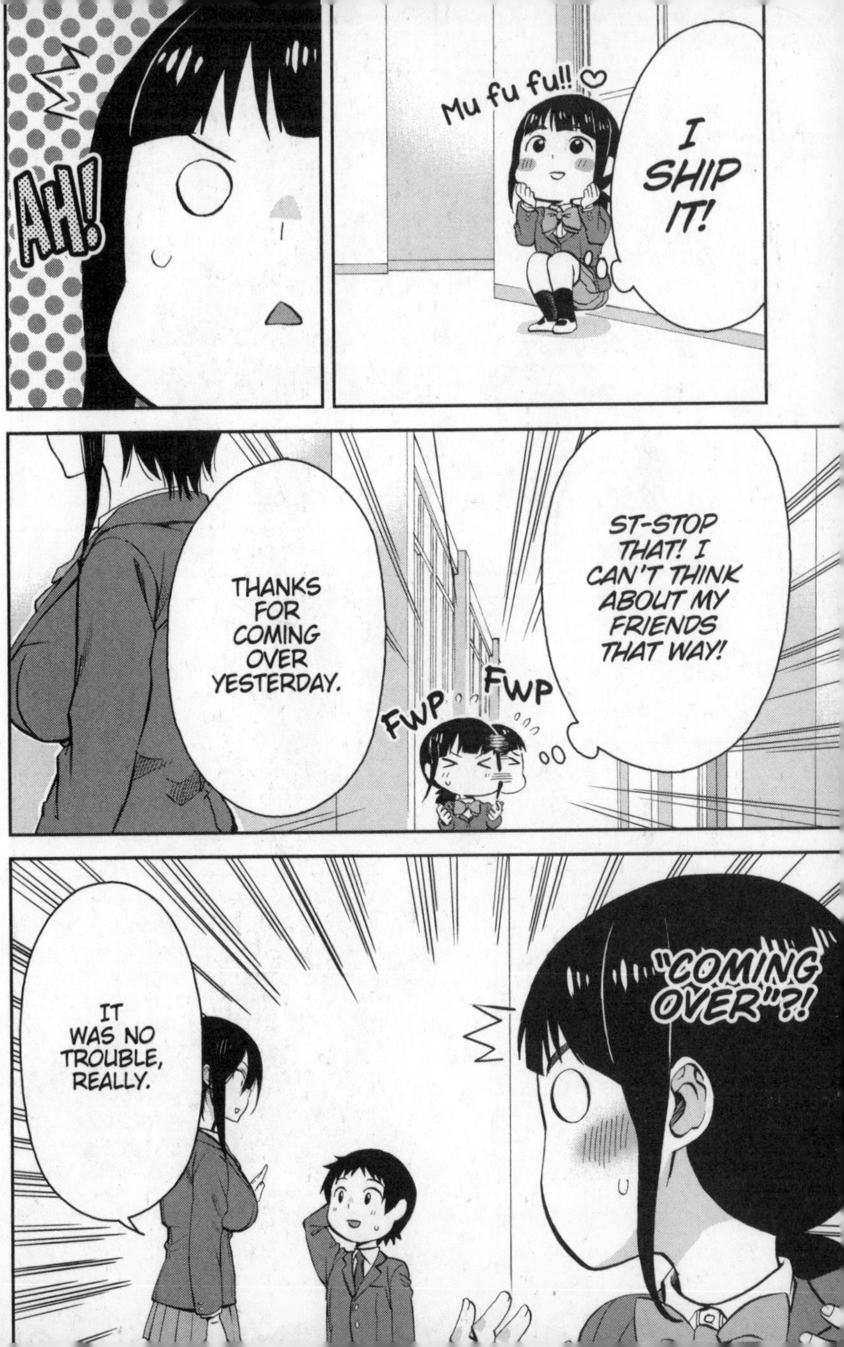
Mu fu fu!! ♡
I SHIP IT!
AH!
ST-STOP THAT! I CAN'T THINK ABOUT MY FRIENDS THAT WAY!
THANKS FOR COMING OVER YESTERDAY.
FWP
FWP
"COMING OVER"?!
IT WAS NO TROUBLE, REALLY.

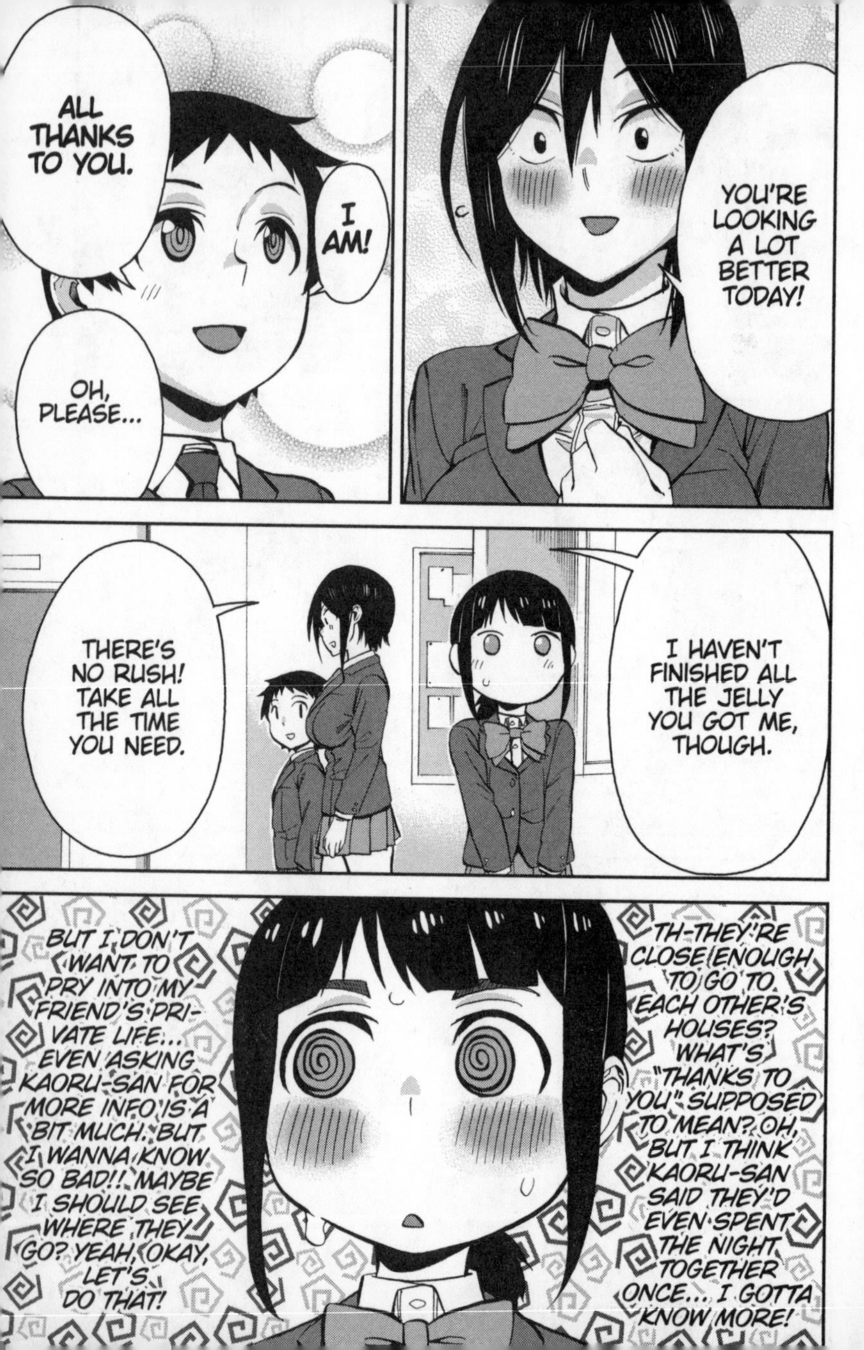
YOU'RE LOOKING A LOT BETTER TODAY!
I AM!
ALL THANKS TO YOU.
OH, PLEASE...
I HAVEN'T FINISHED ALL THE JELLY YOU GOT ME, THOUGH.
THERE'S NO RUSH! TAKE ALL THE TIME YOU NEED.
TH-THEY'RE CLOSE ENOUGH TO GO TO EACH OTHER'S HOUSES? WHAT'S "THANKS TO YOU" SUPPOSED TO MEAN? OH, BUT I THINK KAORU-SAN SAID THEY'D EVEN SPENT THE NIGHT TOGETHER ONCE... I GOTTA KNOW MORE!
BUT I DON'T WANT TO PRY INTO MY FRIEND'S PRI-VATE LIFE... EVEN ASKING KAORU-SAN FOR MORE INFO IS A BIT MUCH. BUT I WANNA KNOW SO BAD!! MAYBE I SHOULD SEE WHERE THEY GO? YEAH, OKAY, LET'S DO THAT!

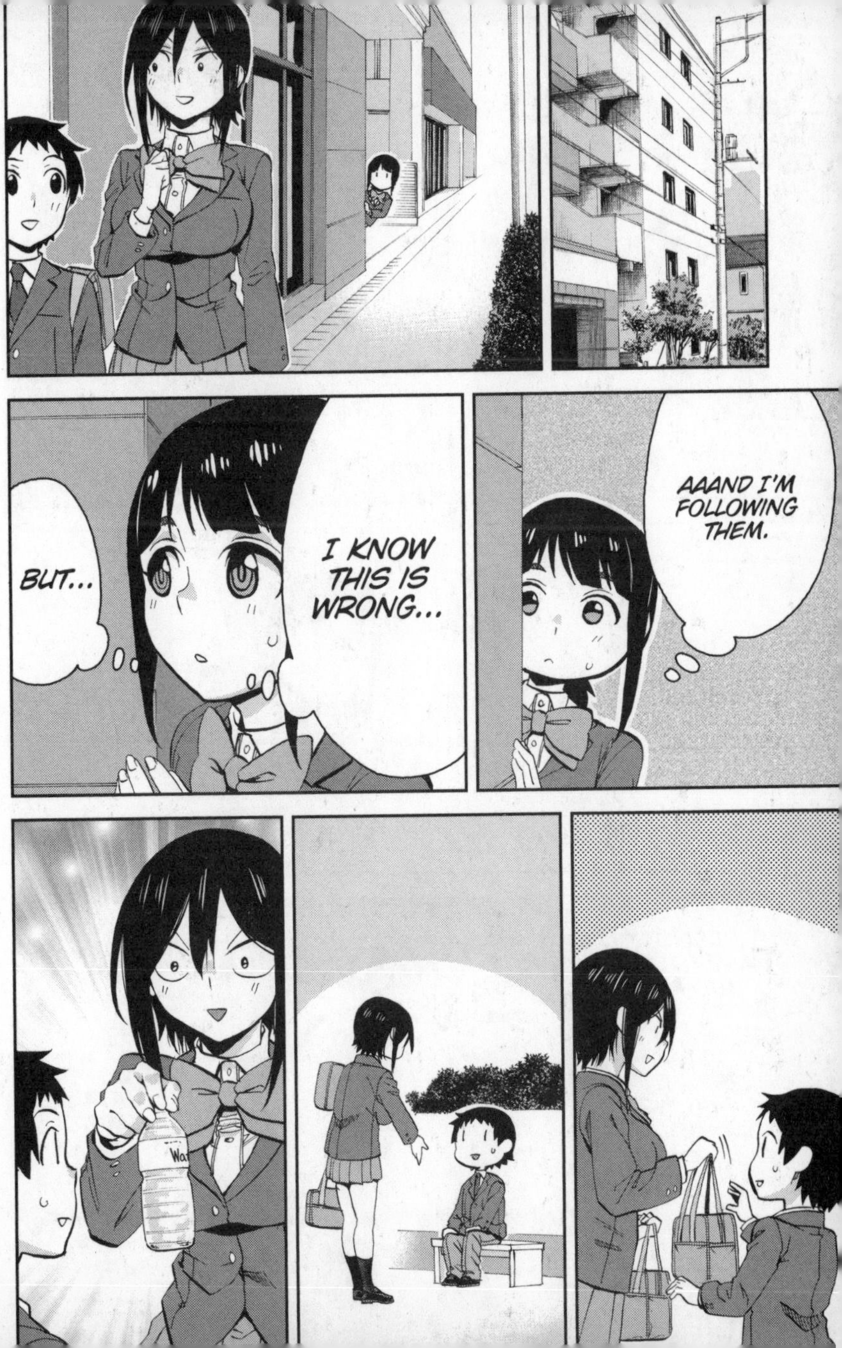
AAAND I'M FOLLOWING THEM.
I KNOW THIS IS WRONG...
BUT...

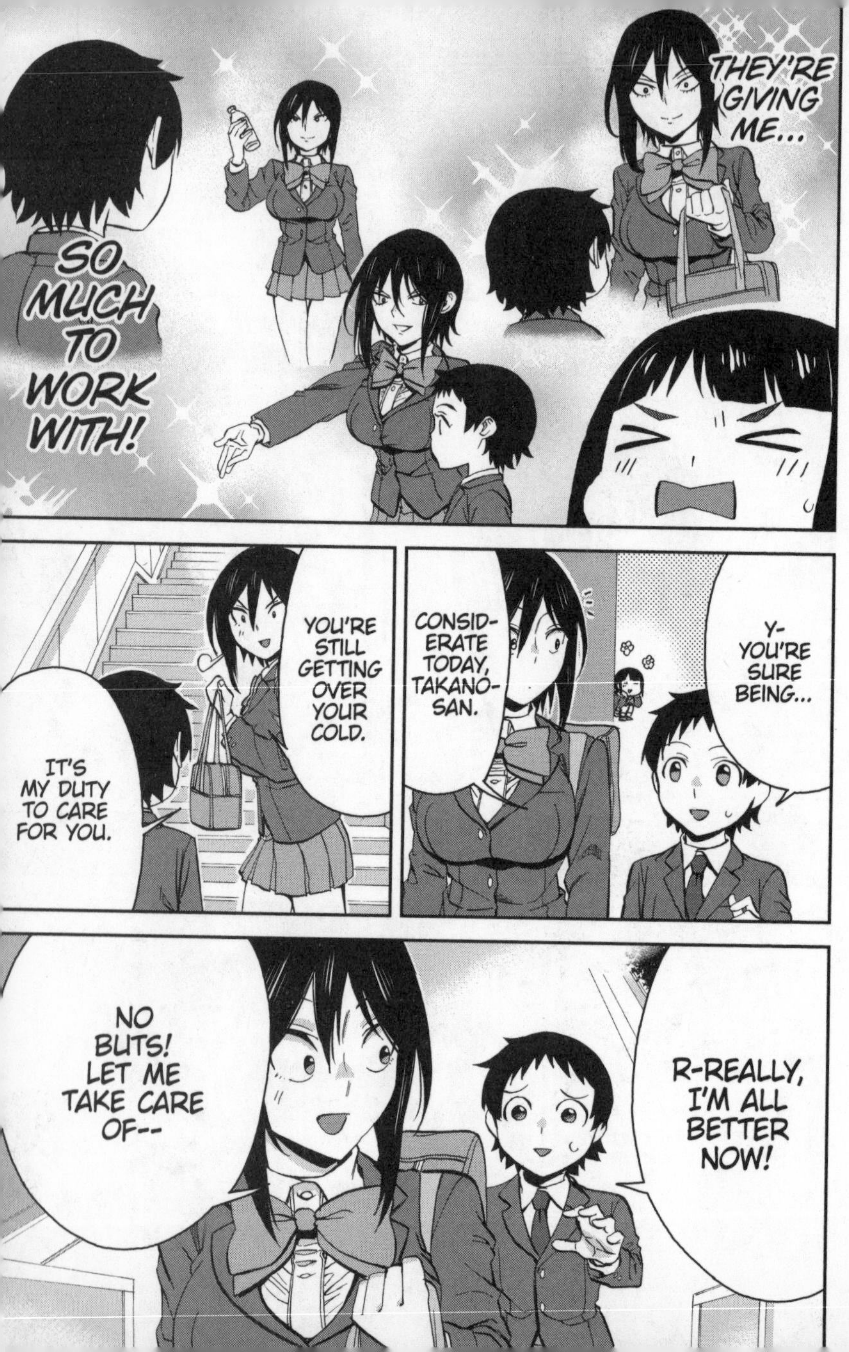
THEY'RE GIVING ME...
SO MUCH TO WORK WITH!
Y- YOU'RE SURE BEING...
CONSID-ERATE TODAY, TAKANO-SAN.
YOU'RE STILL GETTING OVER YOUR COLD.
IT'S MY DUTY TO CARE FOR YOU.
R-REALLY, I'M ALL BETTER NOW!
NO BUTS! LET ME TAKE CARE OF--

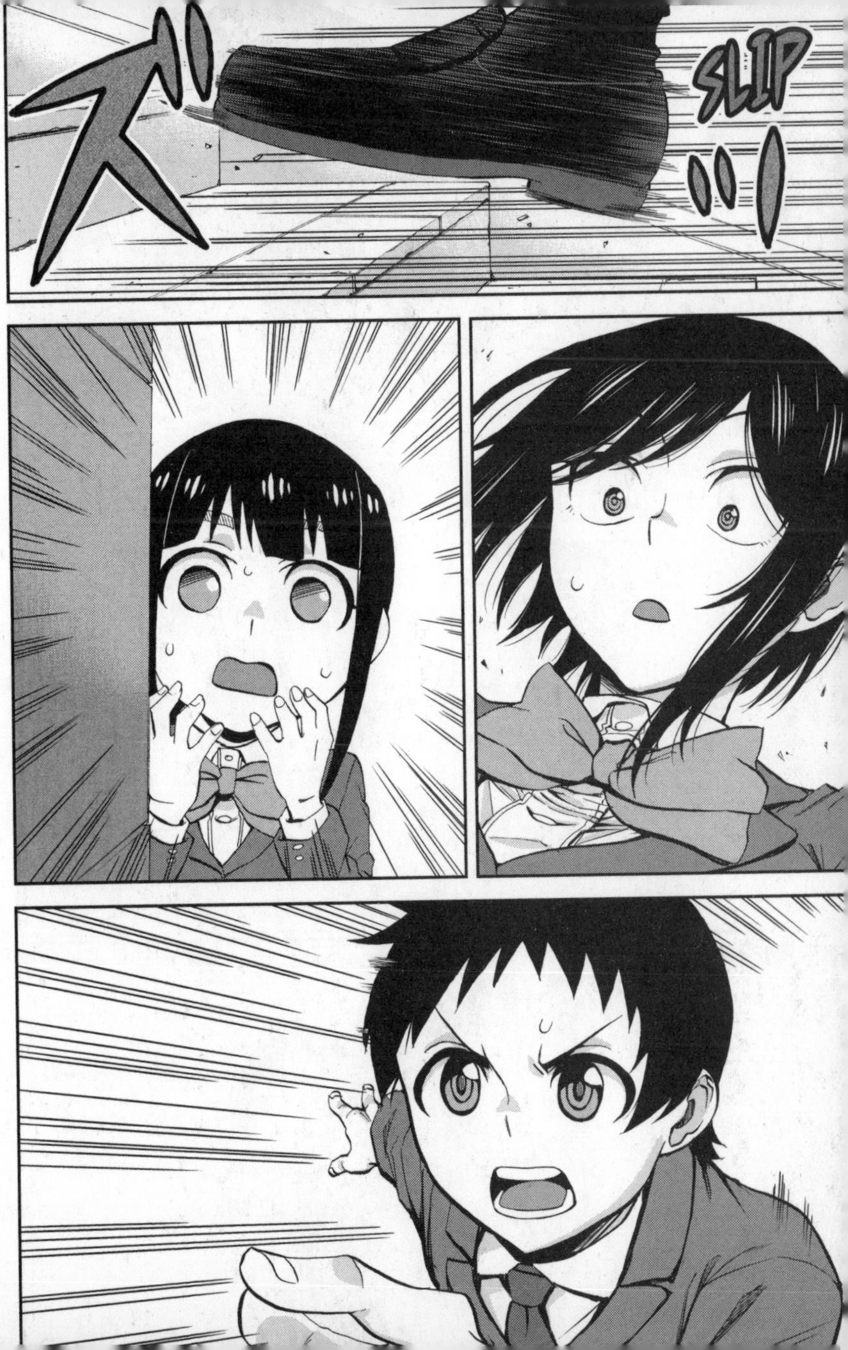
SLIP
ズ

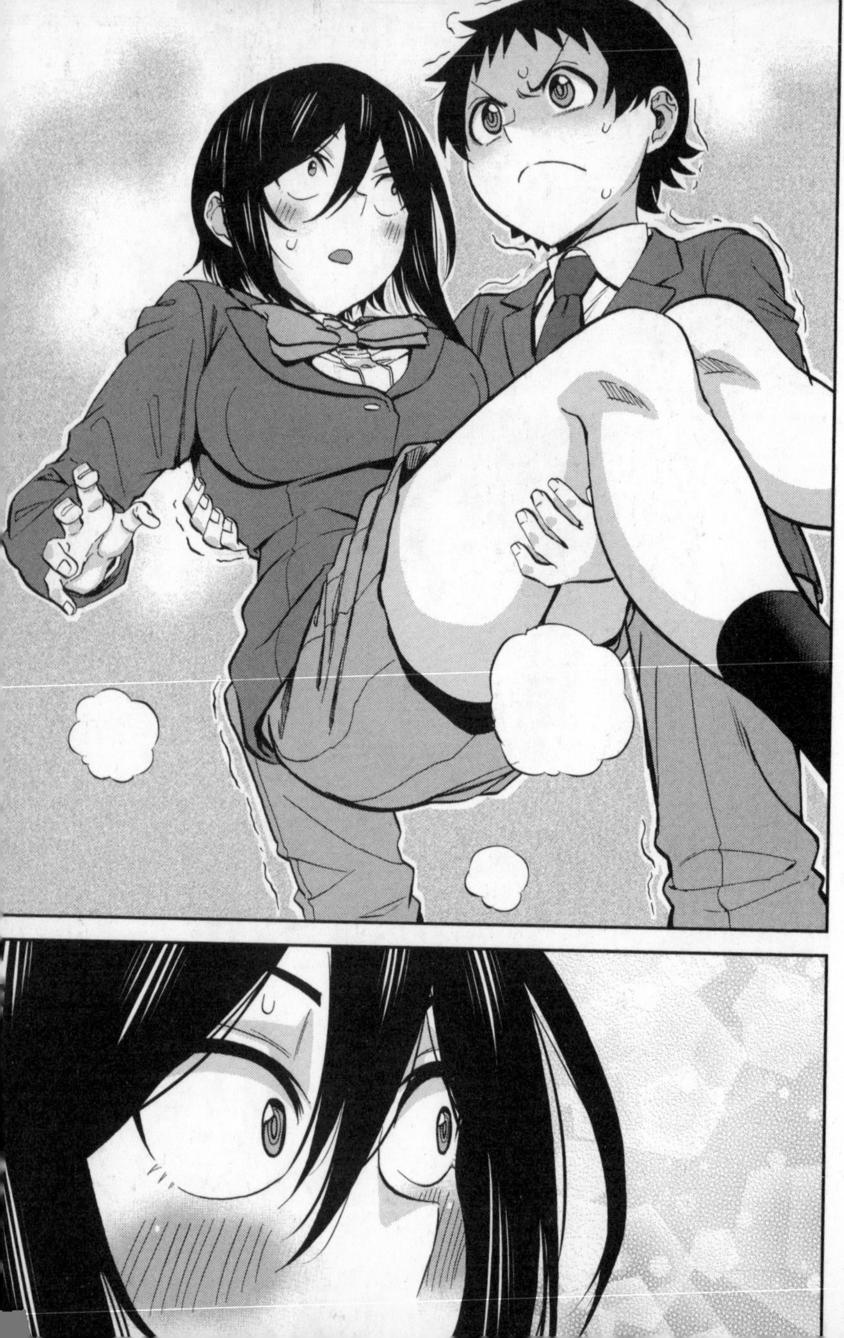

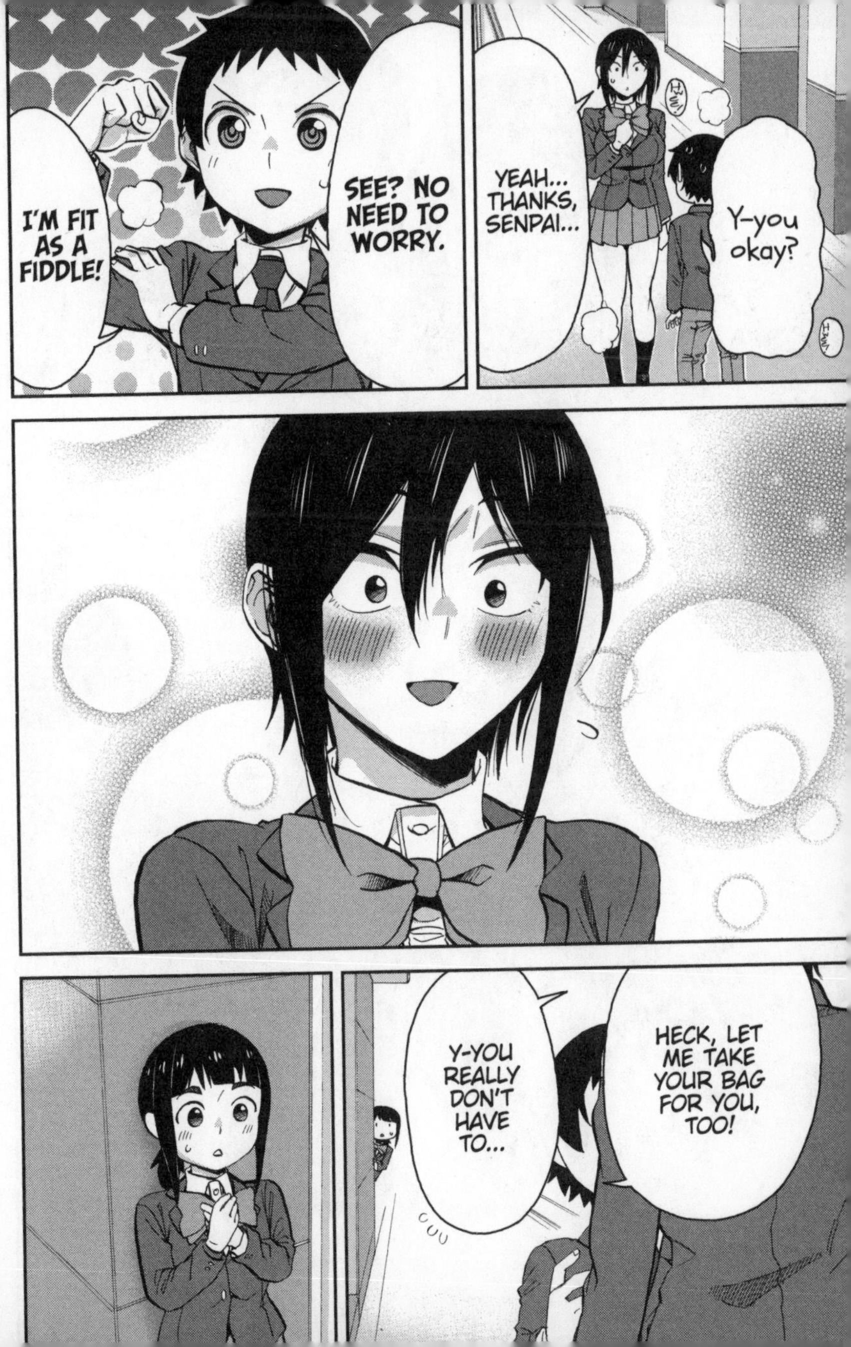
Y-you okay?
YEAH... THANKS, SENPAI...
SEE? NO NEED TO WORRY.
I'M FIT AS A FIDDLE!
HECK, LET ME TAKE YOUR BAG FOR YOU, TOO!
Y-YOU REALLY DON'T HAVE TO...

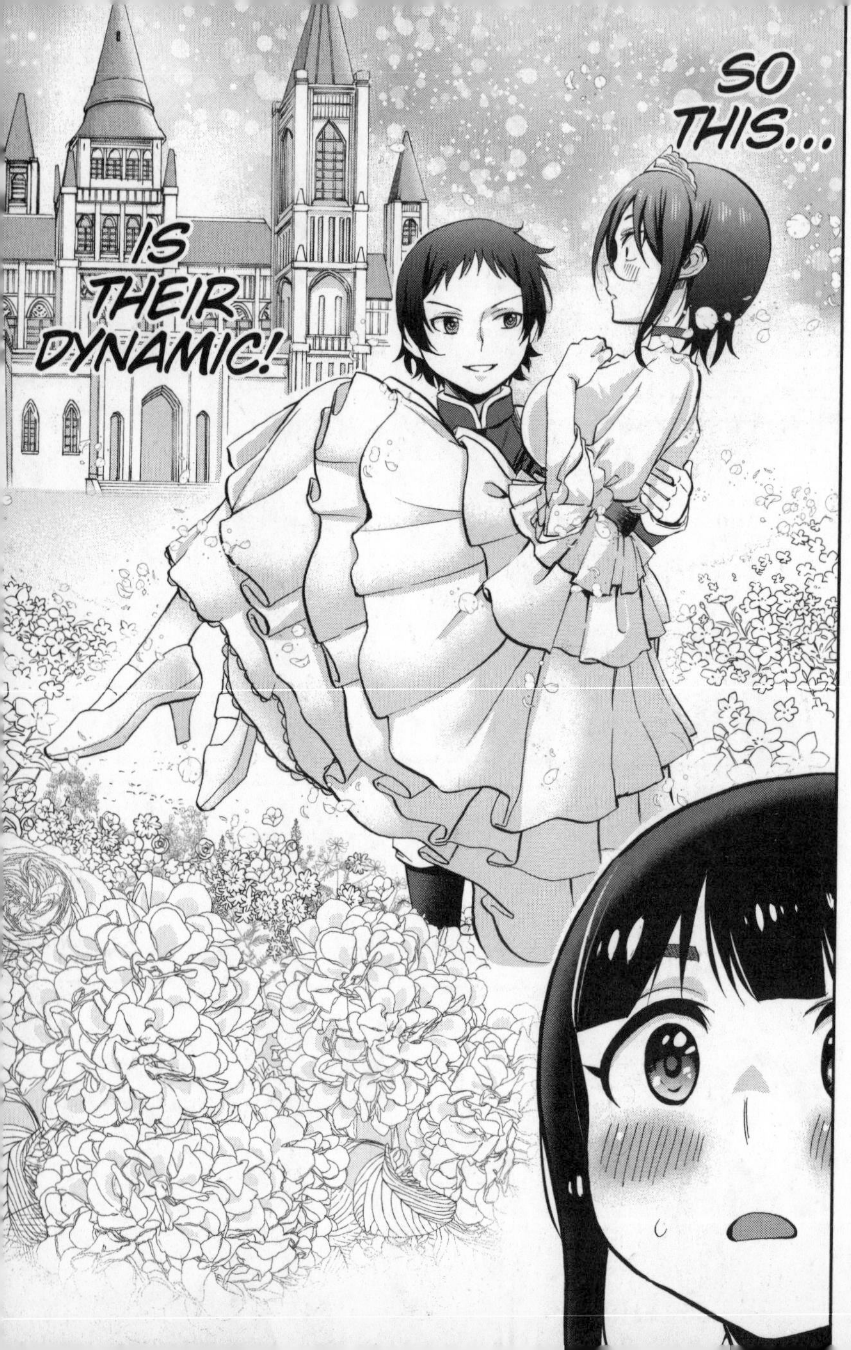
SO THIS...
IS THEIR DYNAMIC!

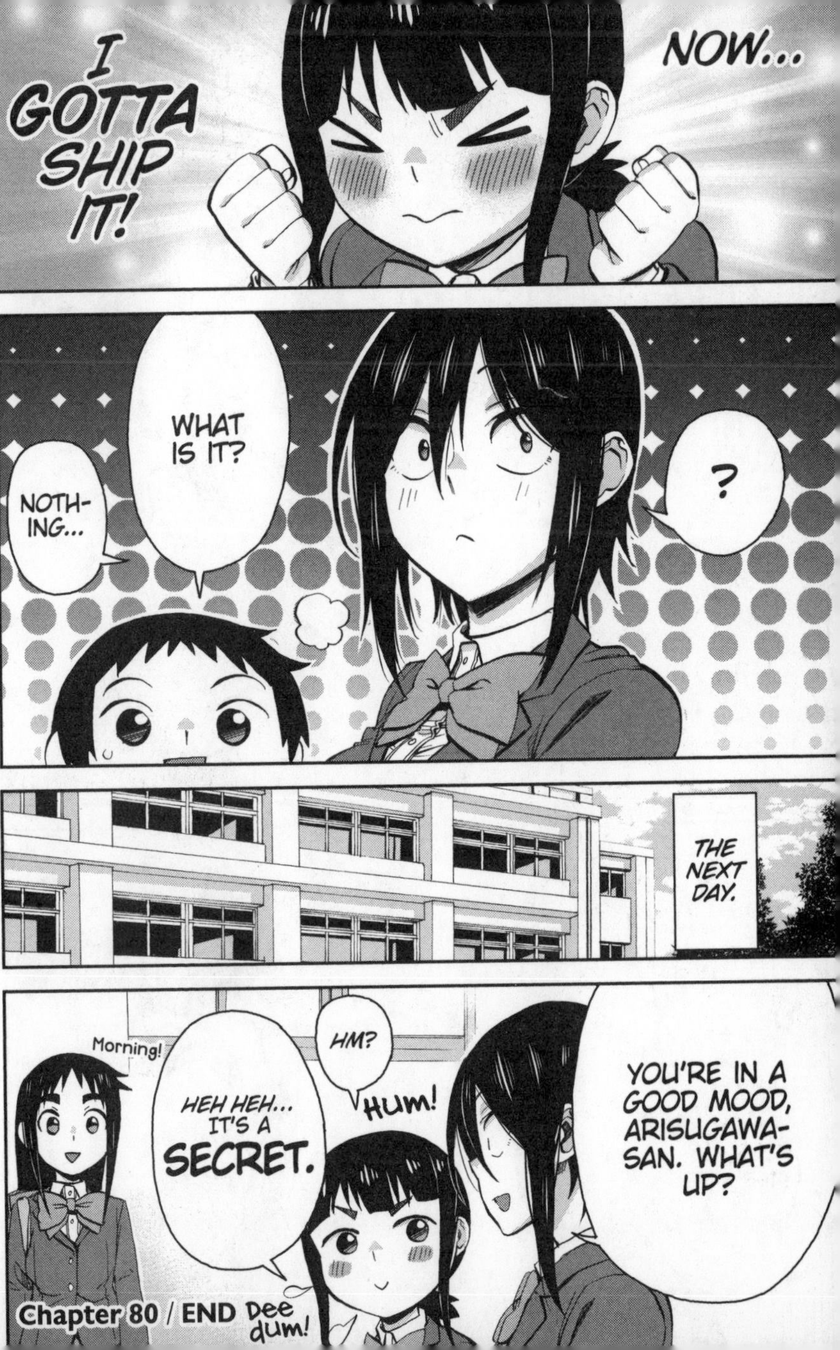
NOW...
I GOTTA SHIP IT!
?
WHAT IS IT?
NOTH-ING...
THE NEXT DAY.
YOU'RE IN A GOOD MOOD, ARISUGAWA-SAN. WHAT'S UP?
HM?
HUM!
HEH HEH... IT'S A SECRET.
Morning!
Dee dum!
Chapter 80 / END

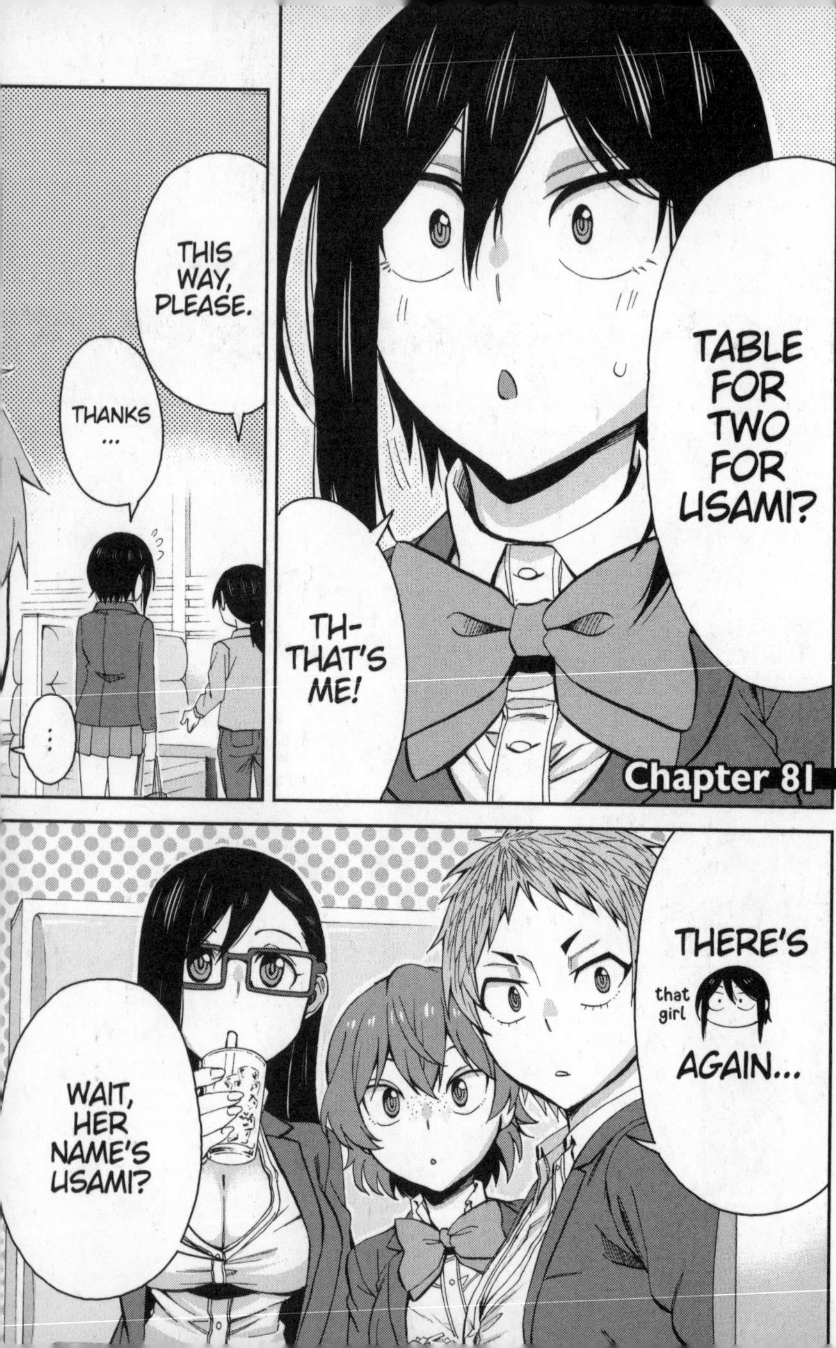
TABLE FOR TWO FOR USAMI?
TH- THAT'S ME!
Chapter 81
THIS WAY, PLEASE.
THANKS ...
...
THERE'S that girl AGAIN...
WAIT, HER NAME'S USAMI?

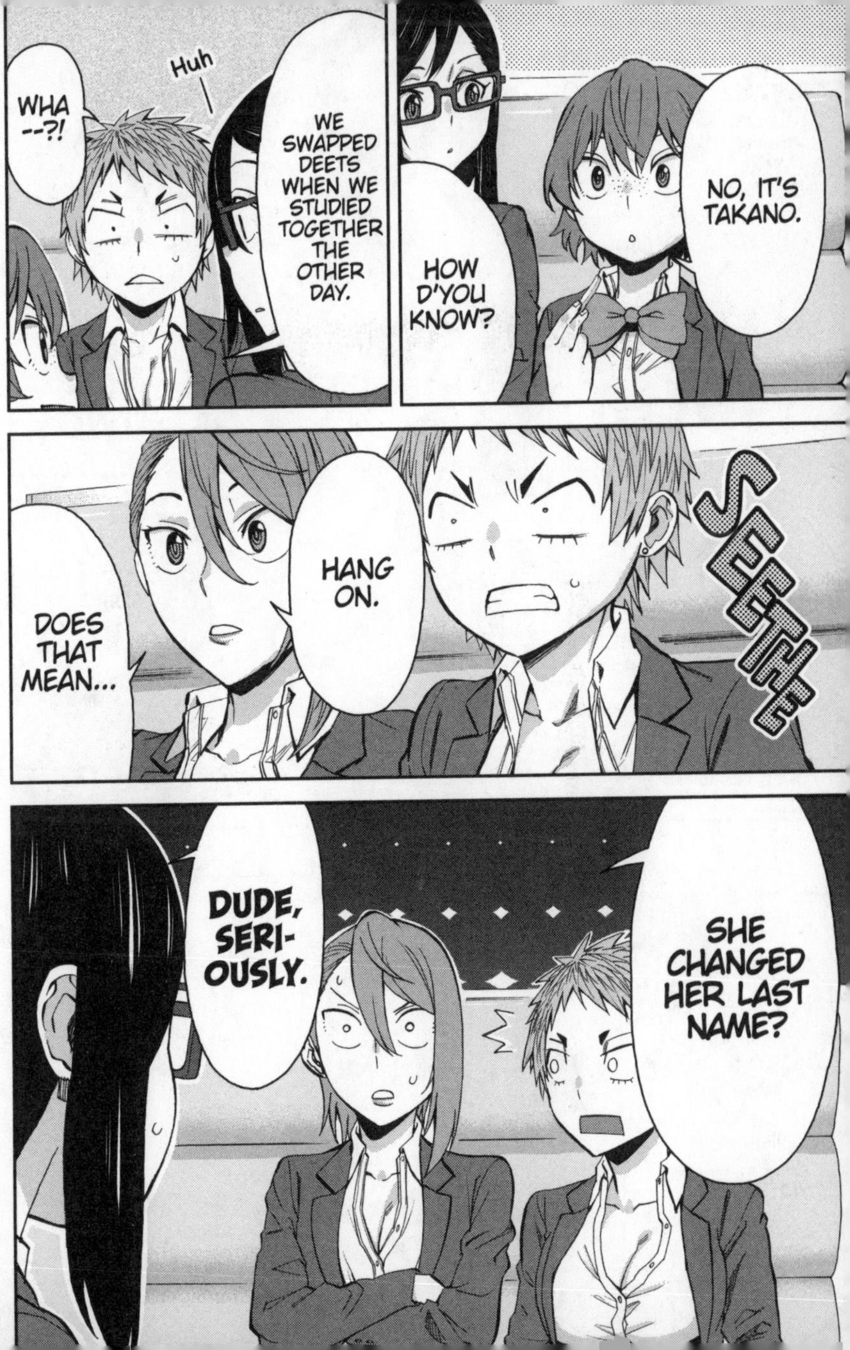
NO, IT'S TAKANO.
HOW D'YOU KNOW?
WE SWAPPED DEETS WHEN WE STUDIED TOGETHER THE OTHER DAY.
Huh
WHA--?!
SEETHE
HANG ON.
DOES THAT MEAN...
SHE CHANGED HER LAST NAME?
DUDE, SERIOUSLY.

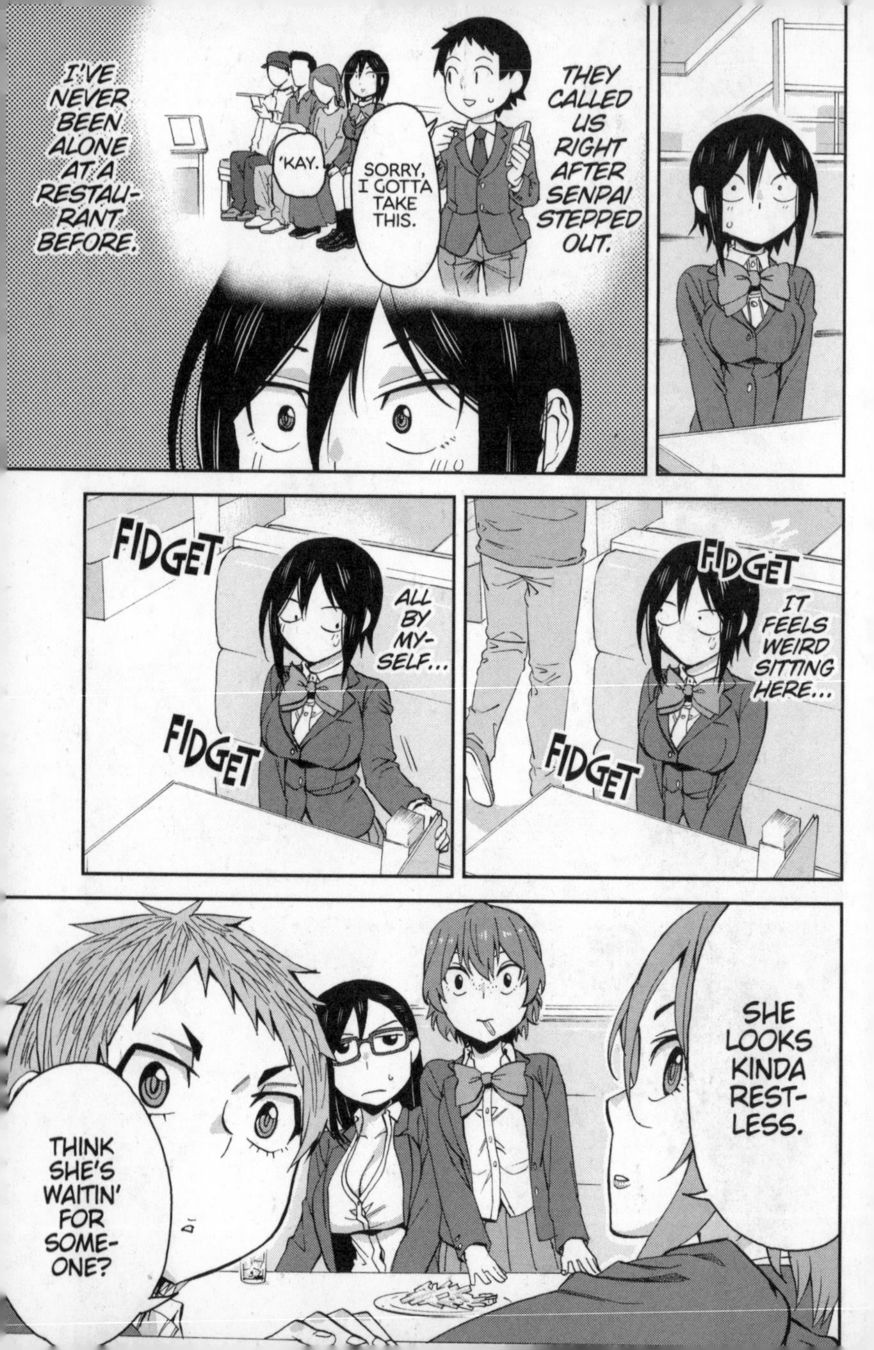
THEY CALLED US RIGHT AFTER SENPAI STEPPED OUT.
SORRY, I GOTTA TAKE THIS.
'KAY.
I'VE NEVER BEEN ALONE AT A RESTAURANT BEFORE.
FIDGET
IT FEELS WEIRD SITTING HERE...
FIDGET
ALL BY MYSELF...
FIDGET
FIDGET
SHE LOOKS KINDA RESTLESS.
THINK SHE'S WAITIN' FOR SOMEONE?

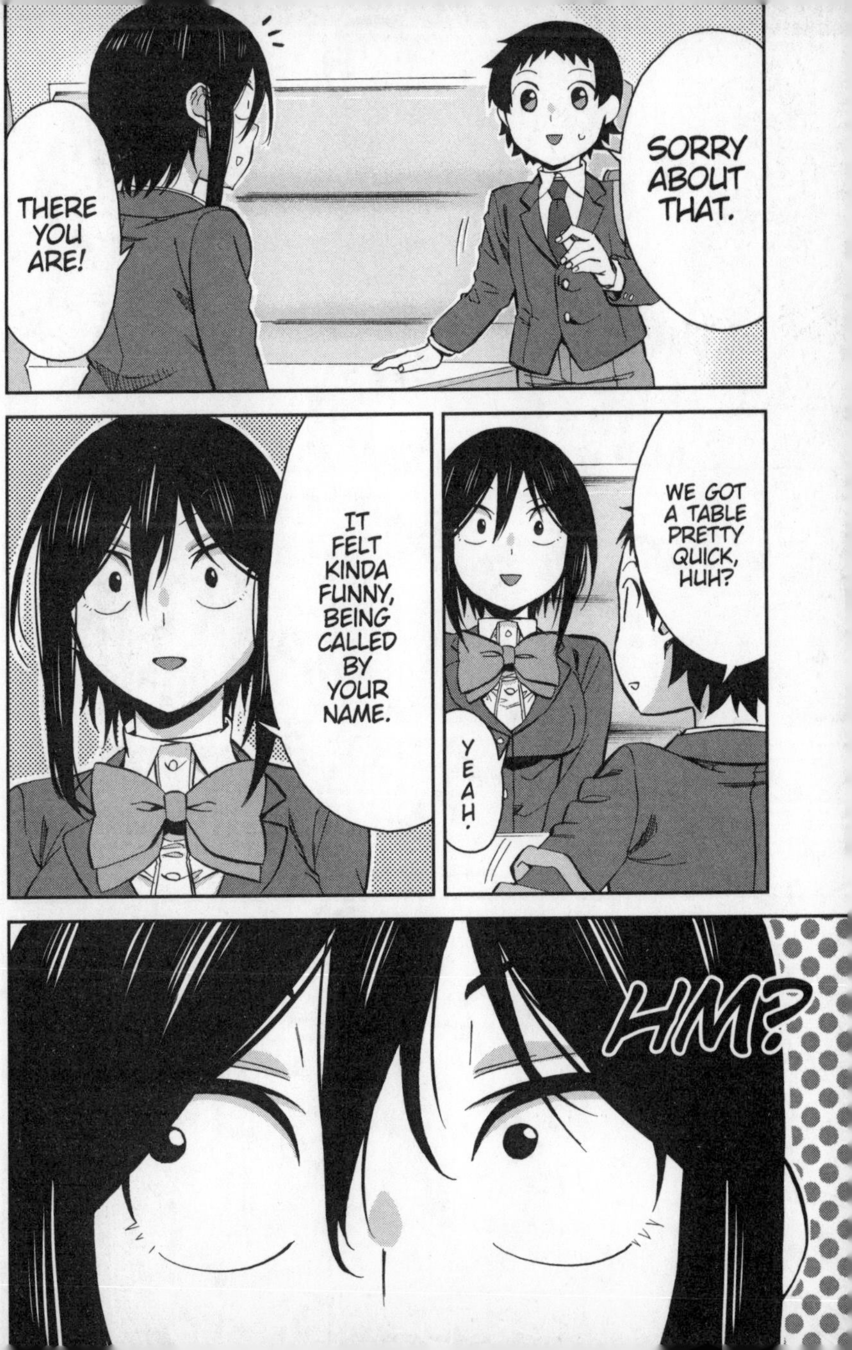
SORRY ABOUT THAT.
THERE YOU ARE!
WE GOT A TABLE PRETTY QUICK, HUH?
YEAH.
IT FELT KINDA FUNNY, BEING CALLED BY YOUR NAME.
HM?

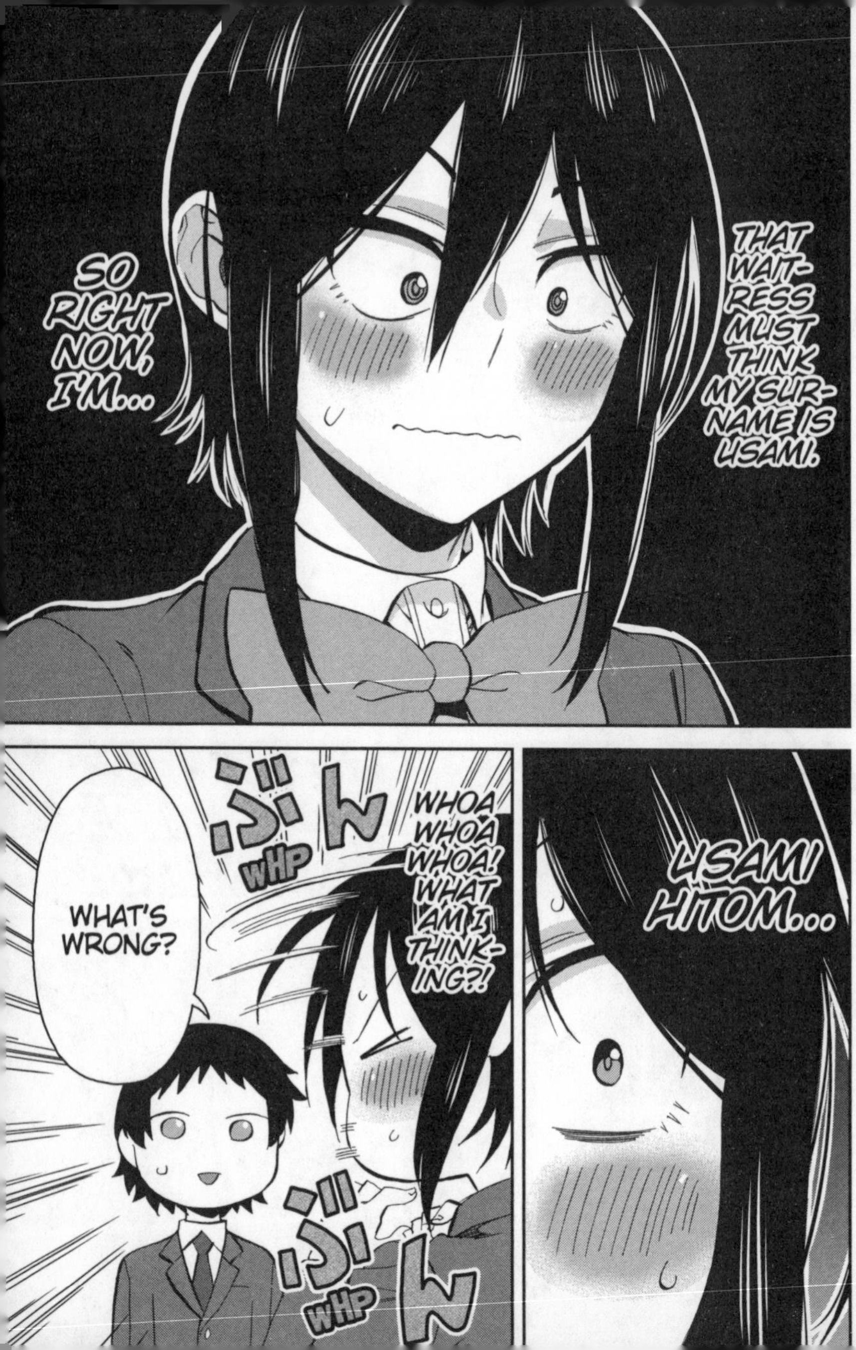
THAT WAIT-RESS MUST THINK MY SUR-NAME IS USAMI.
SO RIGHT NOW, I'M...
USAMI HITOM...
WHOA WHOA WHOA! WHAT AM I THINK-ING?!
ぶん
WHP
WHAT'S WRONG?
ぶん
WHP

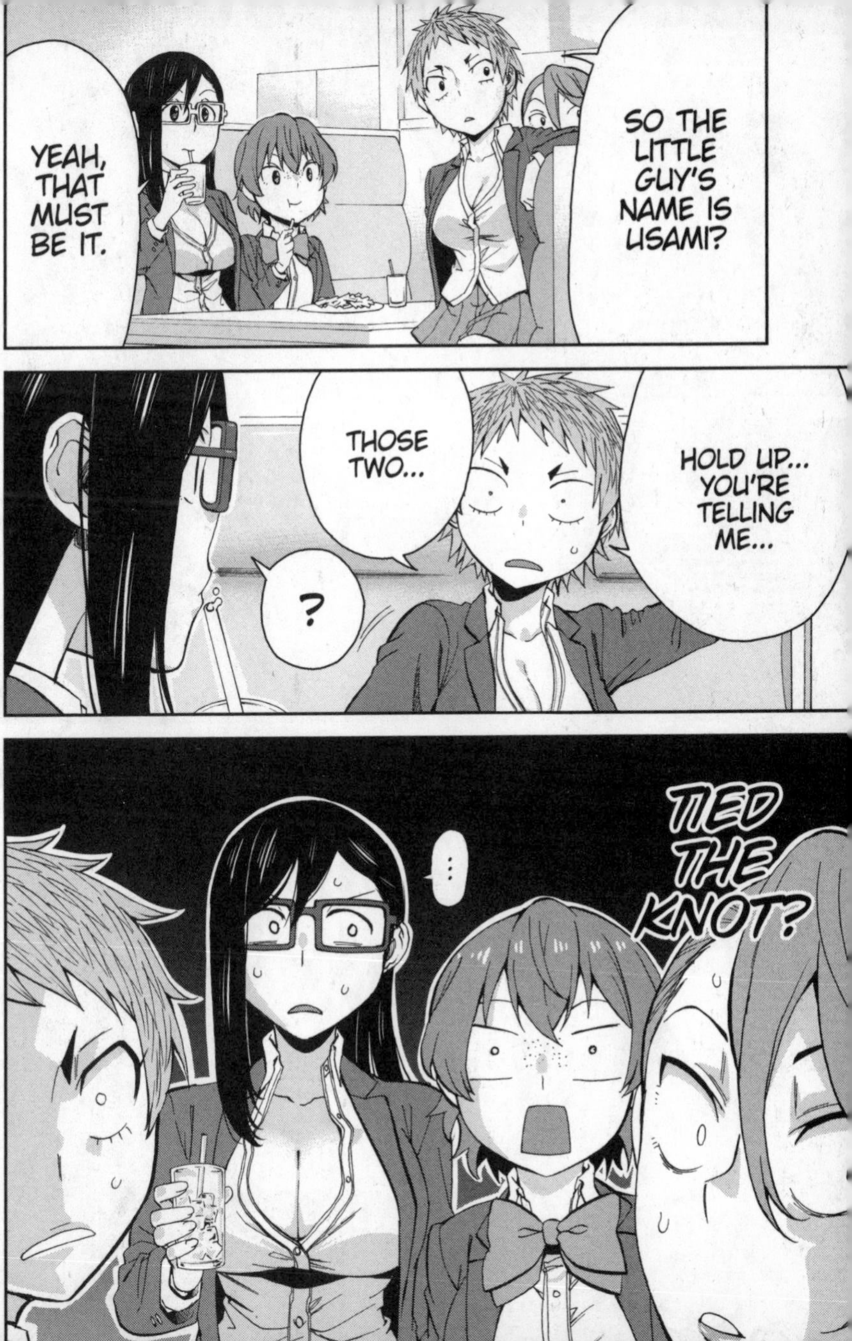
SO THE LITTLE GUY'S NAME IS USAMI?
YEAH, THAT MUST BE IT.
HOLD UP... YOU'RE TELLING ME...
THOSE TWO...
?
TIED THE KNOT?
...

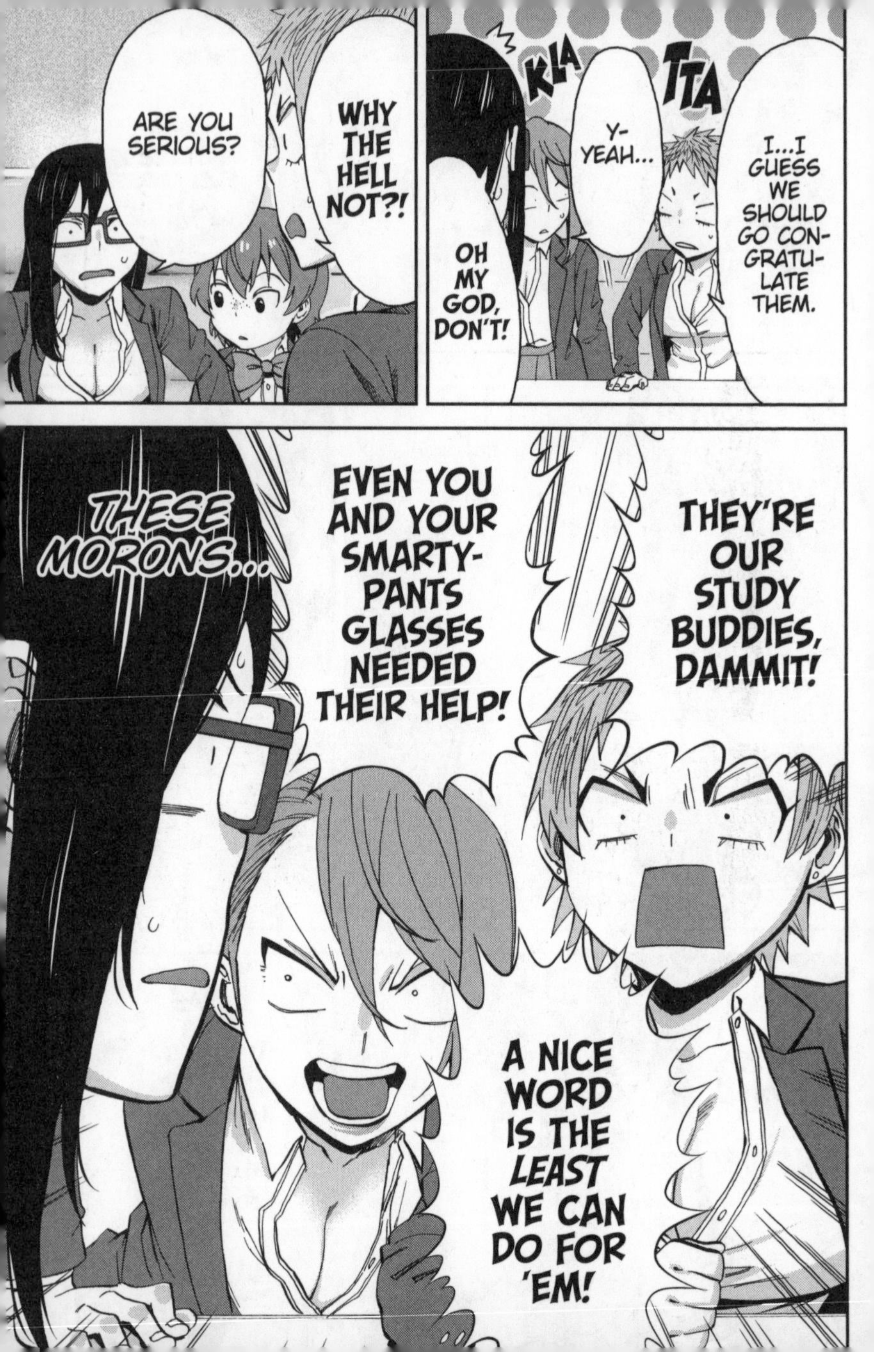
KLA TTA
I...I GUESS WE SHOULD GO CON-GRATU-LATE THEM.
Y-YEAH...
OH MY GOD, DON'T!
WHY THE HELL NOT?!
ARE YOU SERIOUS?
THEY'RE OUR STUDY BUDDIES, DAMMIT!
EVEN YOU AND YOUR SMARTY-PANTS GLASSES NEEDED THEIR HELP!
THESE MORONS...
A NICE WORD IS THE LEAST WE CAN DO FOR 'EM!

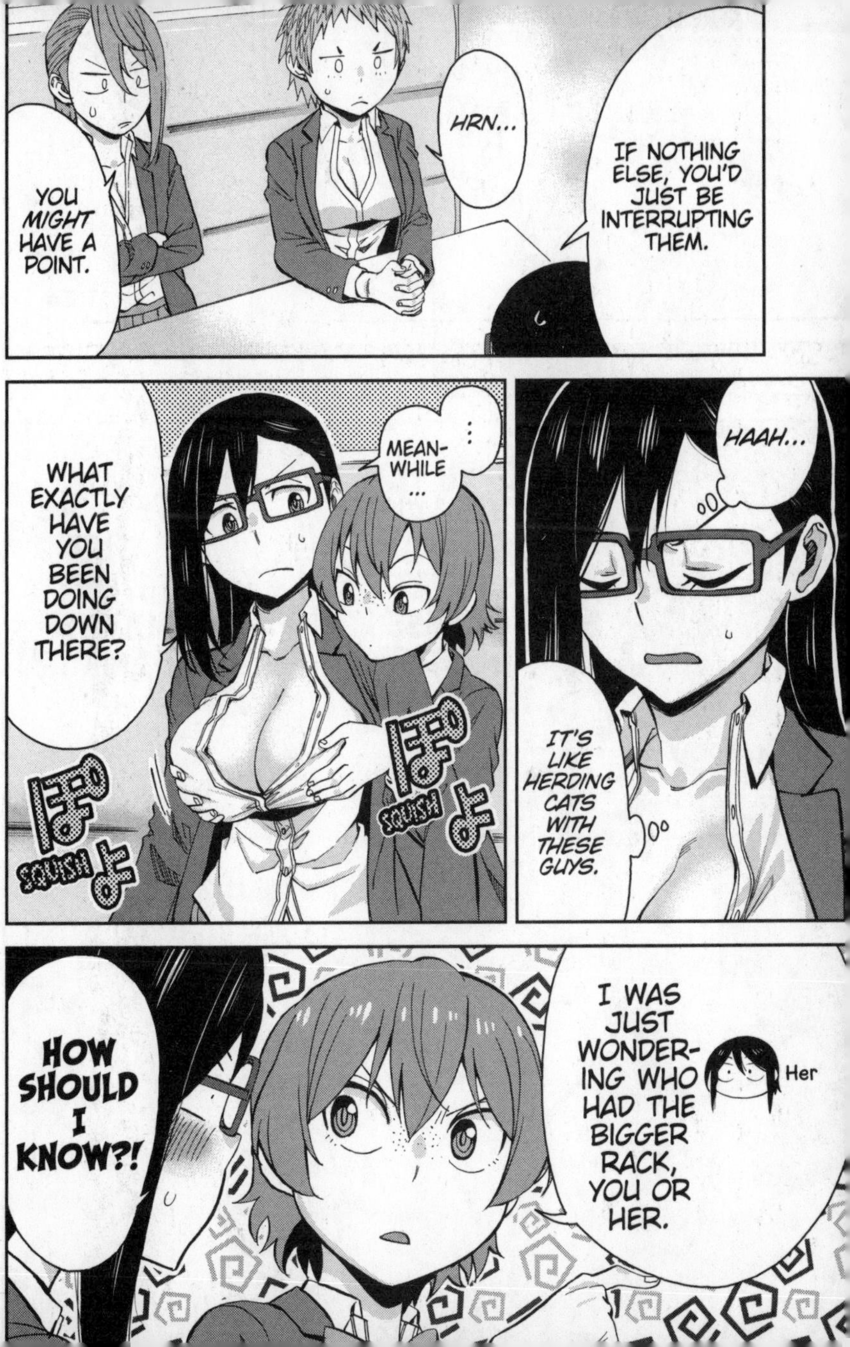
IF NOTHING ELSE, YOU'D JUST BE INTERRUPTING THEM.
HRN...
YOU *MIGHT* HAVE A POINT.
HAAH...
IT'S LIKE HERDING CATS WITH THESE GUYS.
... MEAN-WHILE ...
WHAT EXACTLY HAVE YOU BEEN DOING DOWN THERE?
ぽよ SQUISH
ぽよ SQUISH
I WAS JUST WONDERING WHO HAD THE BIGGER RACK, YOU OR HER.
Her
HOW SHOULD I KNOW?!

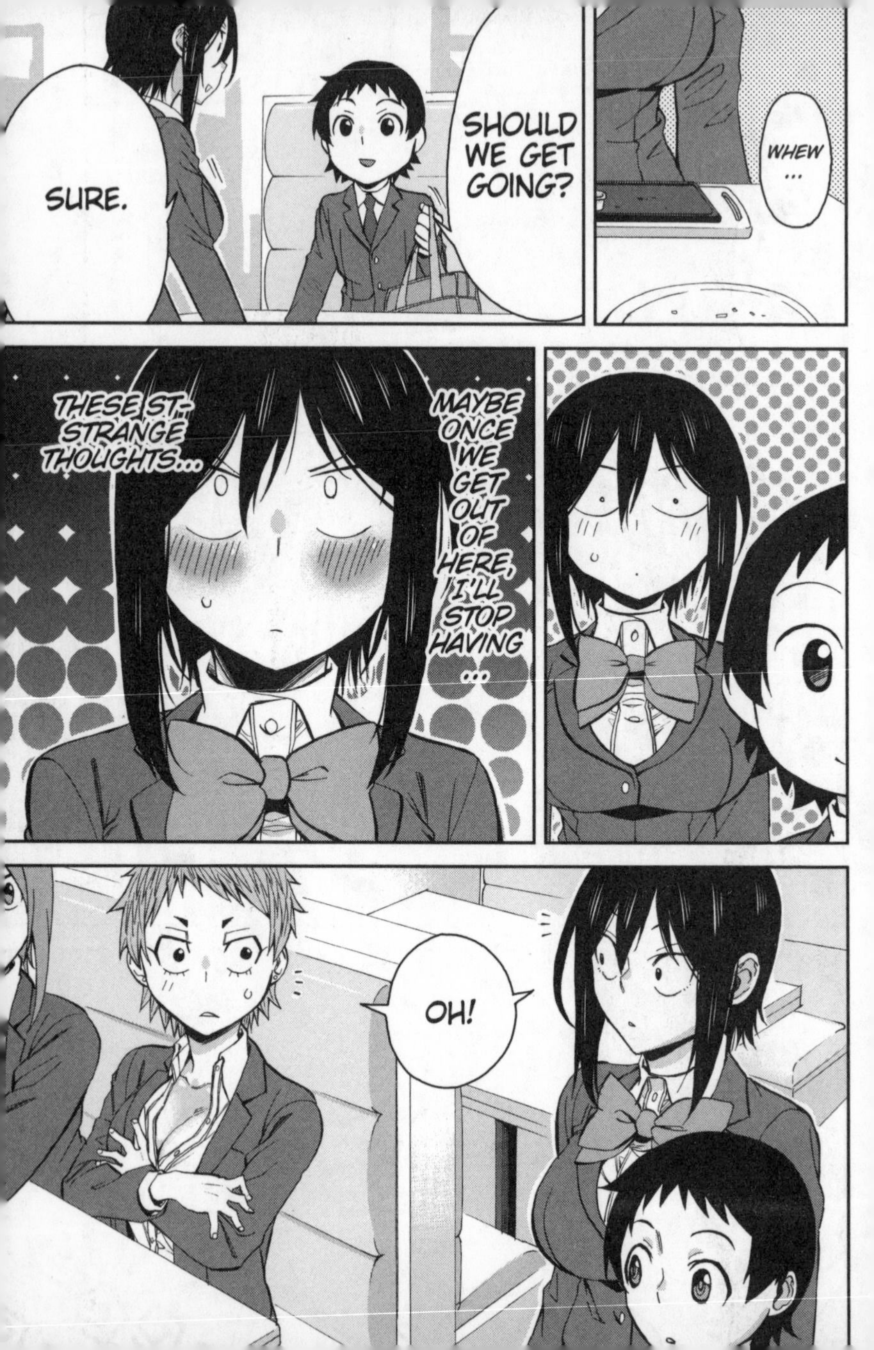
WHEW ...
SHOULD WE GET GOING?
SURE.
MAYBE ONCE WE GET OUT OF HERE, I'LL STOP HAVING ...
THESE ST- STRANGE THOUGHTS...
OH!

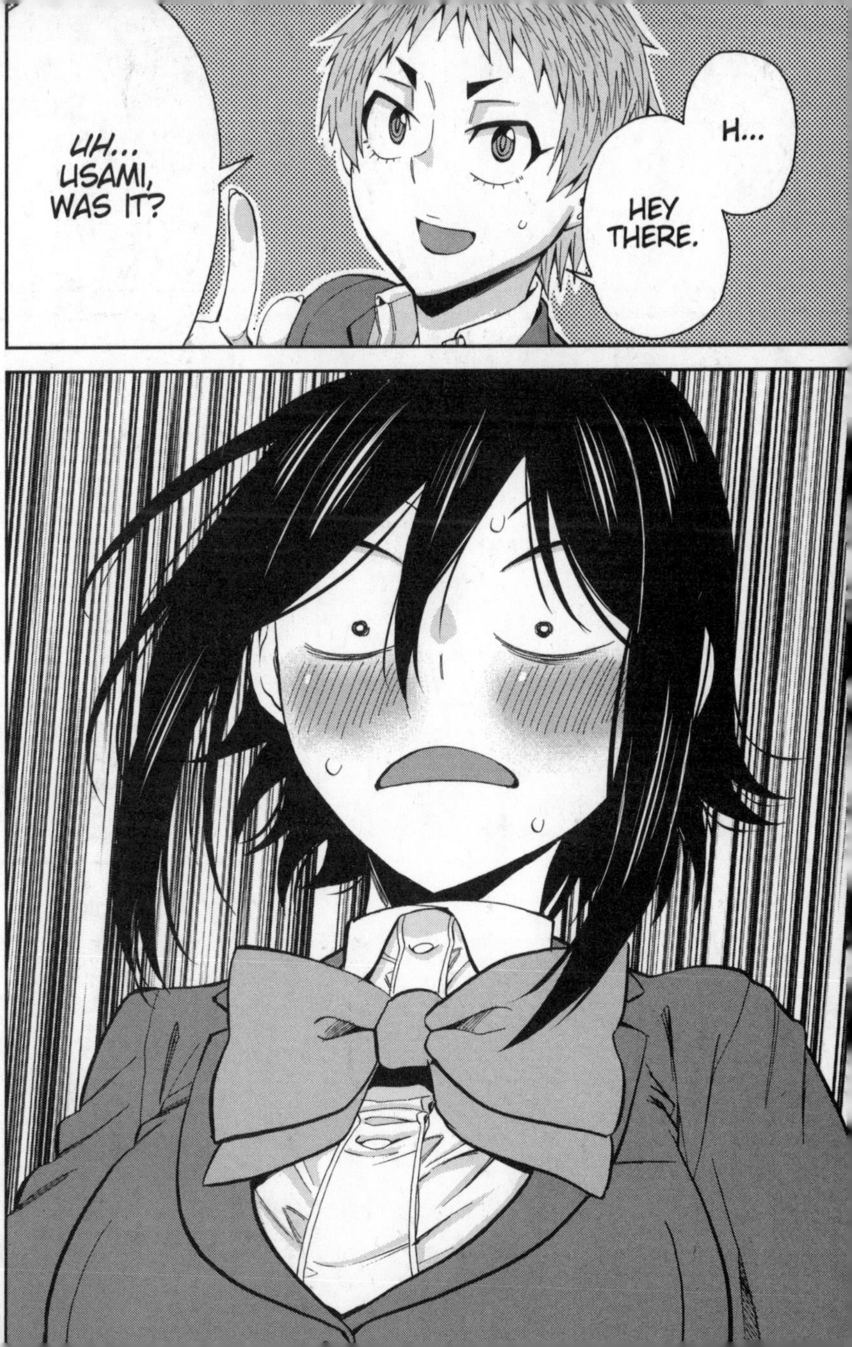
H... HEY THERE.
UH... USAMI, WAS IT?

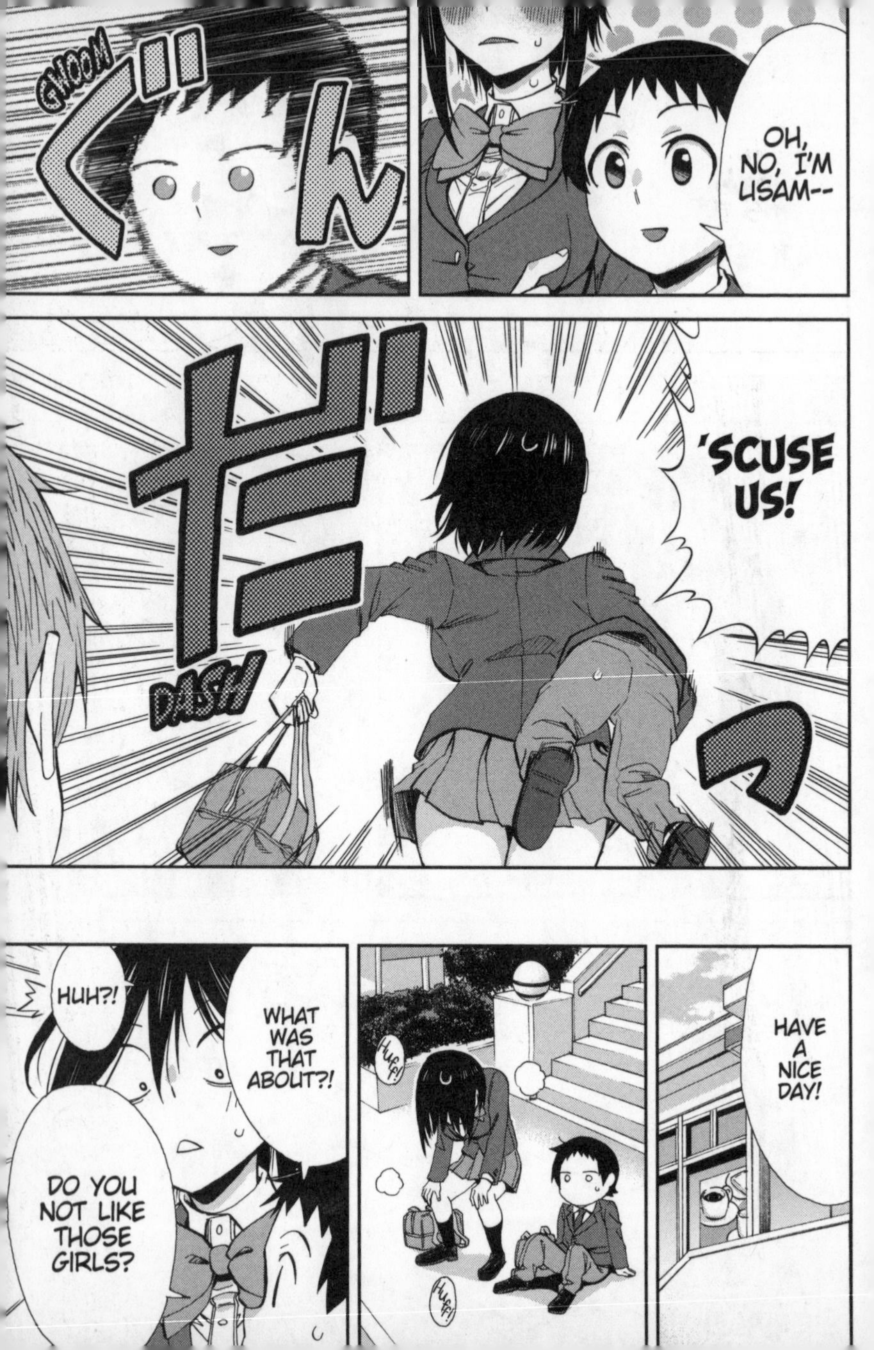
OH, NO, I'M USAM--
GWOOM
'SCUSE US!
DASH
HAVE A NICE DAY!
Huff!
Huff!
WHAT WAS THAT ABOUT?!
HUH?!
DO YOU NOT LIKE THOSE GIRLS?

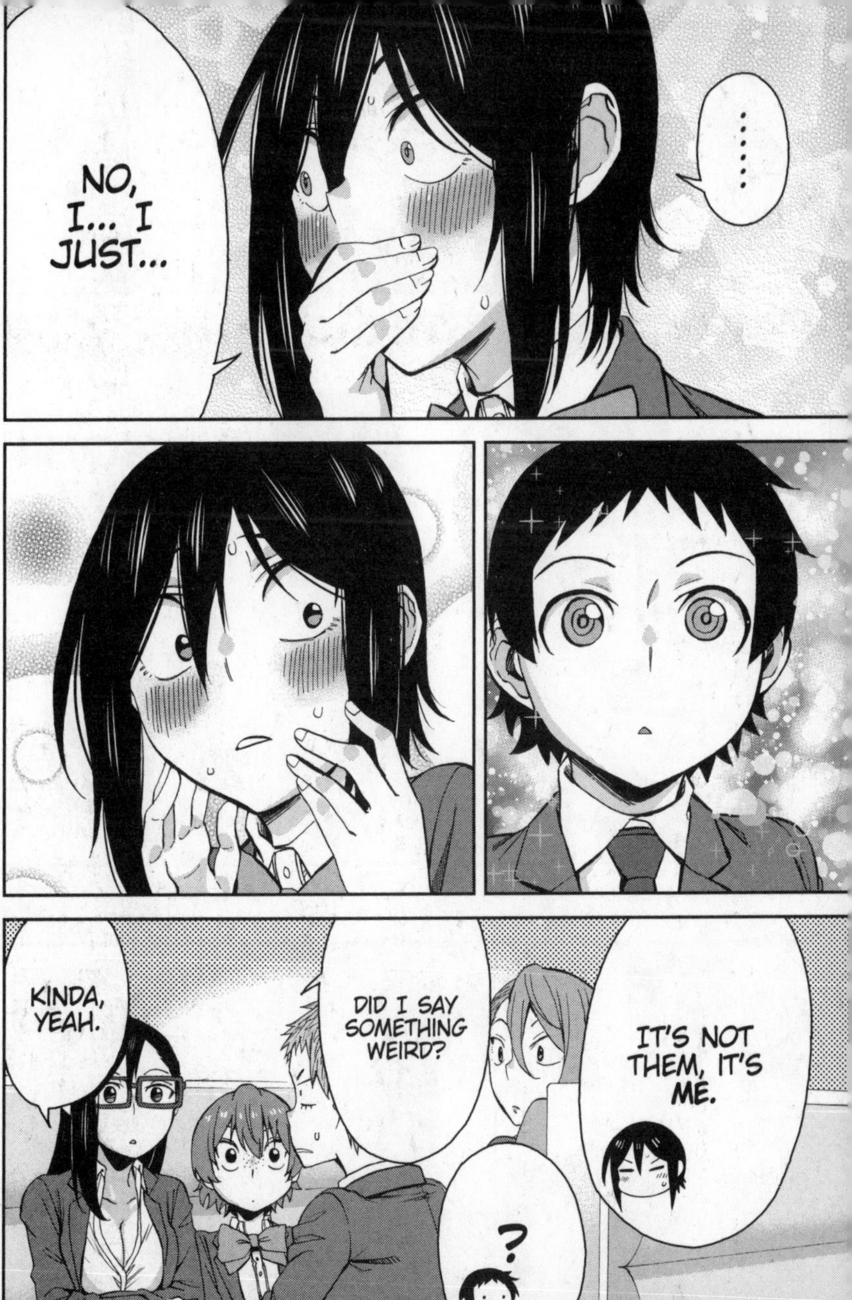
……
NO, I... I JUST...
IT'S NOT THEM, IT'S ME.
?
DID I SAY SOMETHING WEIRD?
KINDA, YEAH.
Chapter 81 / END

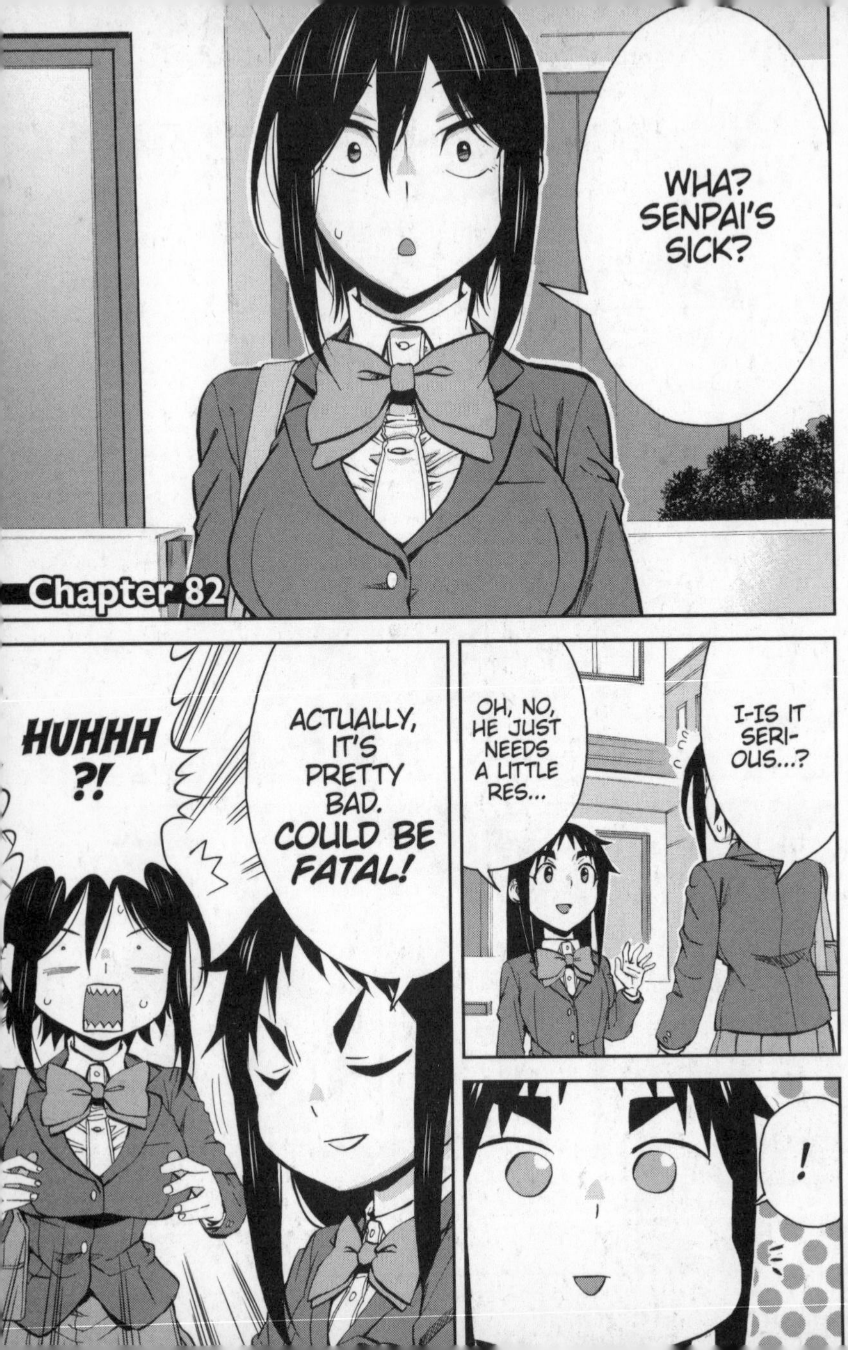
Chapter 82
WHA? SENPAI'S SICK?
I-IS IT SERI-OUS...?
OH, NO, HE JUST NEEDS A LITTLE RES...
!
ACTUALLY, IT'S PRETTY BAD. COULD BE FATAL!
HUHHH ?!

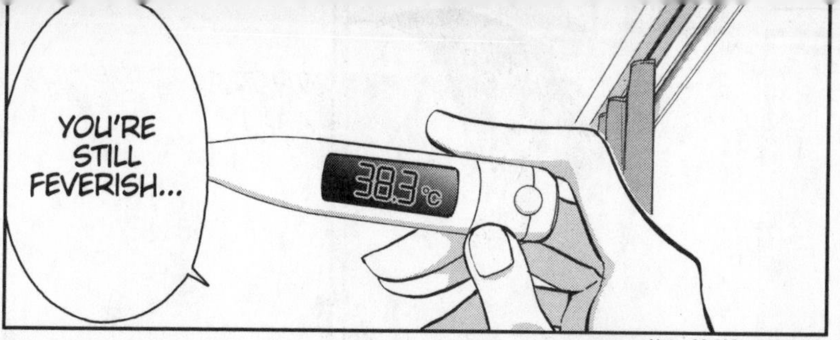
YOU'RE STILL FEVERISH...

Note: 38.3°C = 100.94°F.

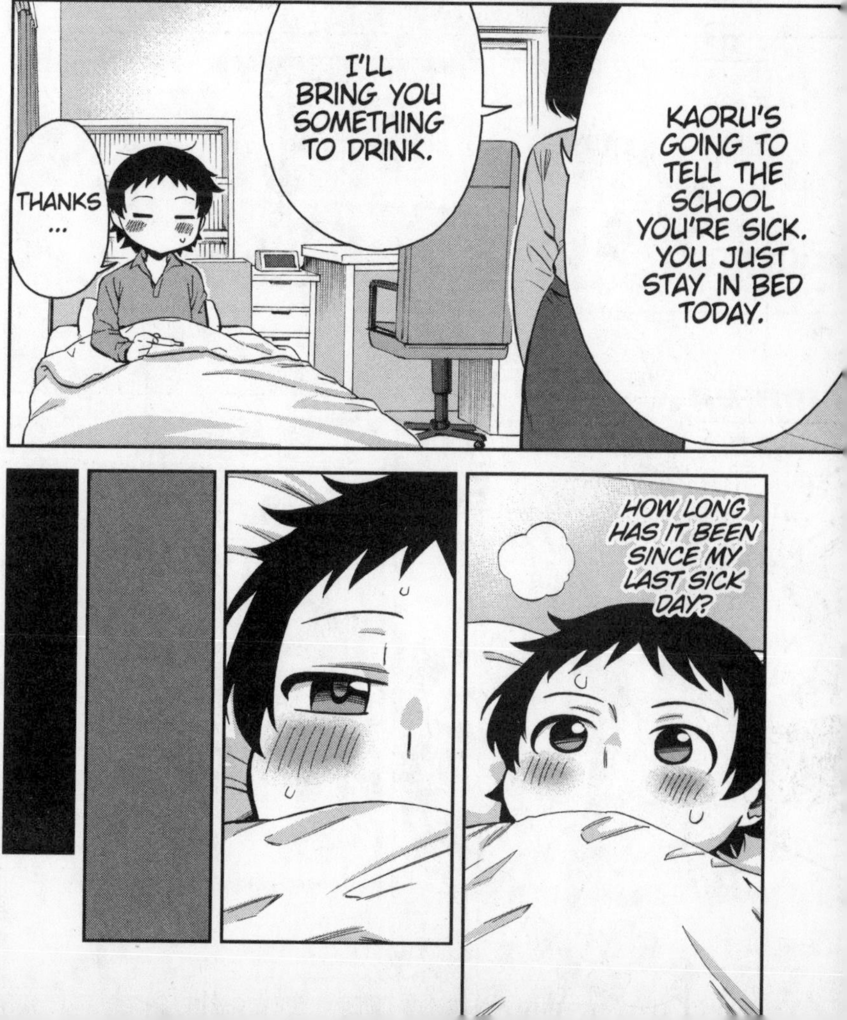
KAORU'S GOING TO TELL THE SCHOOL YOU'RE SICK. YOU JUST STAY IN BED TODAY.
I'LL BRING YOU SOMETHING TO DRINK.
THANKS ...
HOW LONG HAS IT BEEN SINCE MY LAST SICK DAY?

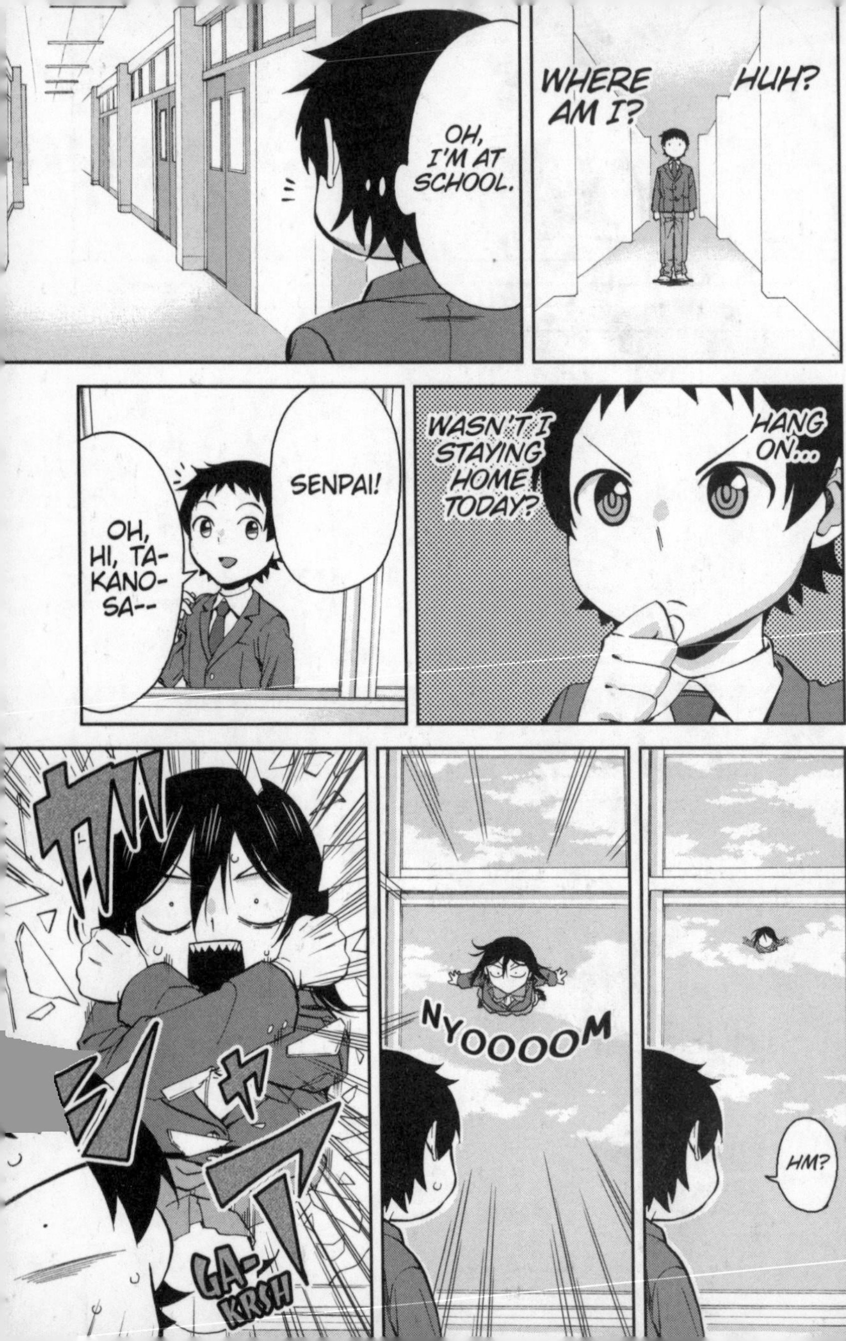
HUH?
WHERE AM I?
OH, I'M AT SCHOOL.
HANG ON...
WASN'T I STAYING HOME TODAY?
SENPAI!
OH, HI, TA-KANO-SA--
HM?
NYOOOOM
GA-KRSH

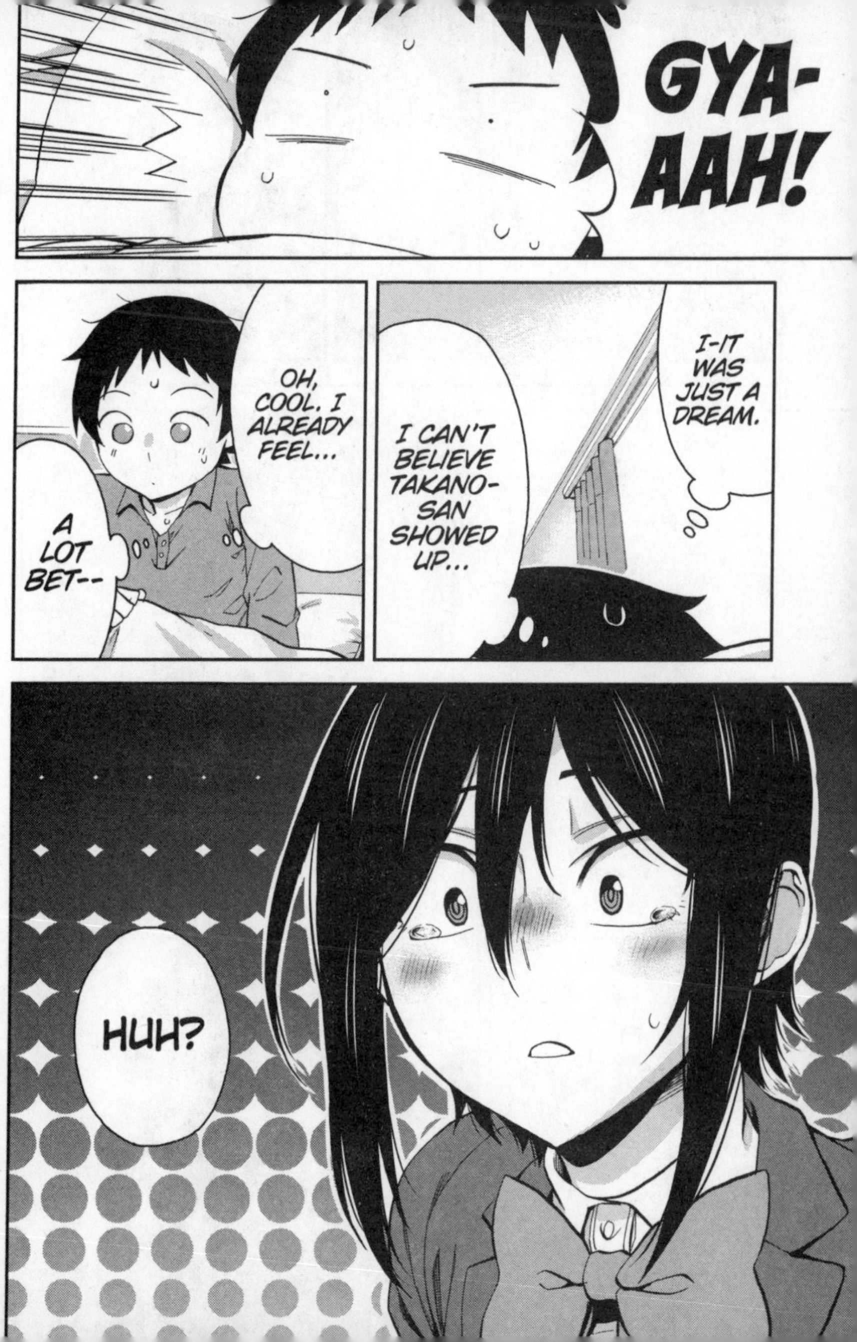
GYA-AAH!
I-IT WAS JUST A DREAM.
I CAN'T BELIEVE TAKANO-SAN SHOWED UP...
OH, COOL. I ALREADY FEEL...
A LOT BET--
HUH?

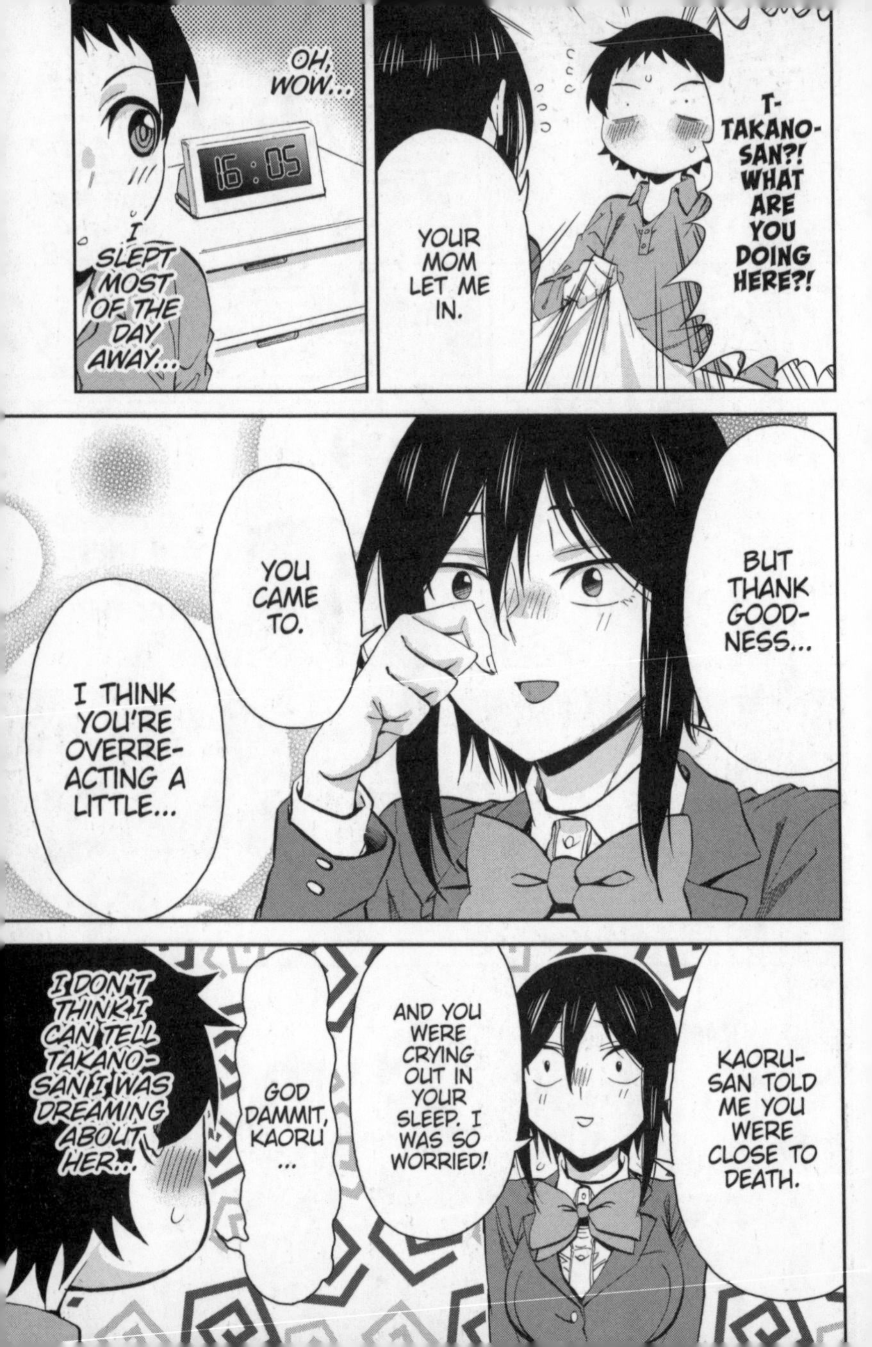
T-TAKANO-SAN?! WHAT ARE YOU DOING HERE?!
YOUR MOM LET ME IN.
OH, WOW...
16:05
I SLEPT MOST OF THE DAY AWAY...
BUT THANK GOODNESS...
YOU CAME TO.
I THINK YOU'RE OVERRE-ACTING A LITTLE...
KAORU-SAN TOLD ME YOU WERE CLOSE TO DEATH.
AND YOU WERE CRYING OUT IN YOUR SLEEP. I WAS SO WORRIED!
GOD DAMMIT, KAORU...
I DON'T THINK I CAN TELL TAKANO-SAN I WAS DREAMING ABOUT HER...

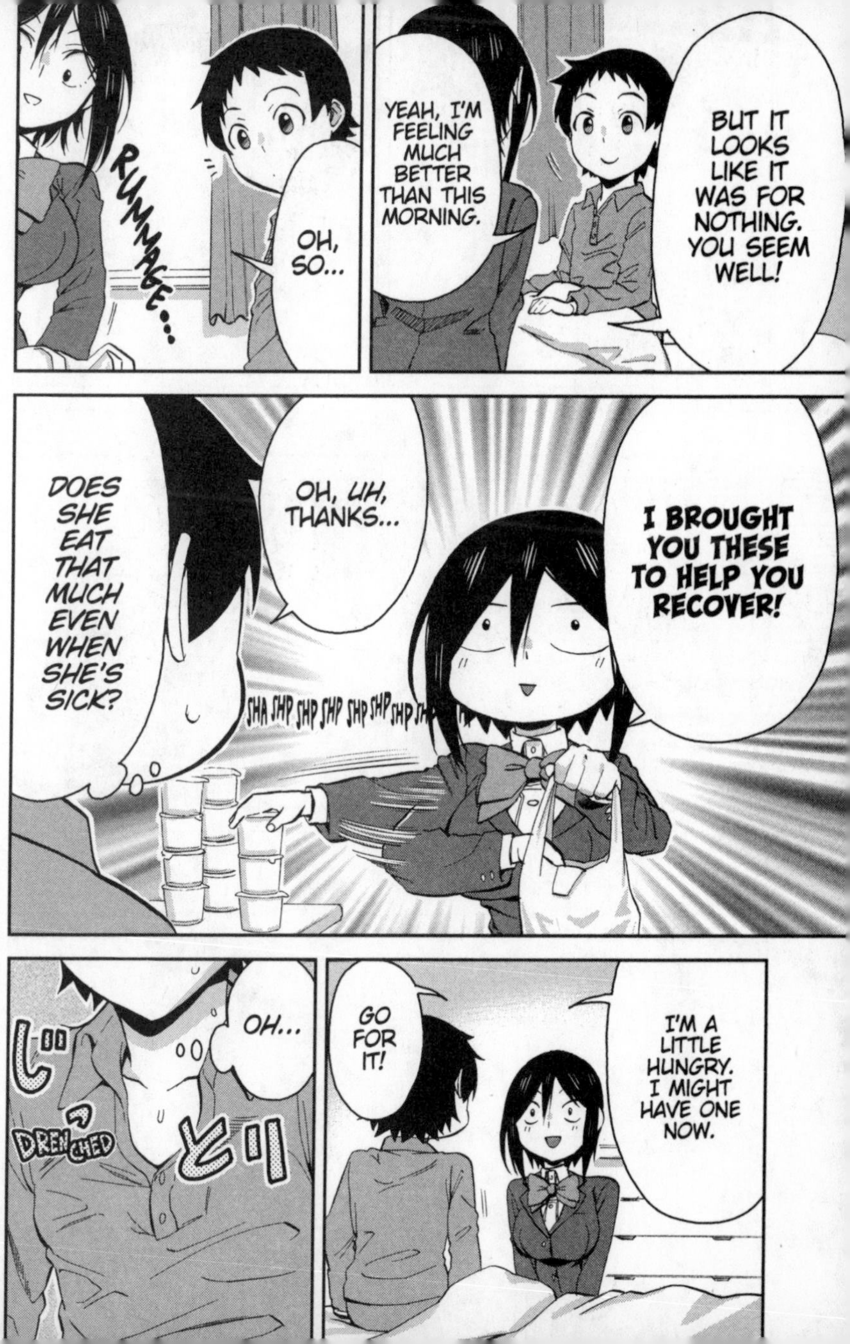
BUT IT LOOKS LIKE IT WAS FOR NOTHING. YOU SEEM WELL!
YEAH, I'M FEELING MUCH BETTER THAN THIS MORNING.
OH, SO...
RUMMAGE...
I BROUGHT YOU THESE TO HELP YOU RECOVER!
OH, UH, THANKS...
SHA SHP SHP SHP SHP SHP SHP SHP
DOES SHE EAT THAT MUCH EVEN WHEN SHE'S SICK?
I'M A LITTLE HUNGRY. I MIGHT HAVE ONE NOW.
GO FOR IT!
OH...
DRENCHED

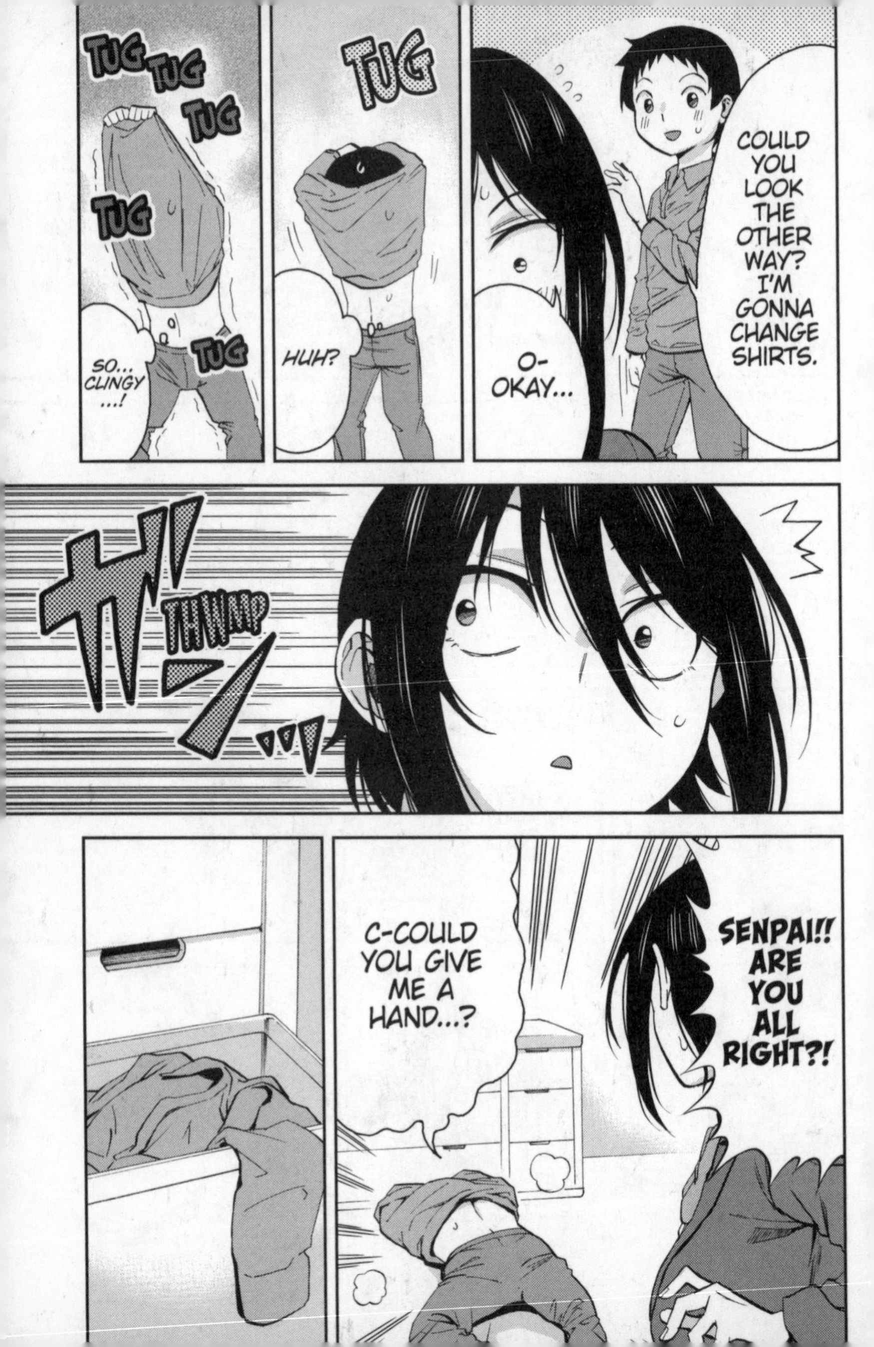
COULD YOU LOOK THE OTHER WAY? I'M GONNA CHANGE SHIRTS.
O-OKAY...
TUG
HUH?
TUG TUG TUG
TUG
TUG
SO... CLINGY ...!
THWMP
SENPAI!! ARE YOU ALL RIGHT?!
C-COULD YOU GIVE ME A HAND...?

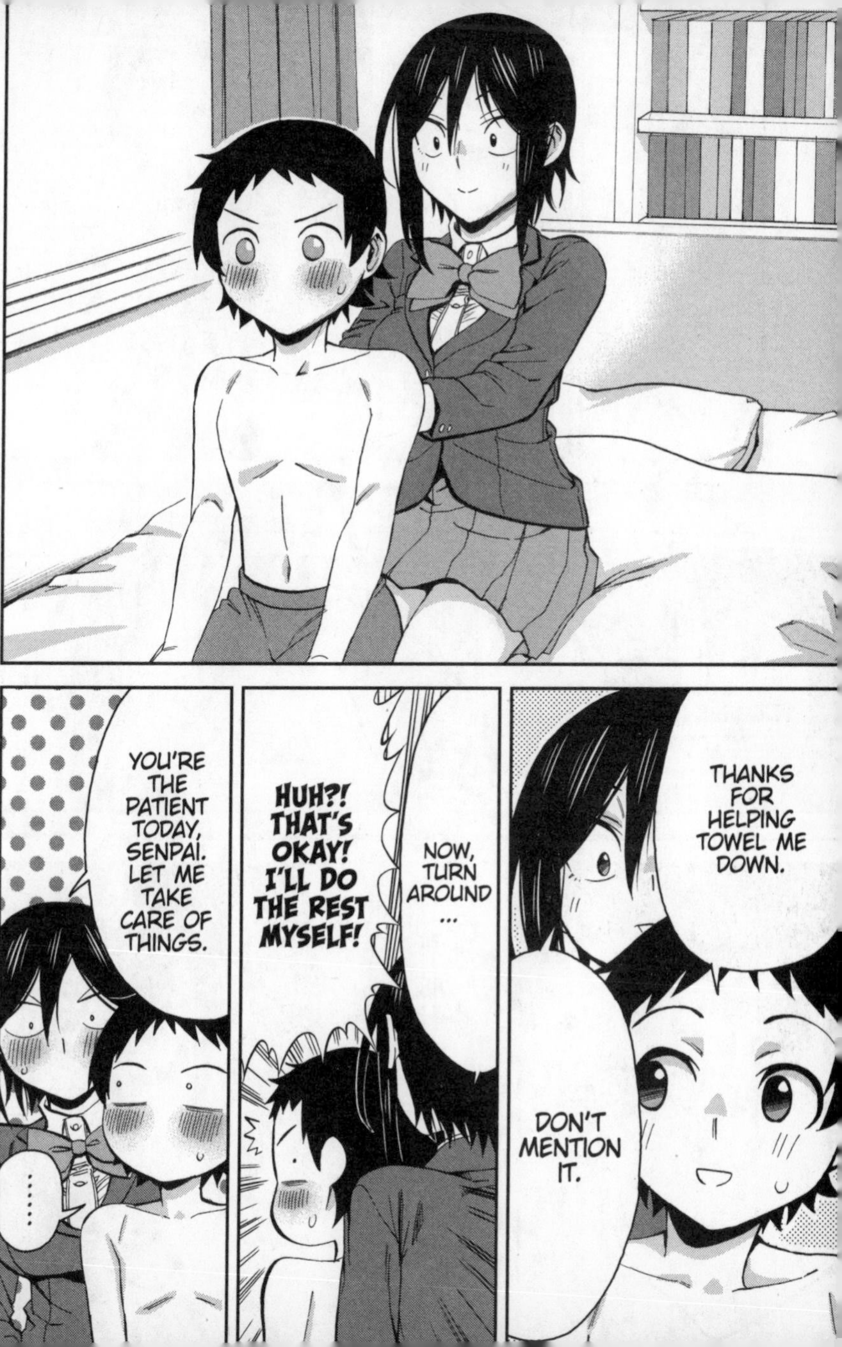
THANKS FOR HELPING TOWEL ME DOWN.
DON'T MENTION IT.
NOW, TURN AROUND ...
HUH?! THAT'S OKAY! I'LL DO THE REST MYSELF!
YOU'RE THE PATIENT TODAY, SENPAI. LET ME TAKE CARE OF THINGS.
......

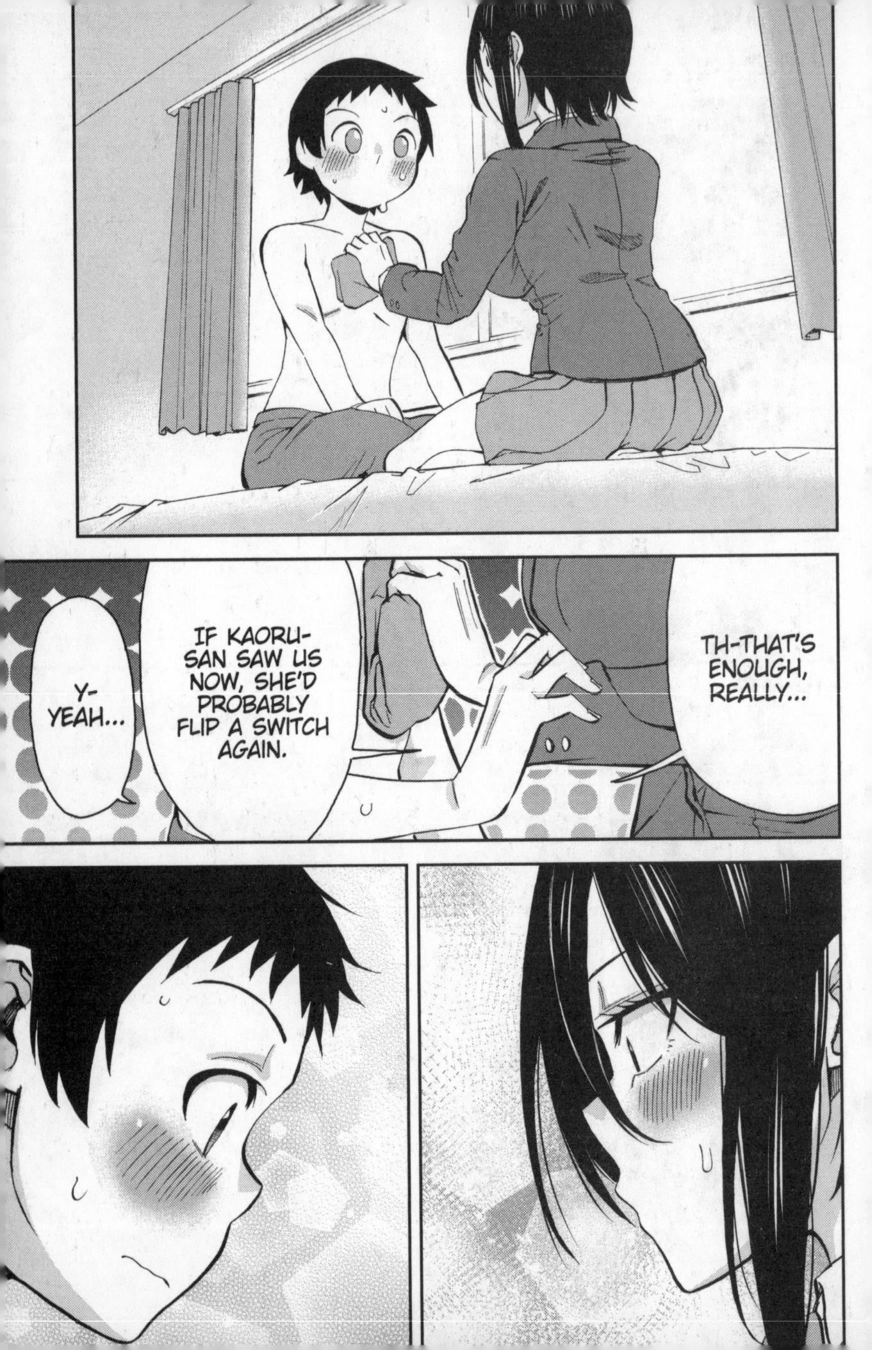
TH-THAT'S ENOUGH, REALLY...
IF KAORU-SAN SAW US NOW, SHE'D PROBABLY FLIP A SWITCH AGAIN.
Y-YEAH...

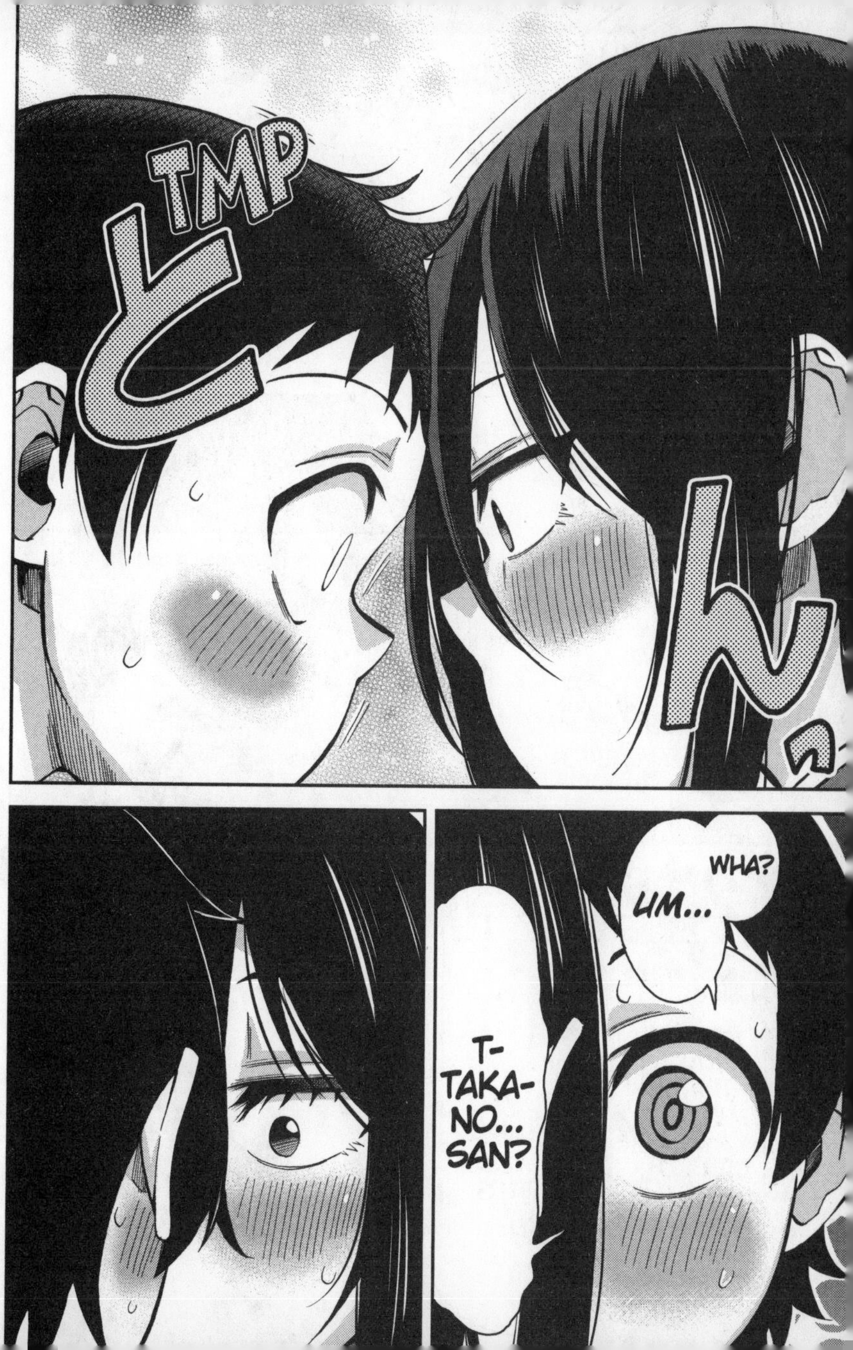
ん
と
TMP
WHA?
UM...
T-TAKANO... SAN?

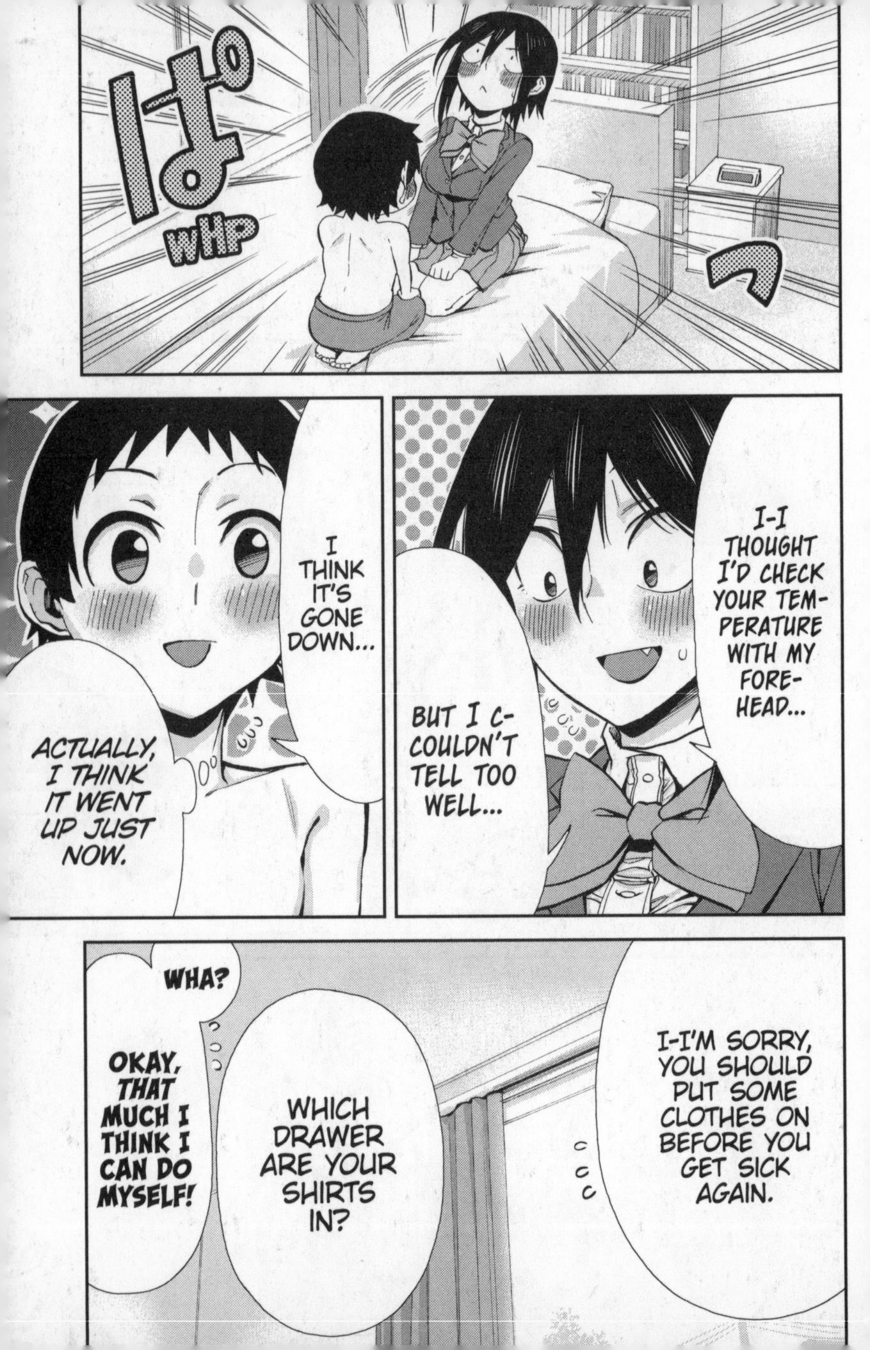

っ
ぱ
WHP
I-I THOUGHT I'D CHECK YOUR TEM-PERATURE WITH MY FORE-HEAD...
BUT I C-COULDN'T TELL TOO WELL...
I THINK IT'S GONE DOWN...
ACTUALLY, I THINK IT WENT UP JUST NOW.
I-I'M SORRY, YOU SHOULD PUT SOME CLOTHES ON BEFORE YOU GET SICK AGAIN.
WHICH DRAWER ARE YOUR SHIRTS IN?
WHA?
OKAY, THAT MUCH I THINK I CAN DO MYSELF!

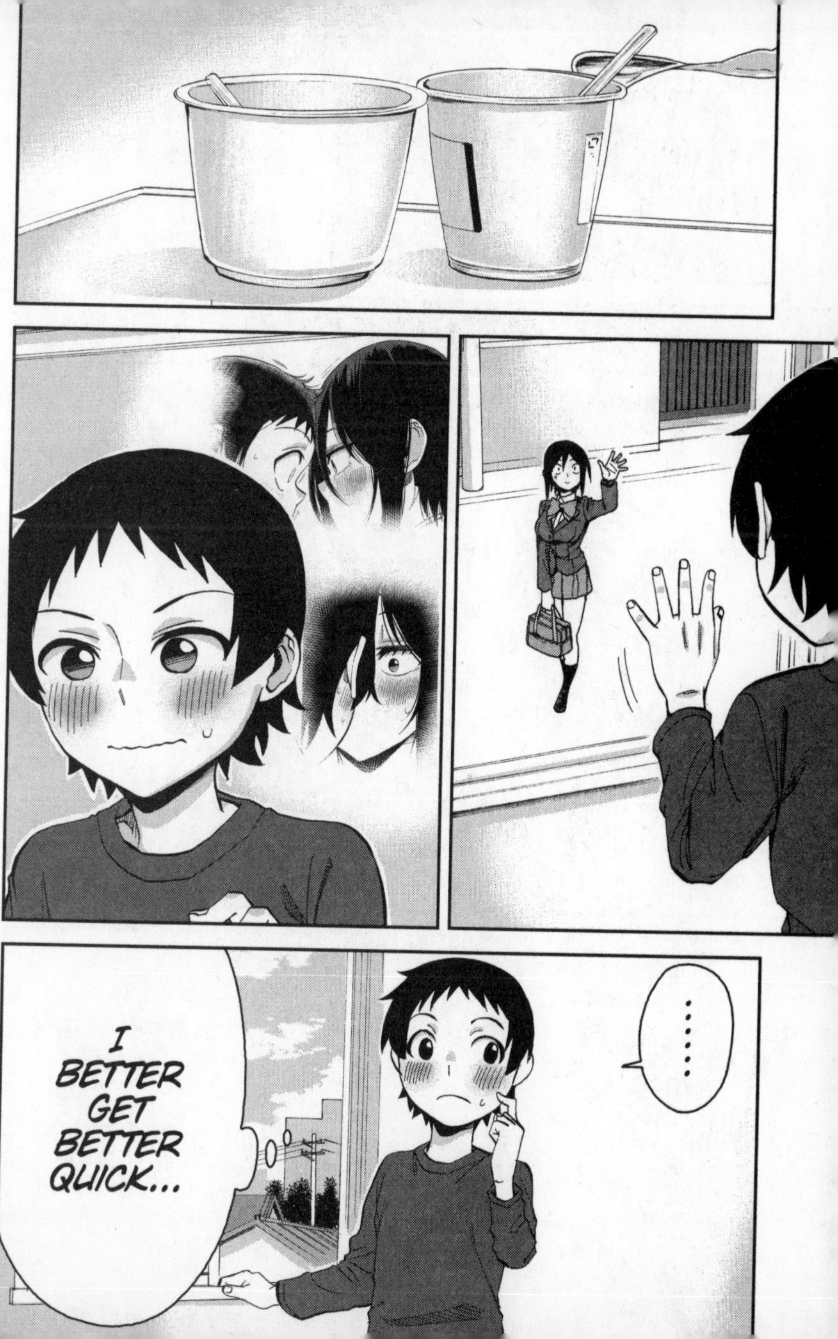
......
I BETTER GET BETTER QUICK...

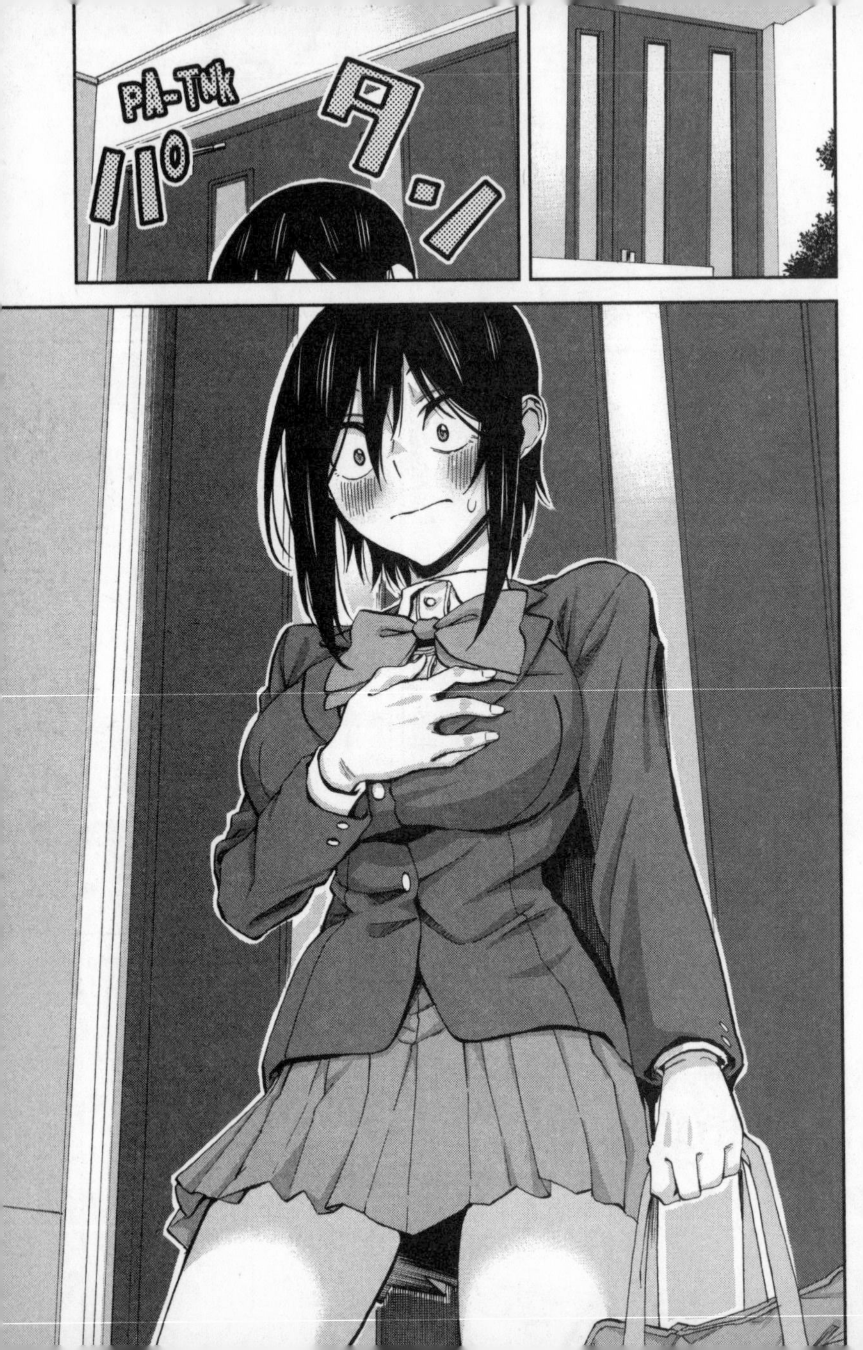
PA-TNK
パタ・ン

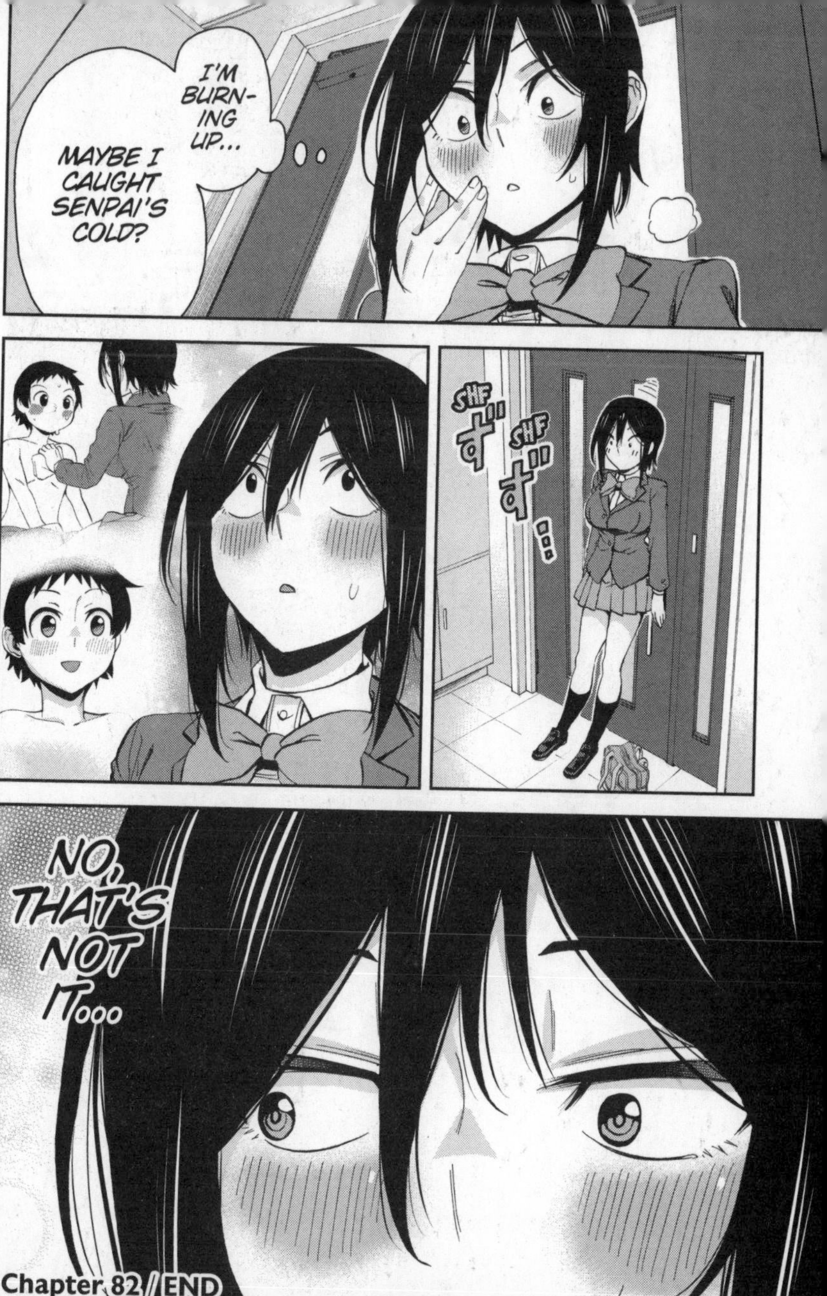
I'M BURNING UP...
MAYBE I CAUGHT SENPAI'S COLD?
SHF
ずず
SHF
ずず...
NO, THAT'S NOT IT...

Chapter 82 / END

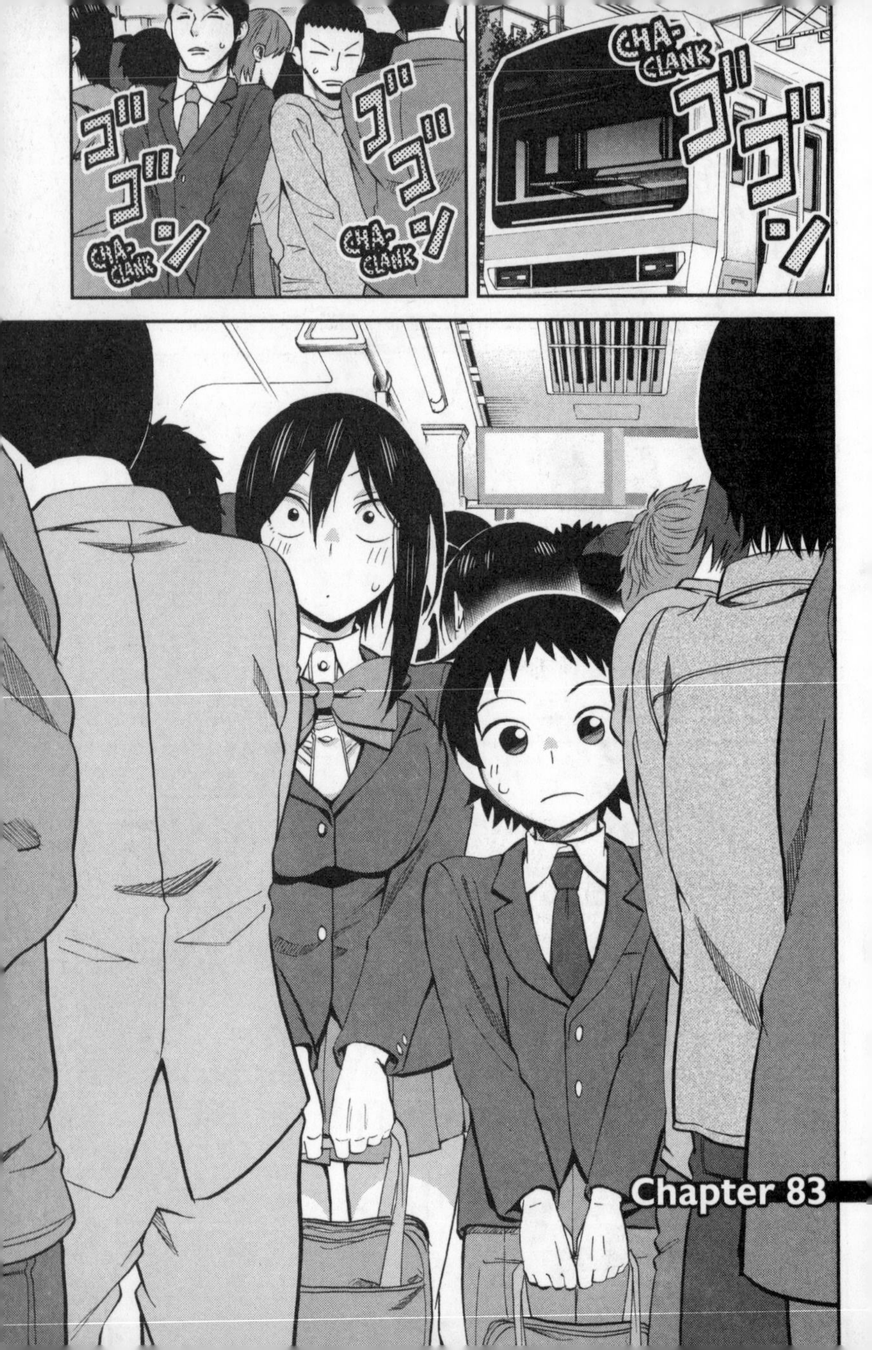
CHA-CLANK
ゴゴン
CHA-CLANK
ゴゴン
CHA-CLANK
ゴゴン
Chapter 83

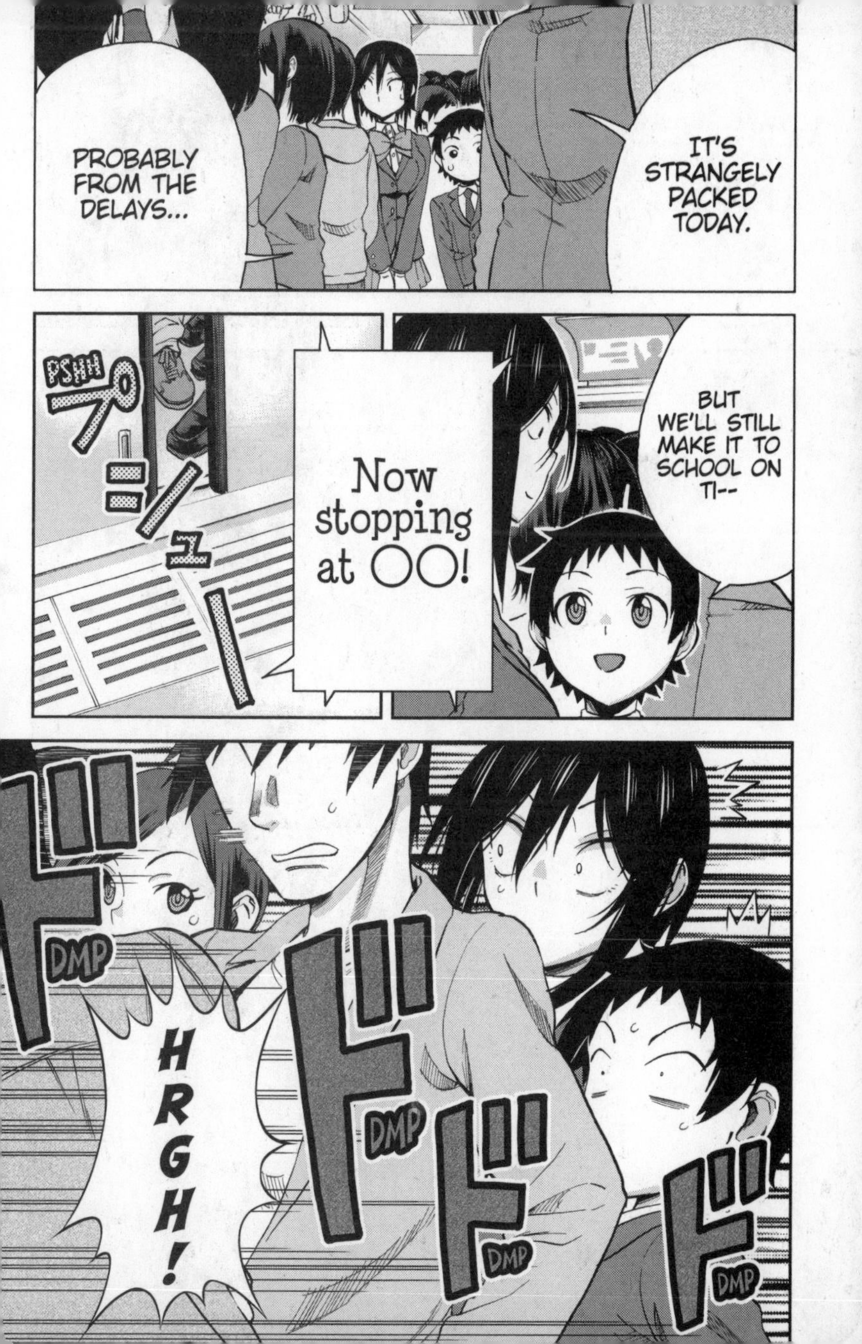
IT'S STRANGELY PACKED TODAY.
PROBABLY FROM THE DELAYS...
BUT WE'LL STILL MAKE IT TO SCHOOL ON TI--
Now stopping at OO!
PSHH
DMP
DMP
DMP
DMP
DMP
HRGH!

YOU ALL RIGHT, SENPAI?

I-IT'S GOTTEN WORSE...

I'm... hanging in there...

....

Please hold on, the train may shake a little.

ど

I CAN DO THI--

WHMP

ん

ONLY TWO STOPS TO GO...

THIS POSTURE IS KILLING ME...

I-IT'S OKAY...

S-S-S-SORRY!

BUT I'M BEING PUSHED FROM BEHIND...

I'VE GOTTA GET MYSELF OUT OF THIS...

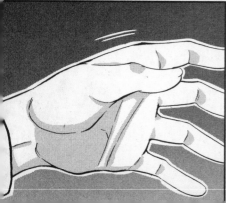

......

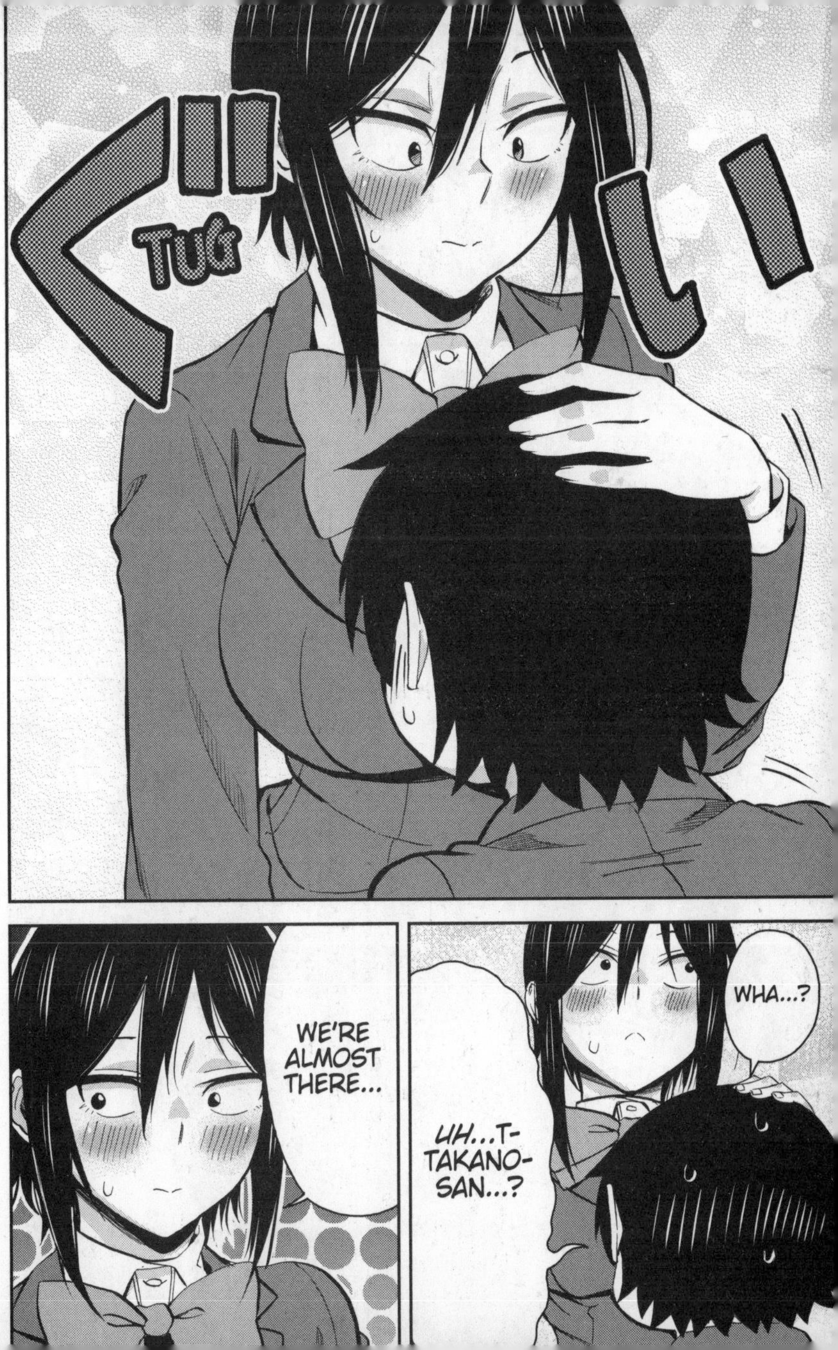
TUG
WHA...?
UH...T-TAKANO-SAN...?
WE'RE ALMOST THERE...

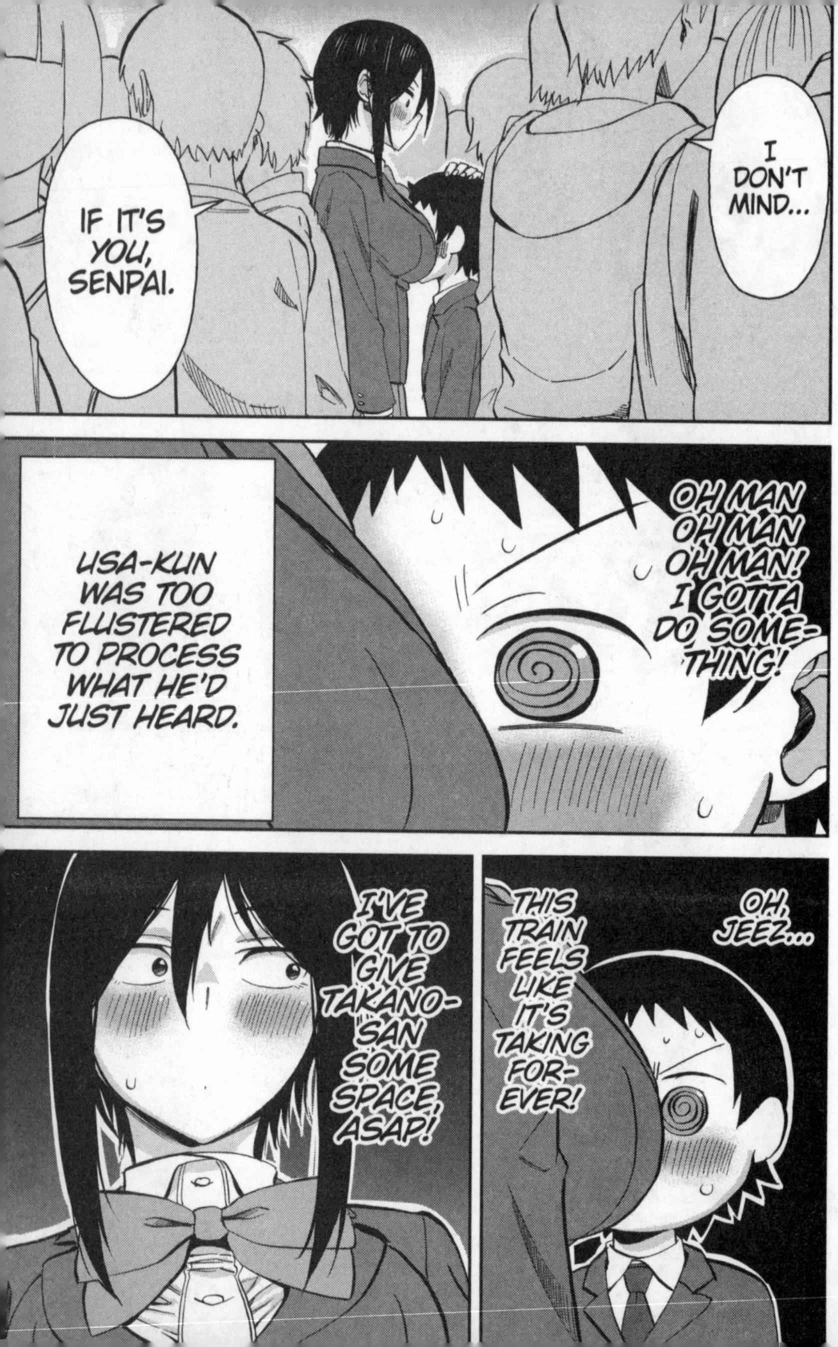
I DON'T MIND...
IF IT'S YOU, SENPAI.
OH MAN OH MAN OH MAN! I GOTTA DO SOME-THING!
USA-KUN WAS TOO FLUSTERED TO PROCESS WHAT HE'D JUST HEARD.
OH, JEEZ...
THIS TRAIN FEELS LIKE IT'S TAKING FOR-EVER!
I'VE GOT TO GIVE TAKANO-SAN SOME SPACE, ASAP!

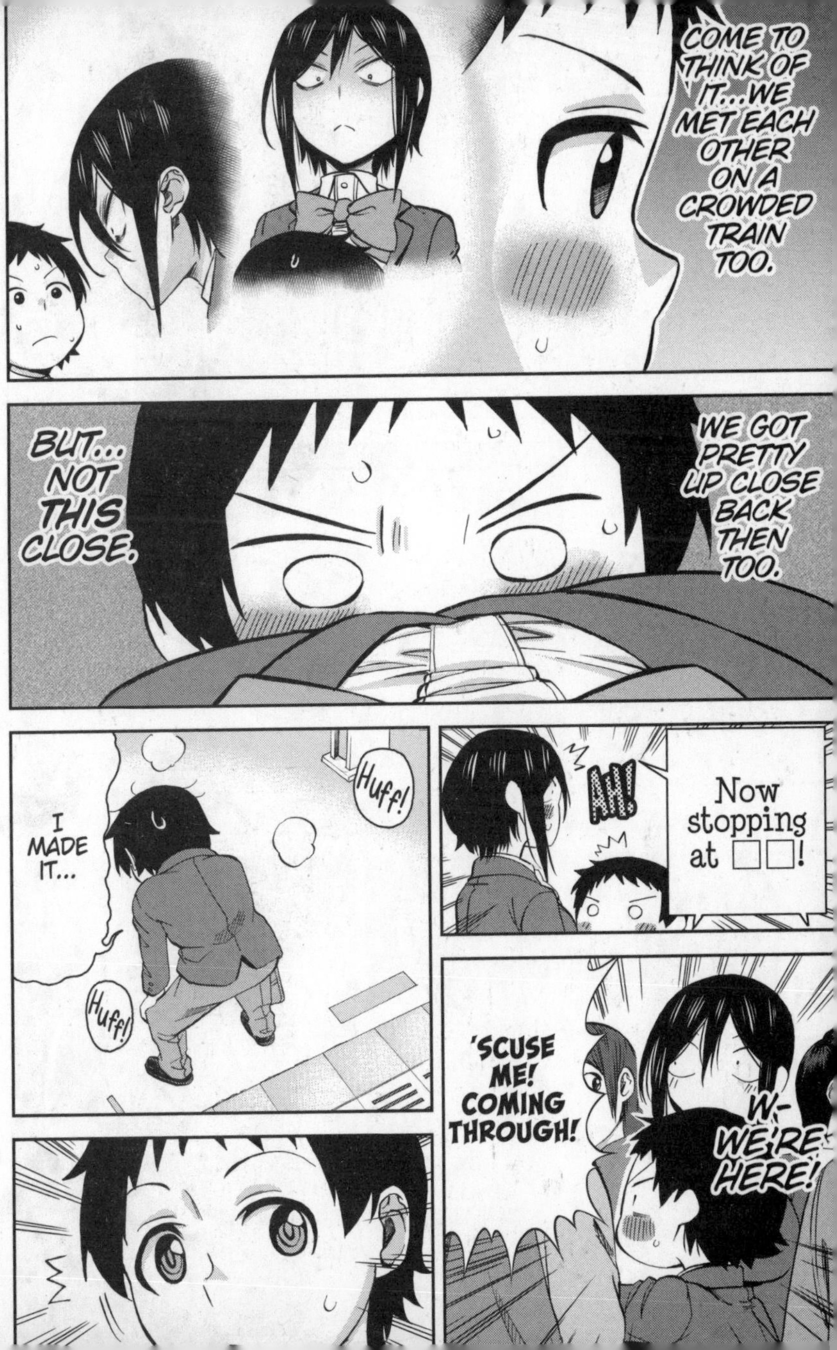
COME TO THINK OF IT...WE MET EACH OTHER ON A CROWDED TRAIN TOO.
WE GOT PRETTY UP CLOSE BACK THEN TOO.
BUT... NOT THIS CLOSE.
Now stopping at □□!
AH!
W-WE'RE HERE!
'SCUSE ME! COMING THROUGH!
Huff!
I MADE IT...
Huff!

Stand
clear,
doors
closing.

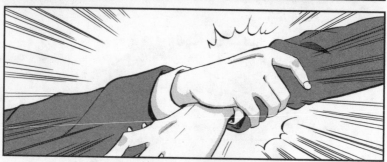

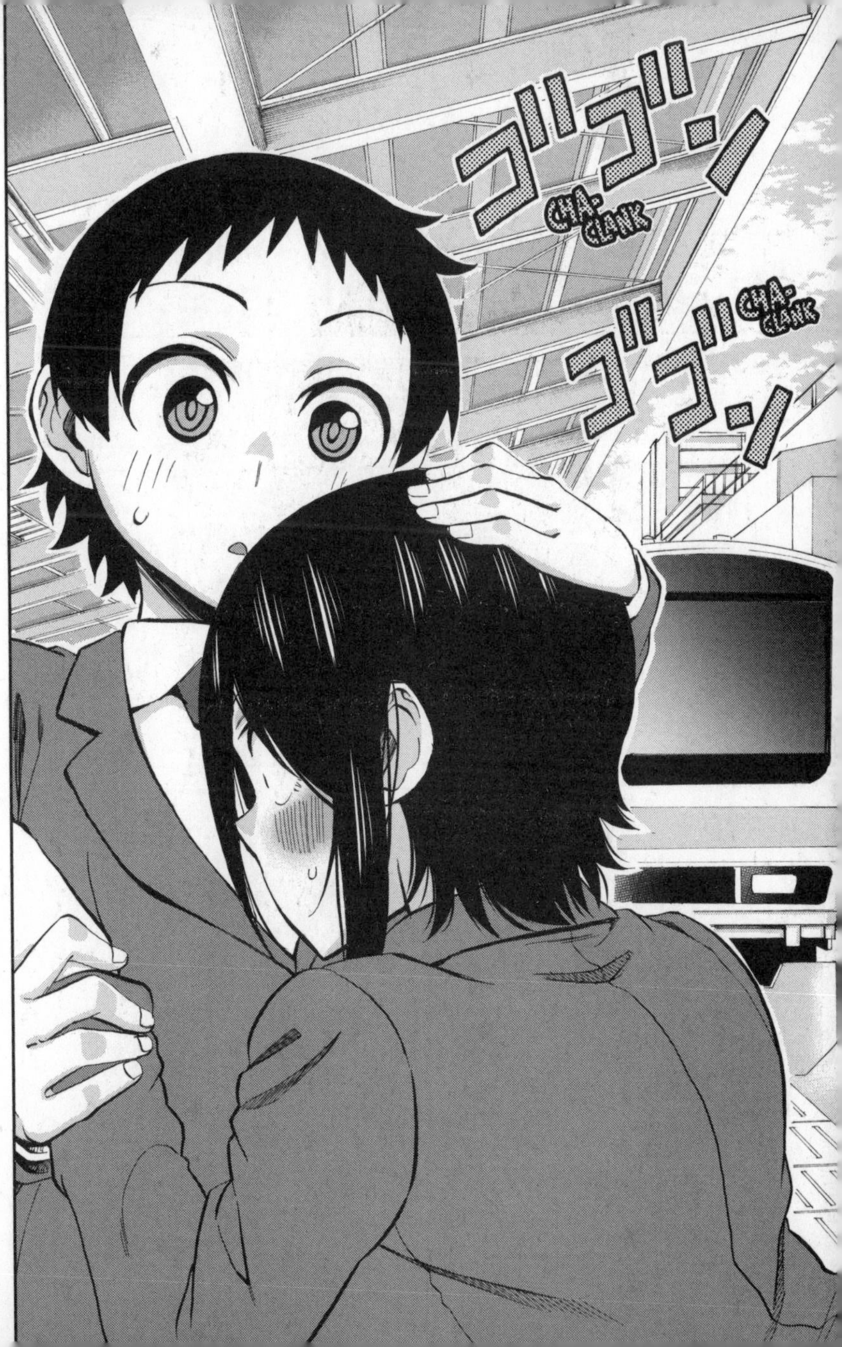
ゴゴン
CHA-CLANK
ゴゴン
CHA-CLANK

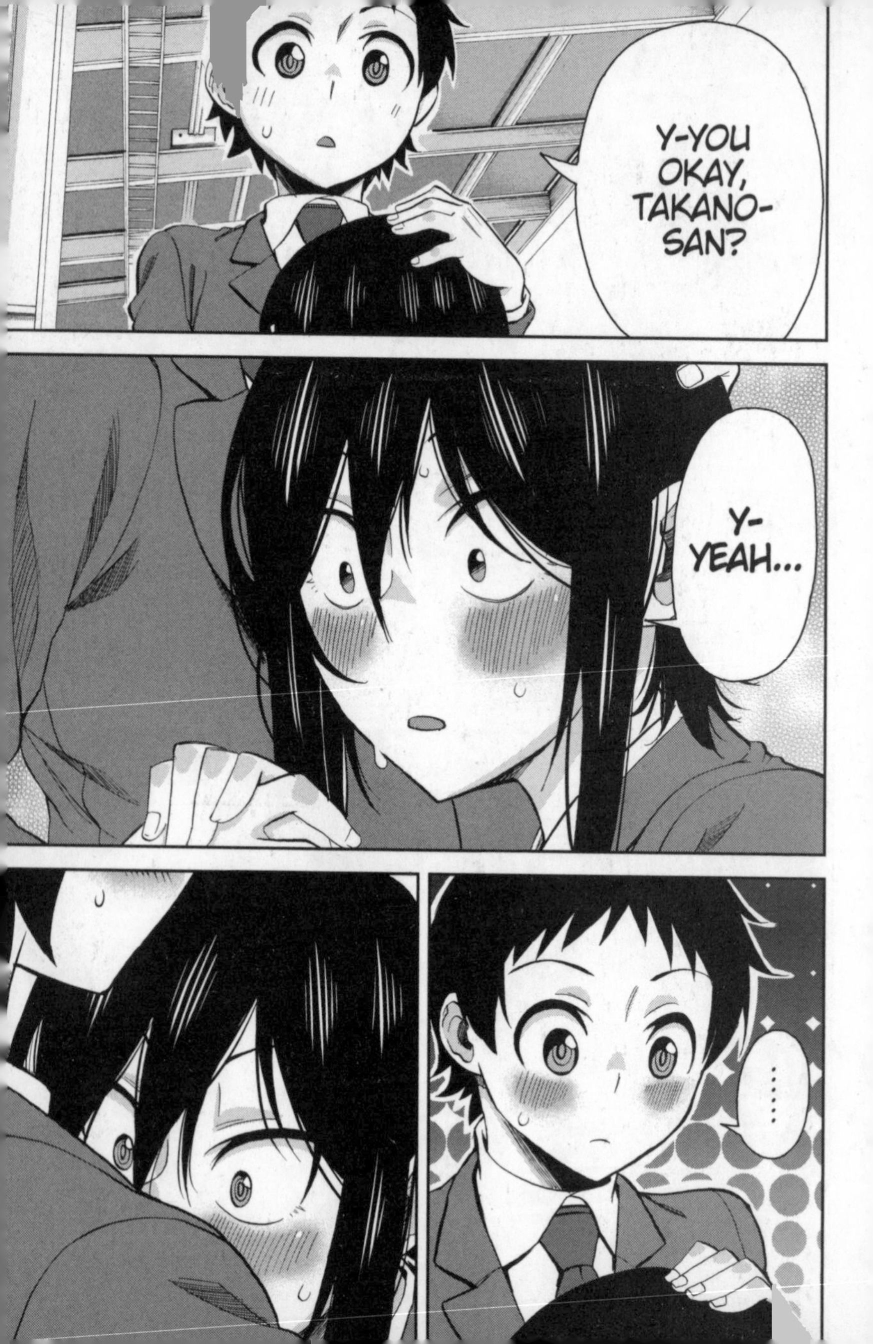
Y-YOU OKAY, TAKANO-SAN?
Y-YEAH...
......

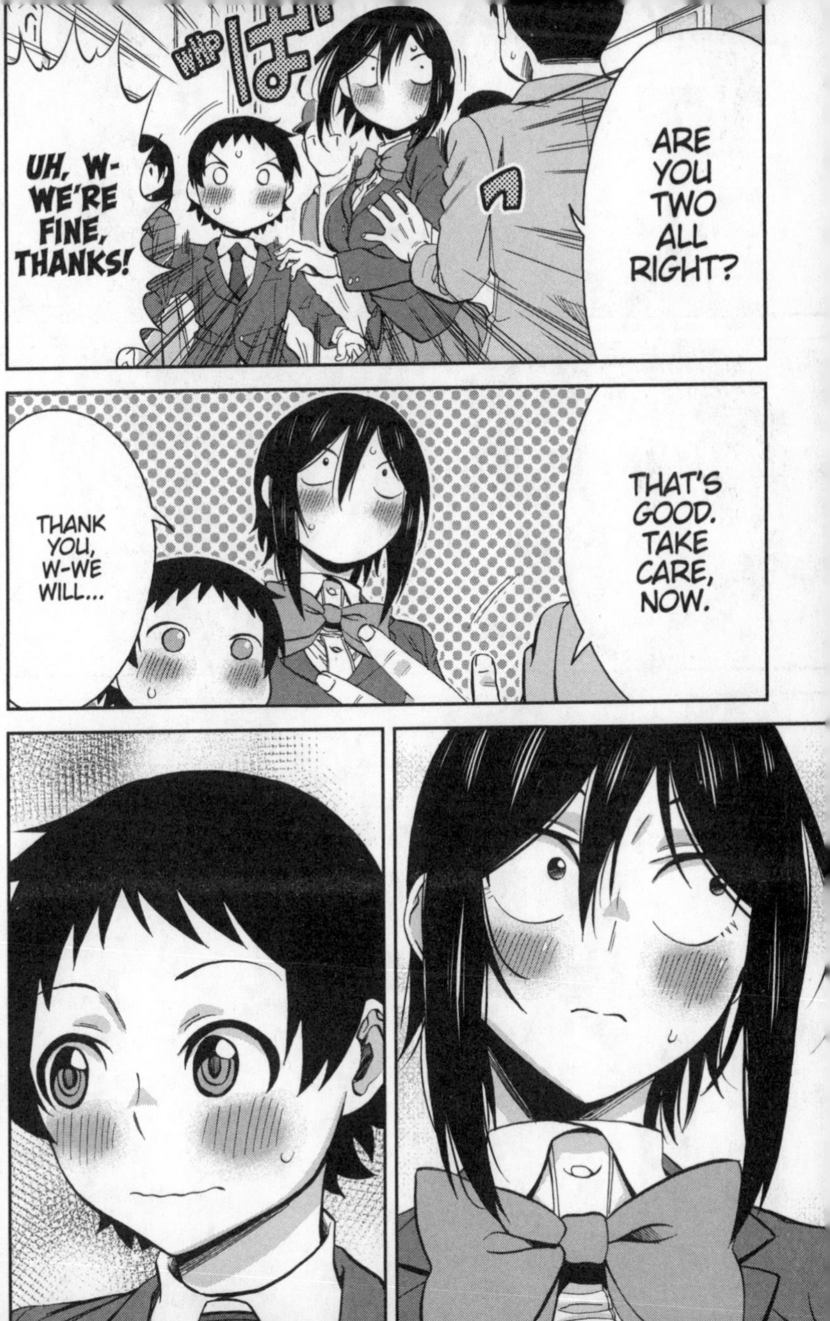
ARE YOU TWO ALL RIGHT?
ぱ
WHIP
UH, W-WE'RE FINE, THANKS!
THAT'S GOOD. TAKE CARE, NOW.
THANK YOU, W-WE WILL...

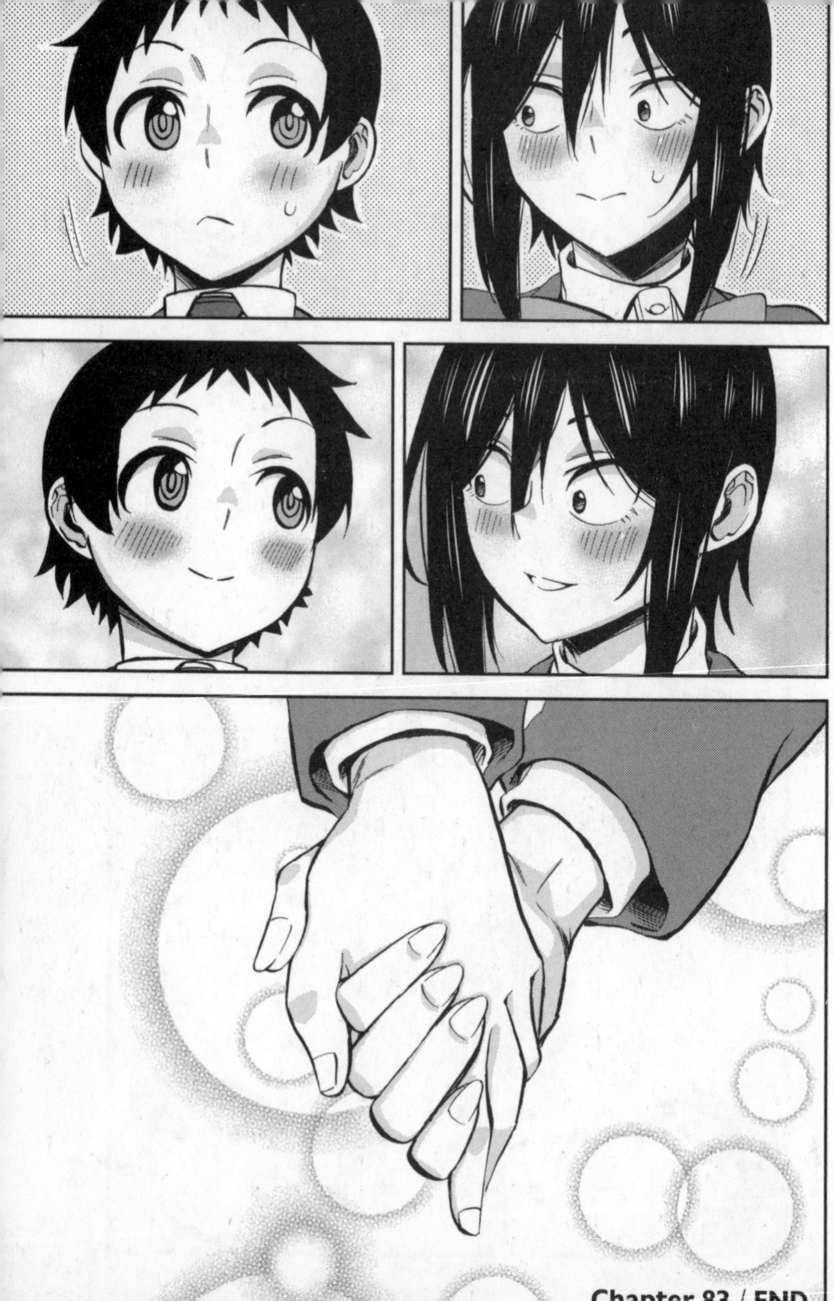

Chapter 83 / END

Hitomi-chan is Shy With Strangers

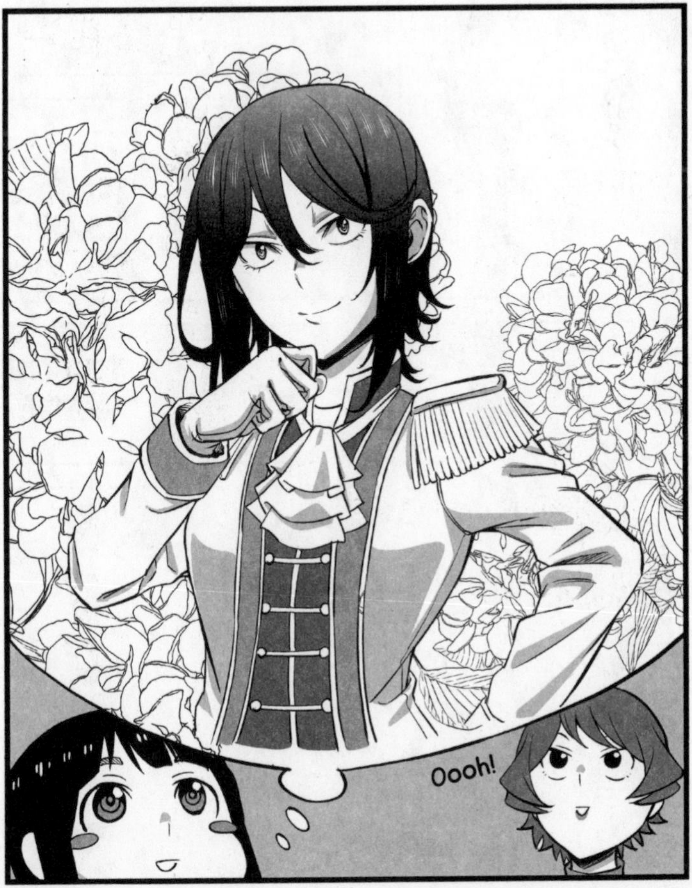
Oooh!

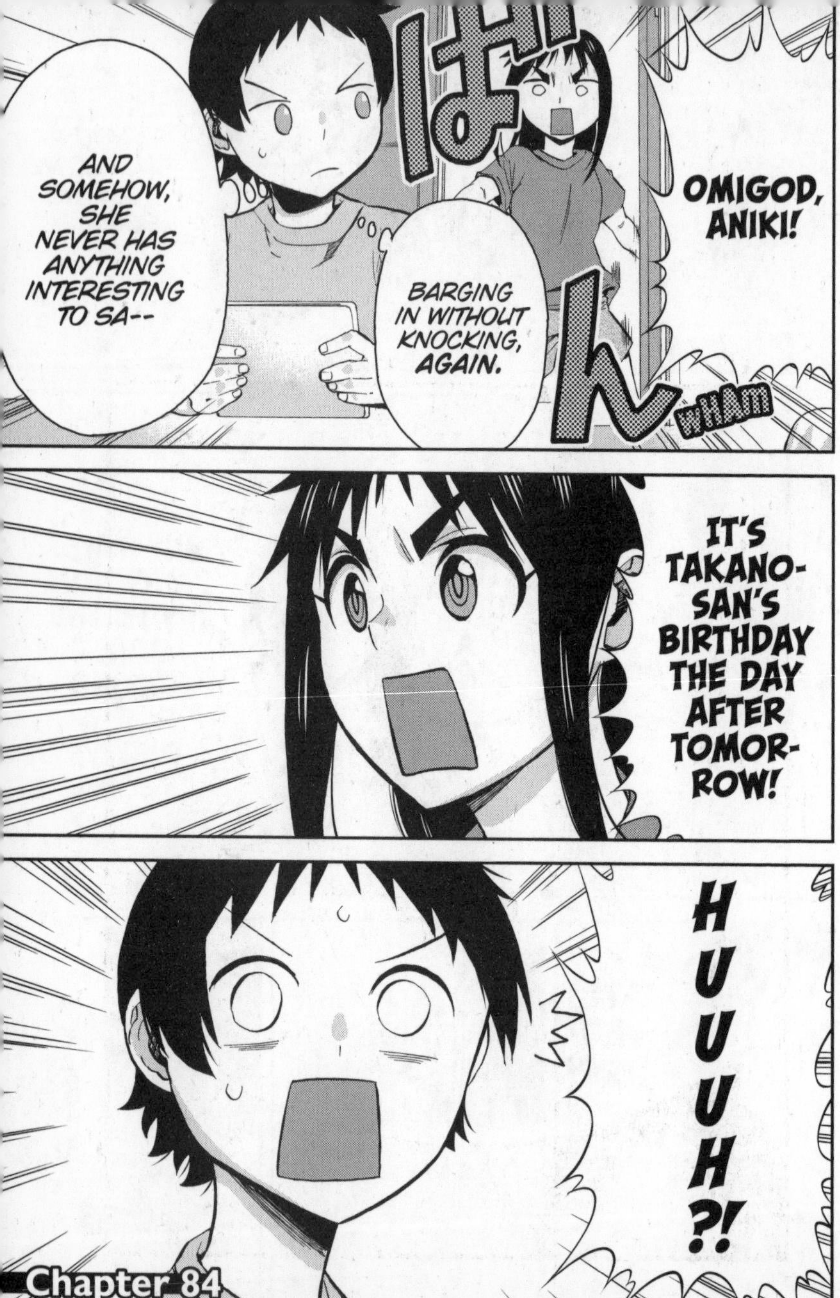
OMIGOD, ANIKI!
WHAM
BARGING IN WITHOUT KNOCKING, AGAIN.
AND SOMEHOW, SHE NEVER HAS ANYTHING INTERESTING TO SA--
IT'S TAKANO-SAN'S BIRTHDAY THE DAY AFTER TOMOR-ROW!
HUUUUH?!
Chapter 84

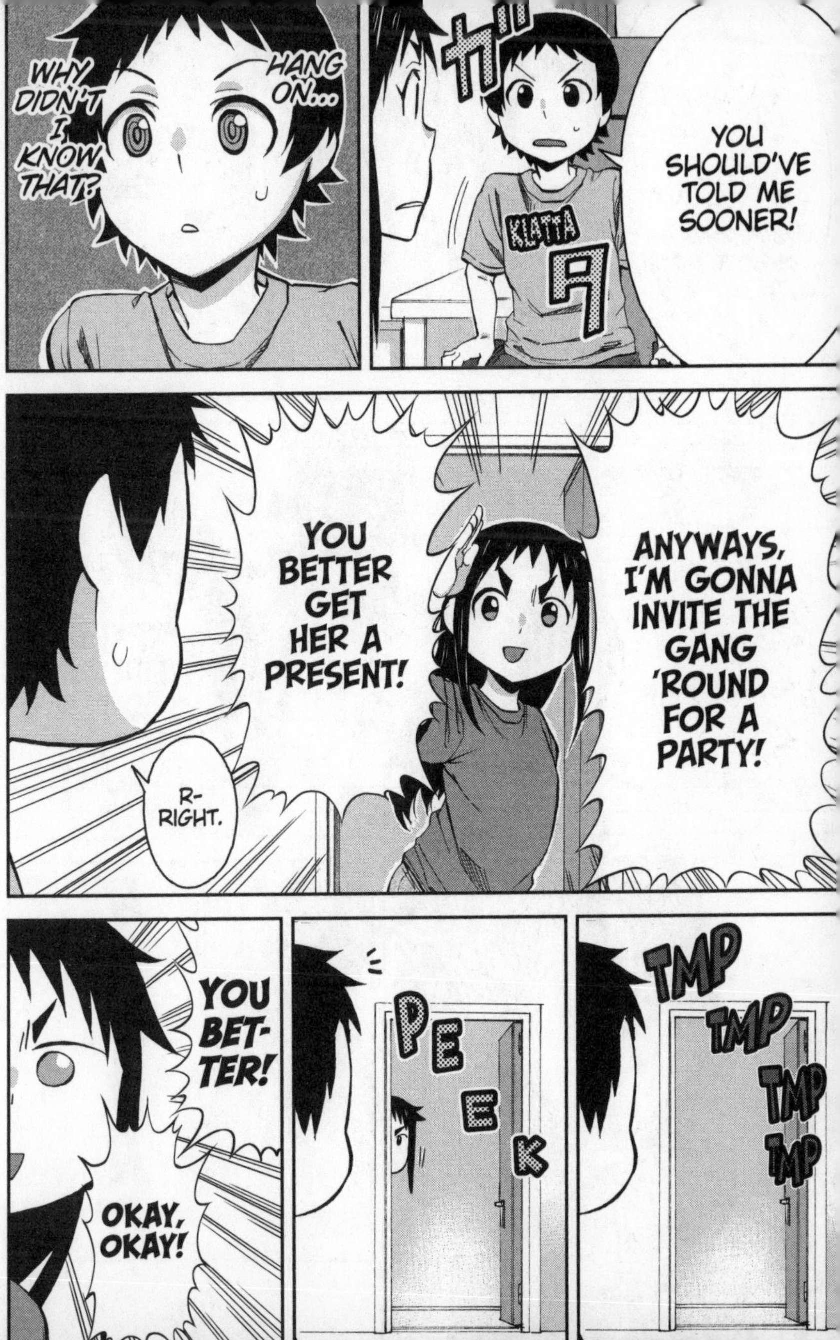
ガ
YOU SHOULD'VE TOLD ME SOONER!
KIATTA 9
HANG ON...
WHY DIDN'T I KNOW THAT?
ANYWAYS, I'M GONNA INVITE THE GANG 'ROUND FOR A PARTY!
YOU BETTER GET HER A PRESENT!
R-RIGHT.
TMP TMP TMP TMP
PEEK
YOU BET-TER!
OKAY, OKAY!

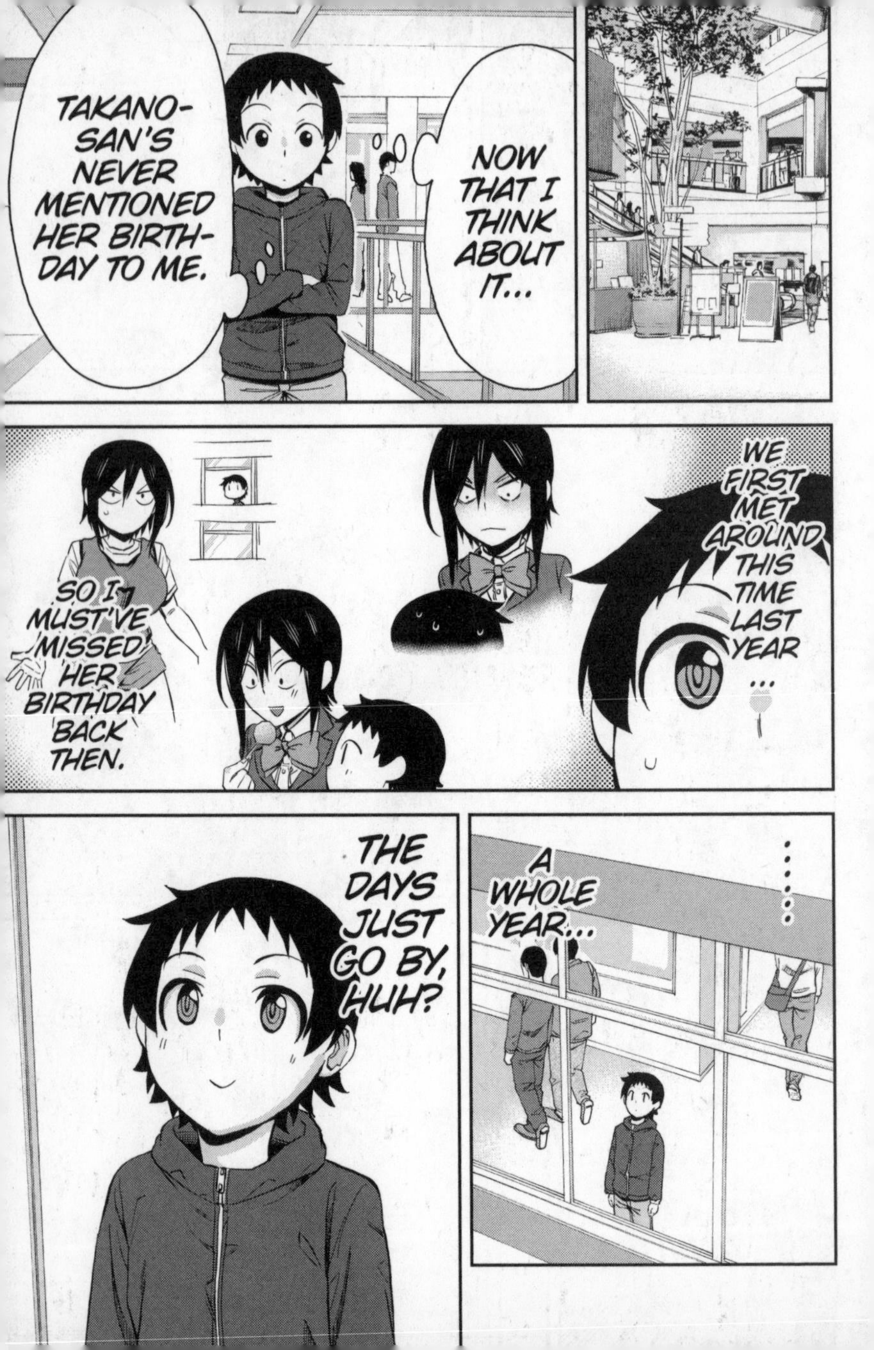
NOW THAT I THINK ABOUT IT...
TAKANO-SAN'S NEVER MENTIONED HER BIRTHDAY TO ME.
WE FIRST MET AROUND THIS TIME LAST YEAR ...
SO I MUST'VE MISSED HER BIRTHDAY BACK THEN.
......
A WHOLE YEAR...
THE DAYS JUST GO BY, HUH?

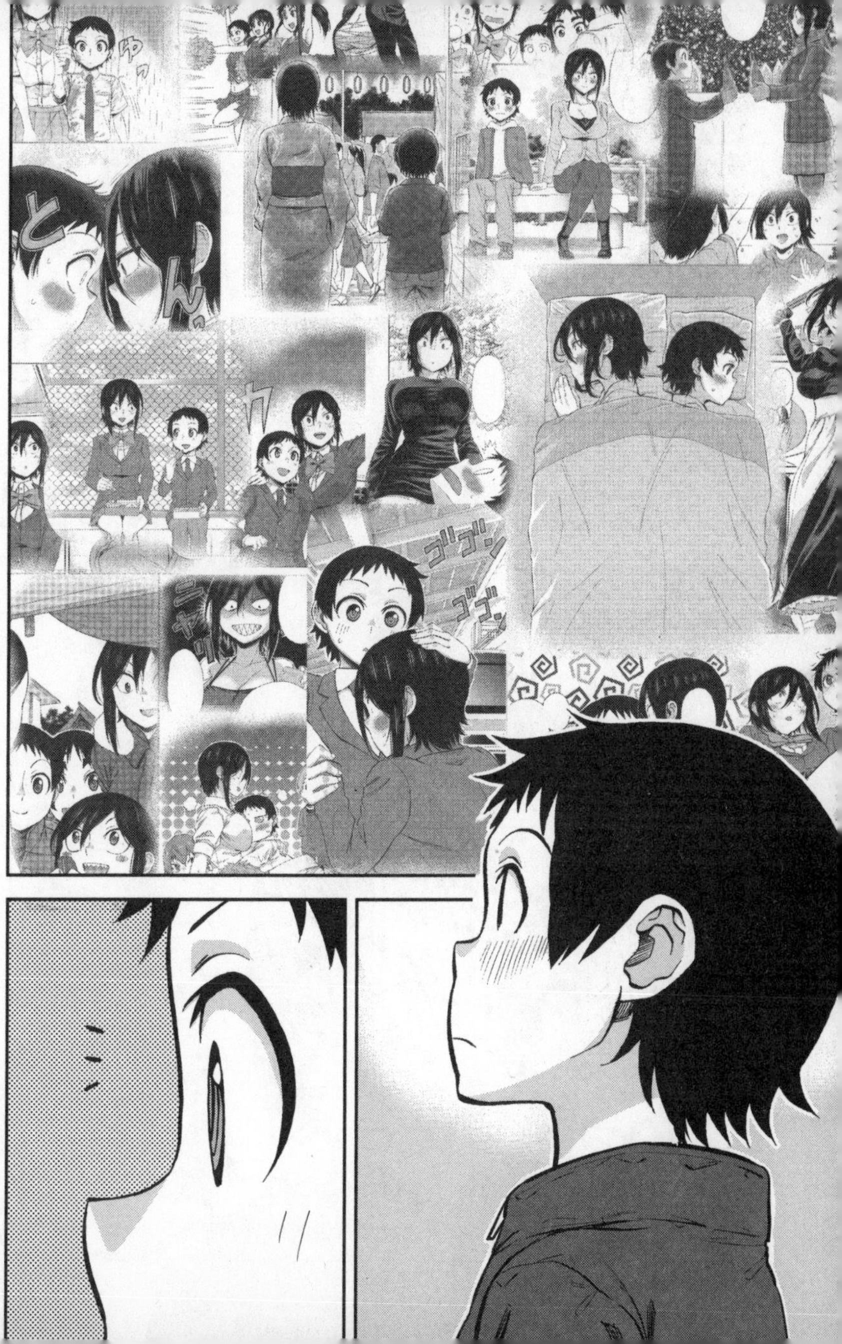

ゆっ
とん
ワ
ゴゴン
ゴゴ
ニヤリ

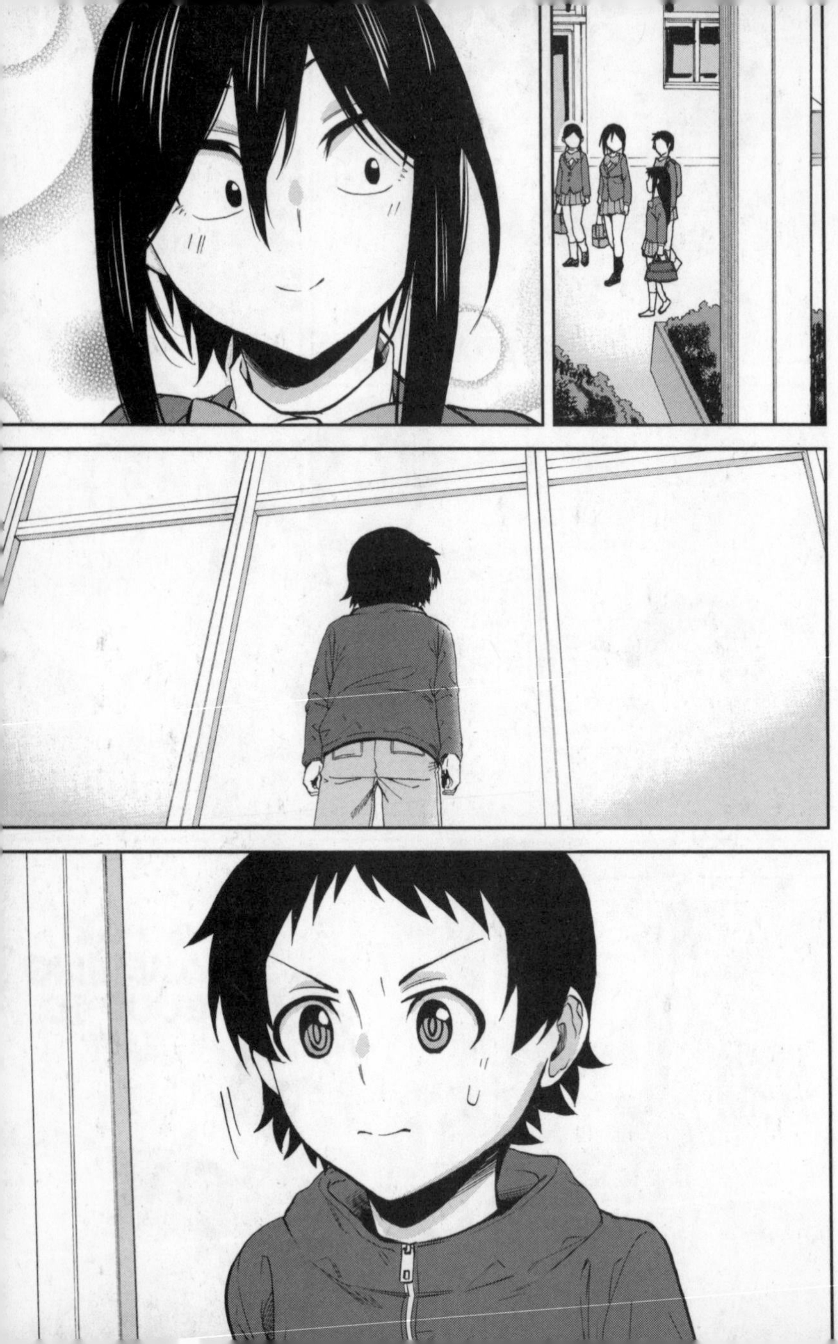

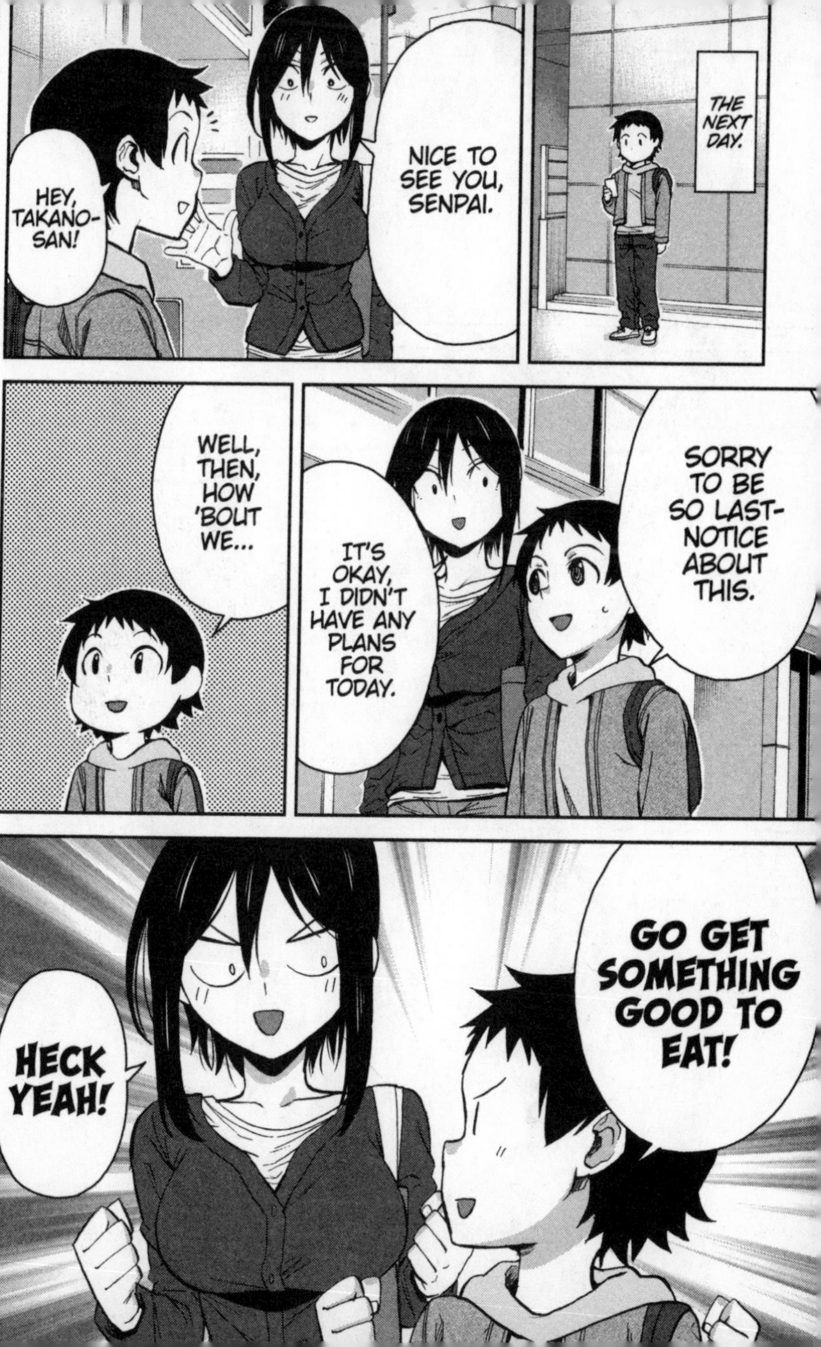
THE NEXT DAY.
NICE TO SEE YOU, SENPAI.
HEY, TAKANO-SAN!
SORRY TO BE SO LAST-NOTICE ABOUT THIS.
IT'S OKAY, I DIDN'T HAVE ANY PLANS FOR TODAY.
WELL, THEN, HOW 'BOUT WE...
GO GET SOMETHING GOOD TO EAT!
HECK YEAH!

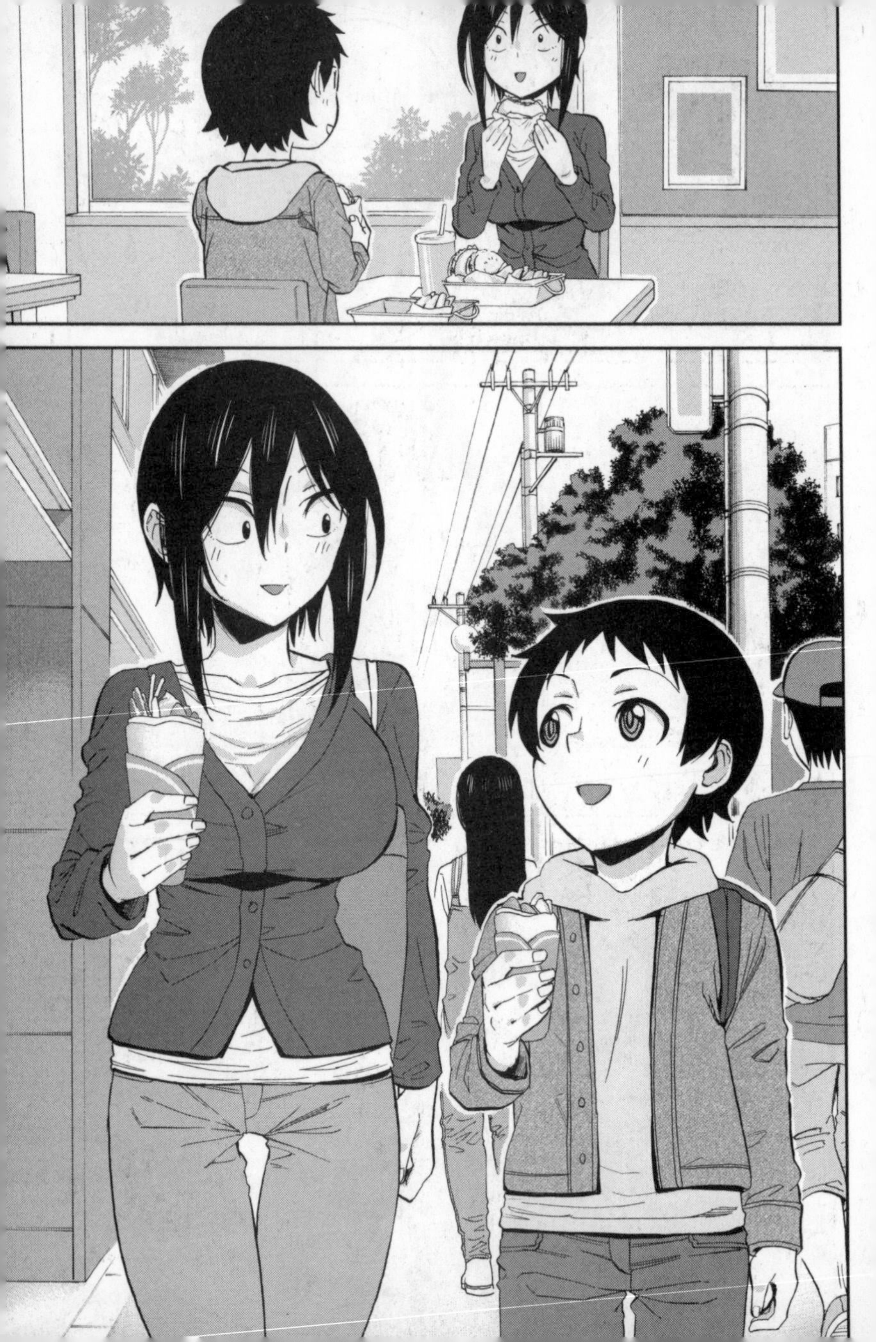

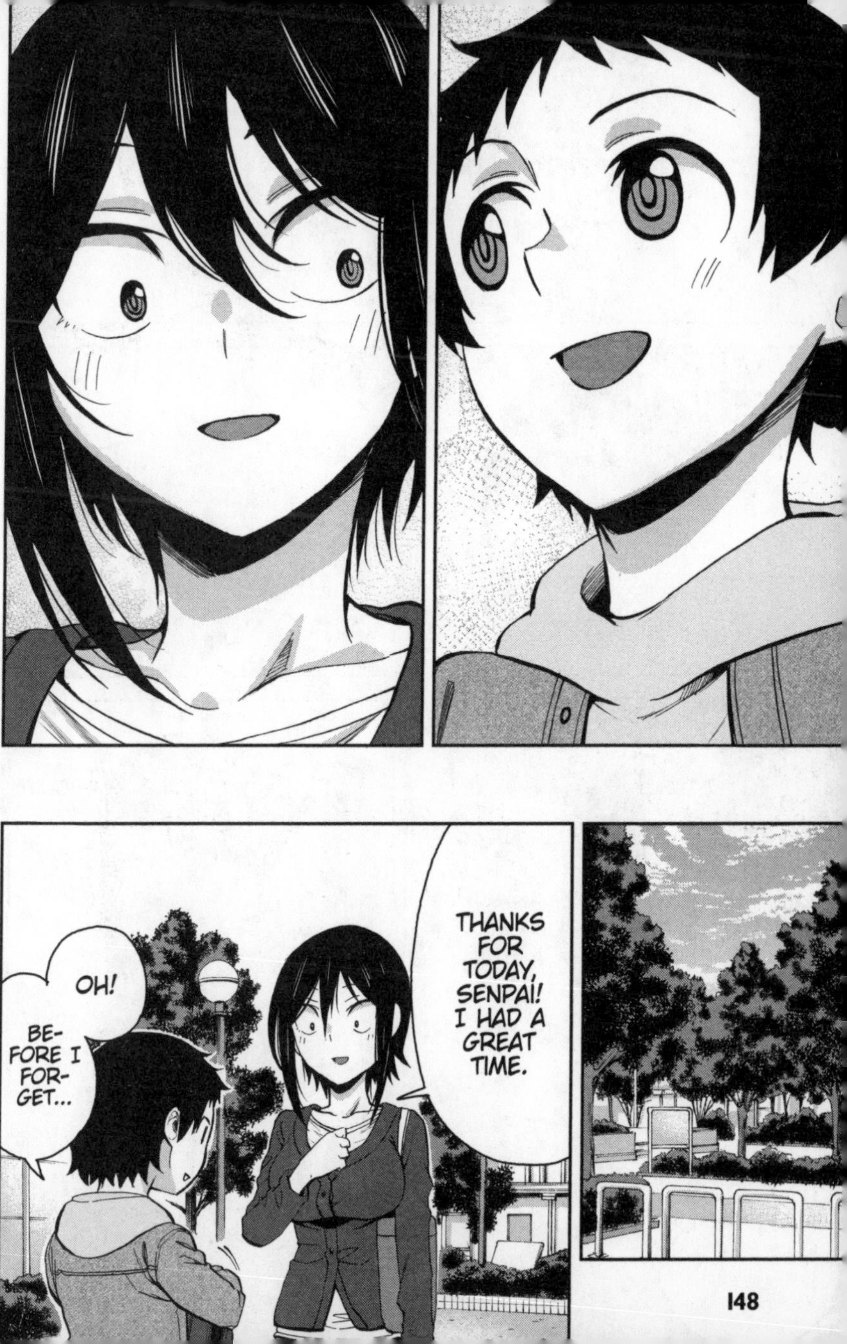
THANKS FOR TODAY, SENPAI! I HAD A GREAT TIME.
OH!
BEFORE I FORGET...

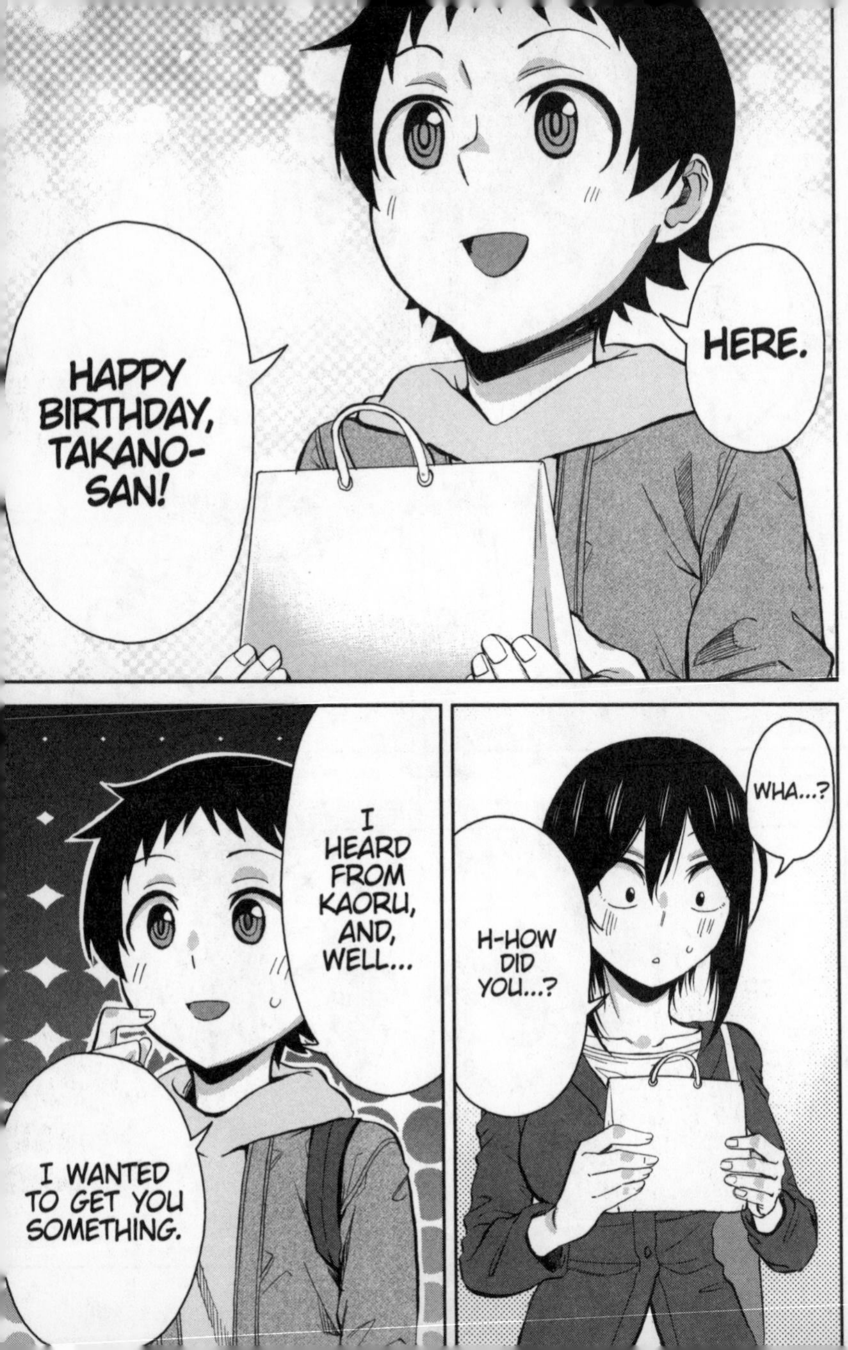
HERE.
HAPPY BIRTHDAY, TAKANO-SAN!
WHA...?
H-HOW DID YOU...?
I HEARD FROM KAORU, AND, WELL...
I WANTED TO GET YOU SOMETHING.

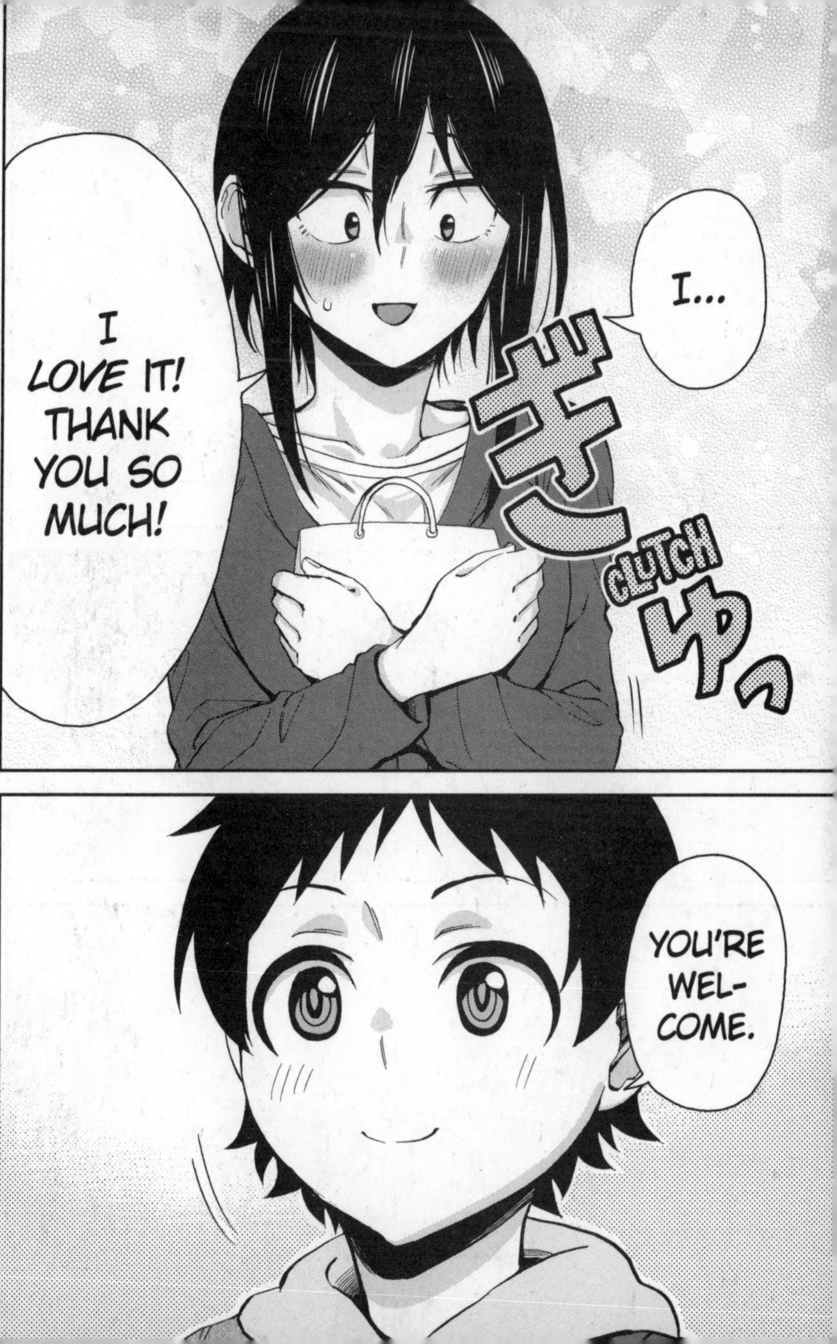
I...
ぎゅっ
CLUTCH
I LOVE IT! THANK YOU SO MUCH!
YOU'RE WEL-COME.

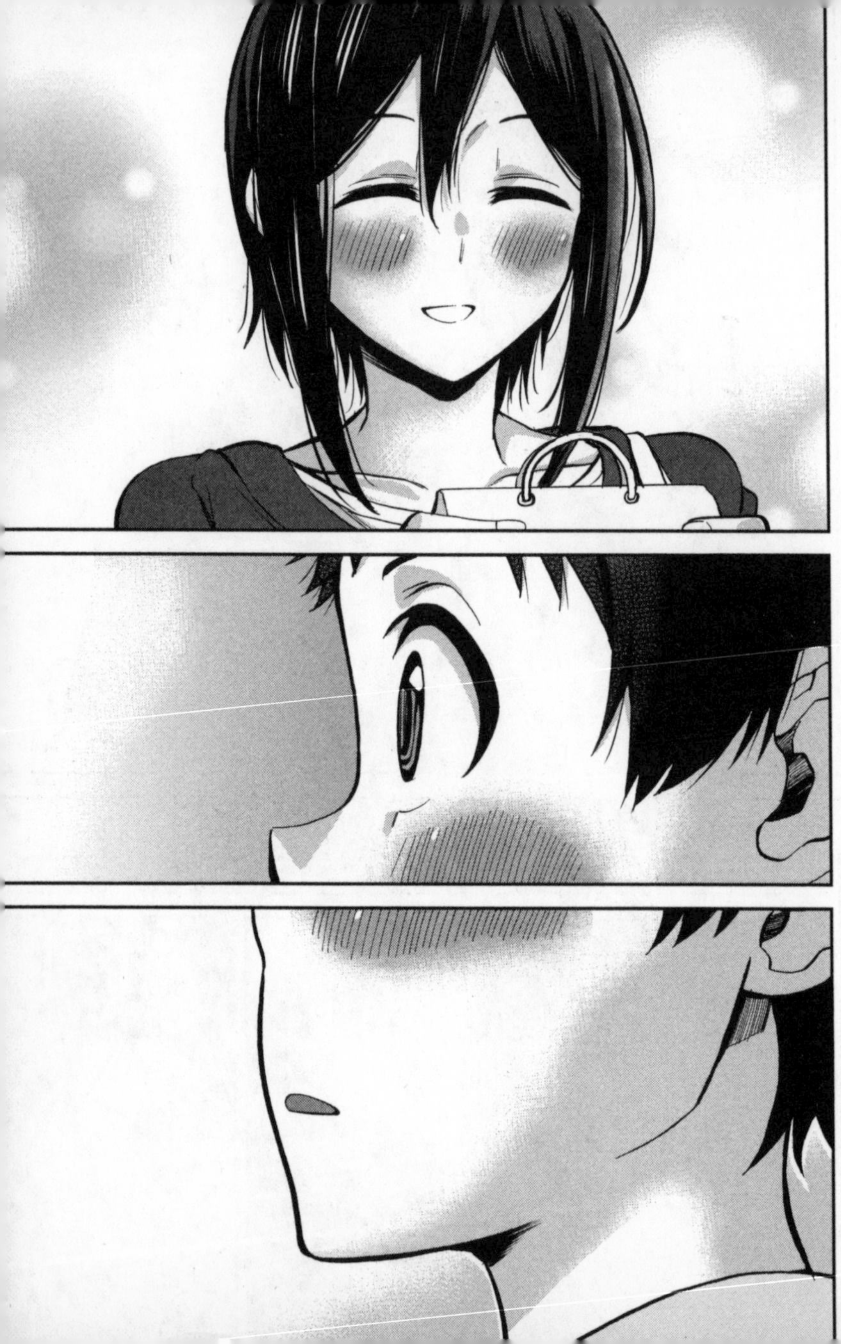

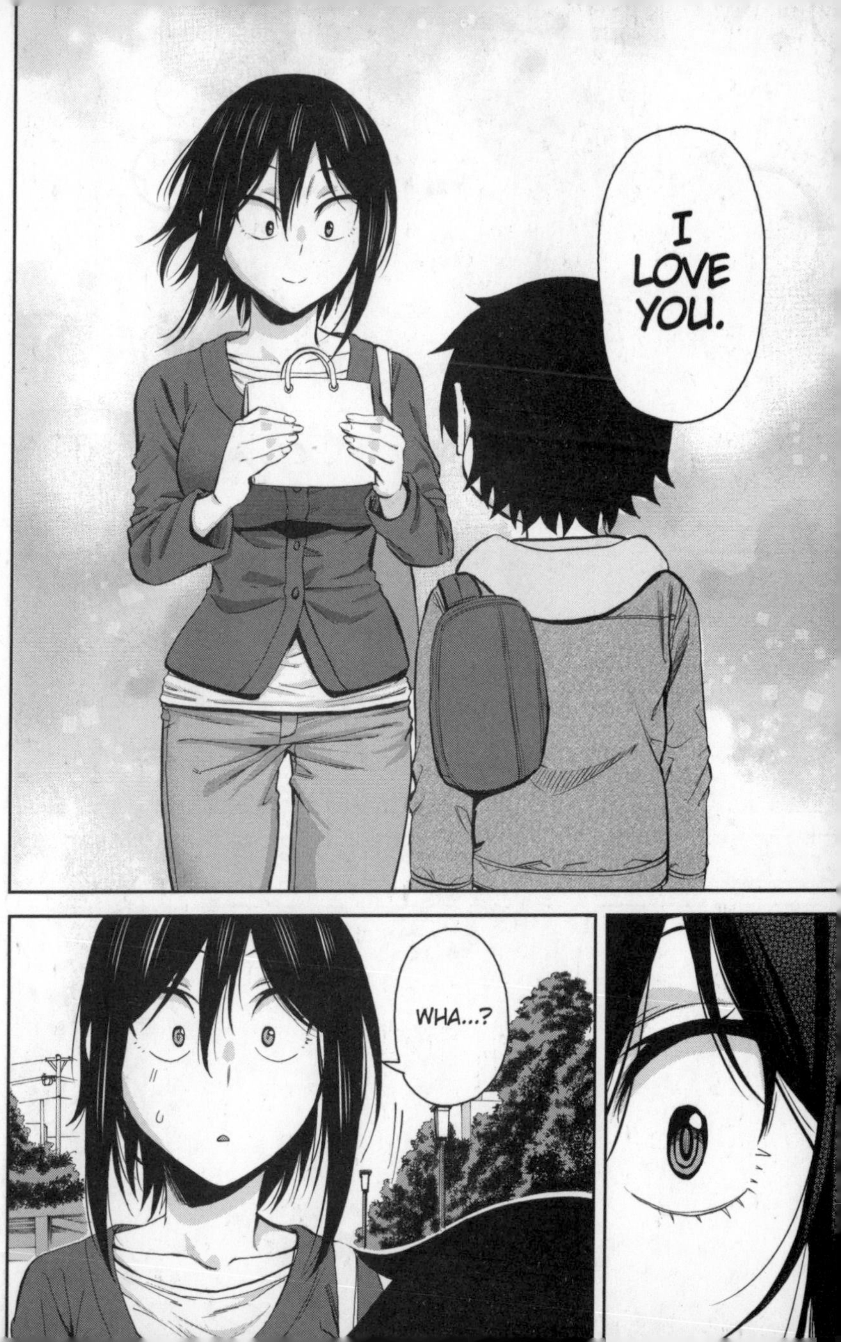
I LOVE YOU.
WHA...?

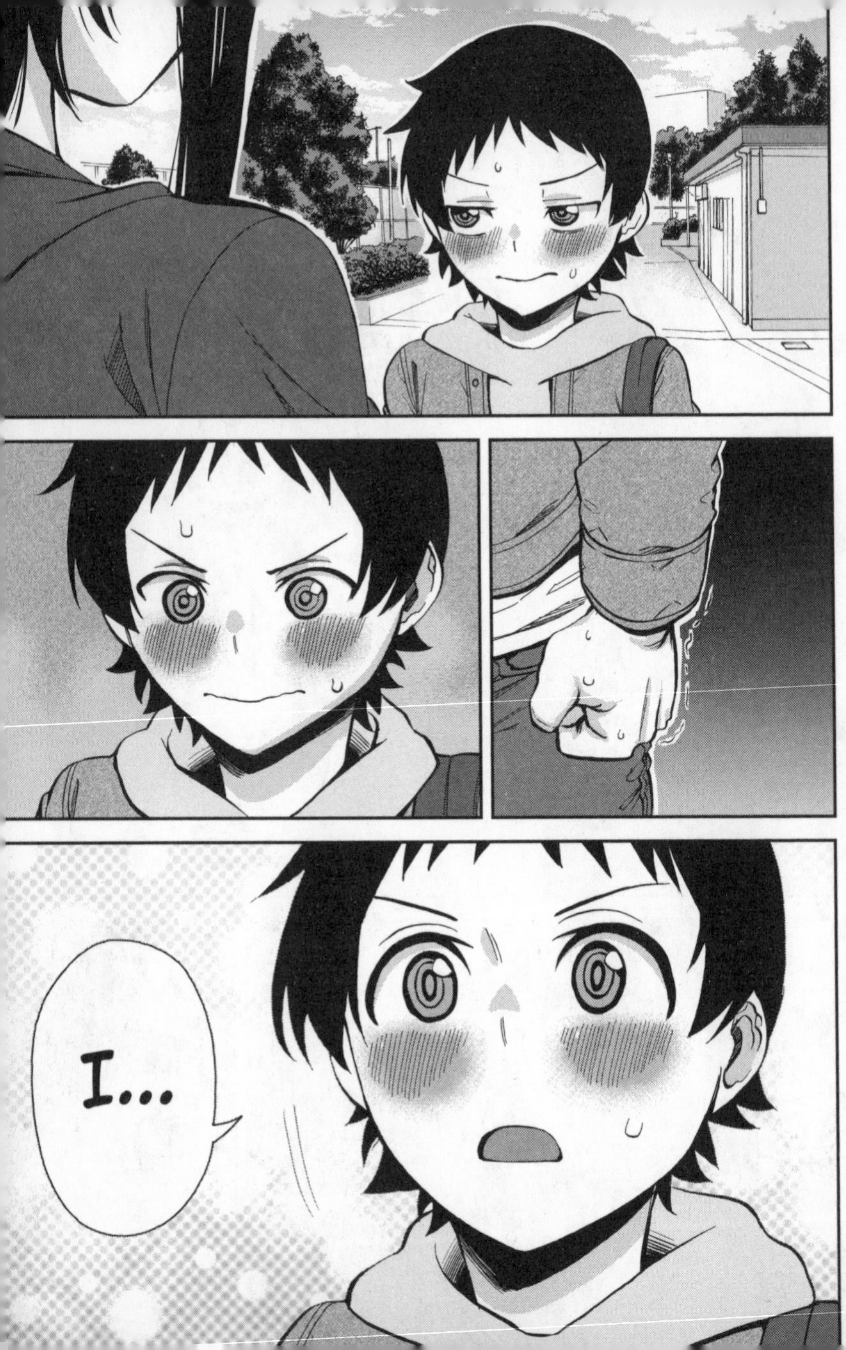
I...

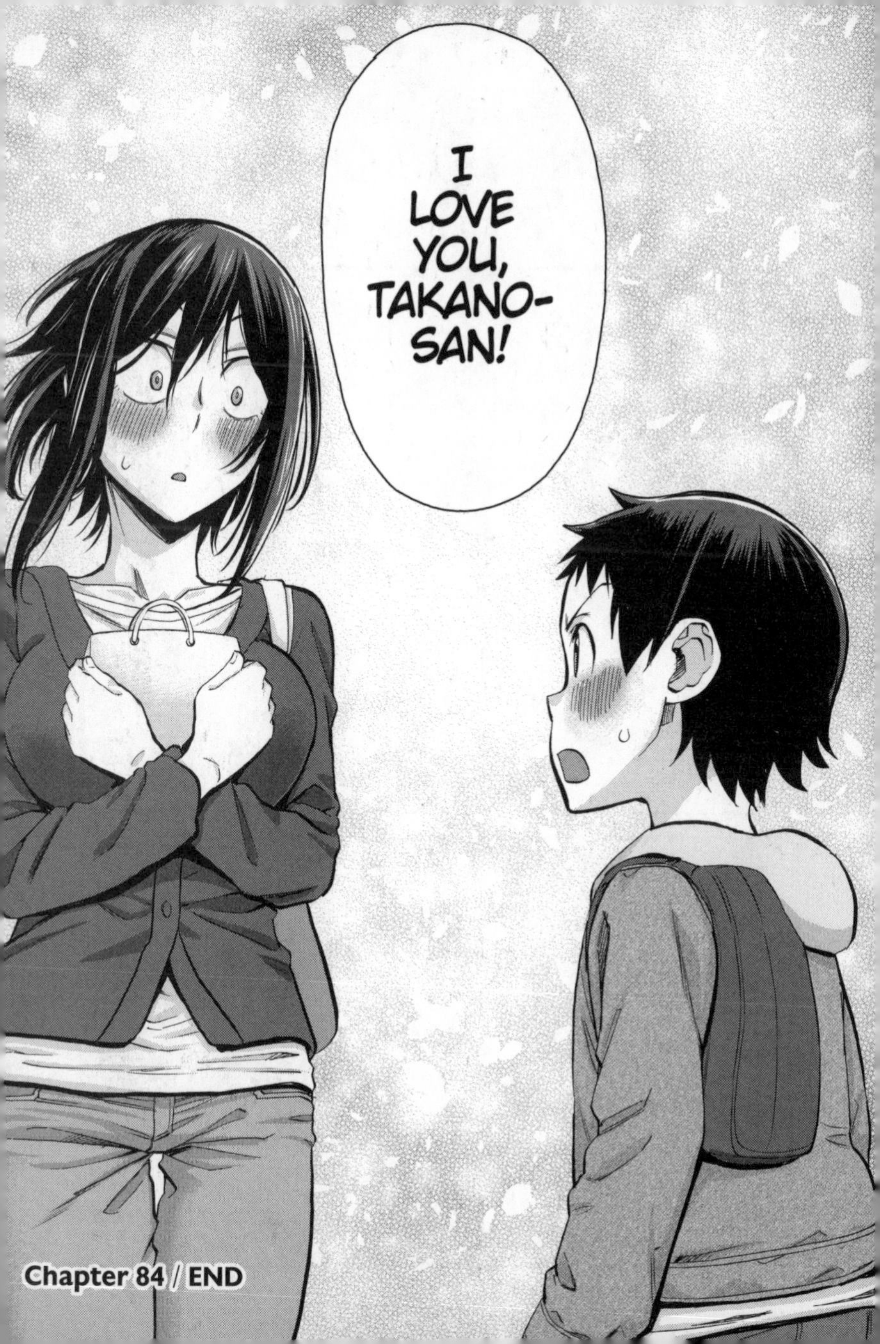
I LOVE YOU, TAKANO-SAN!
Chapter 84 / END

Hitomi-chan is Shy With Strangers

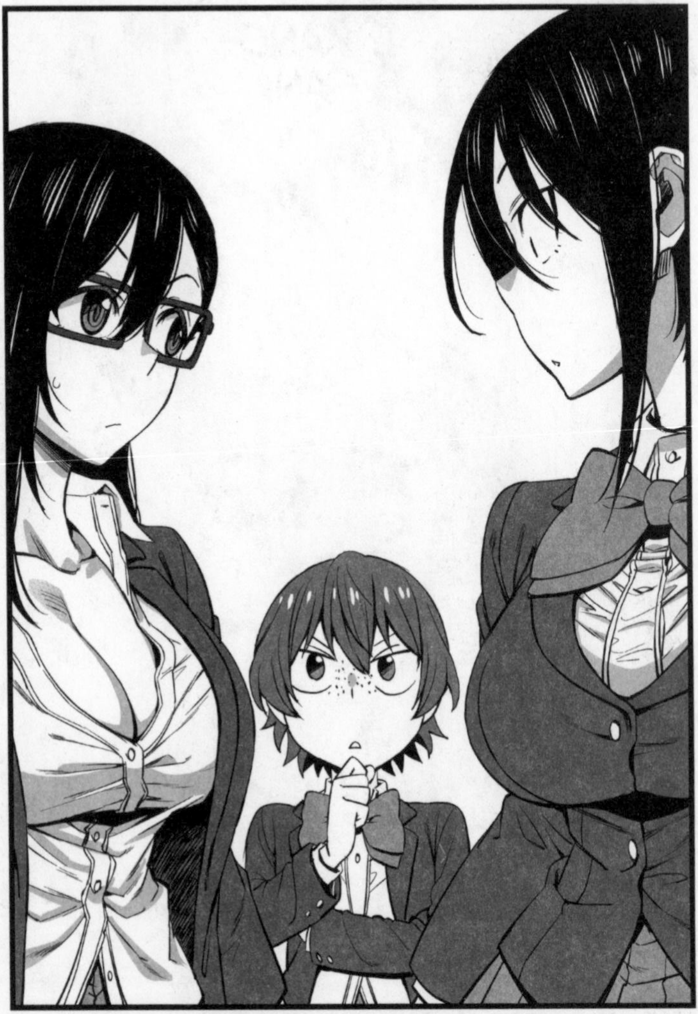

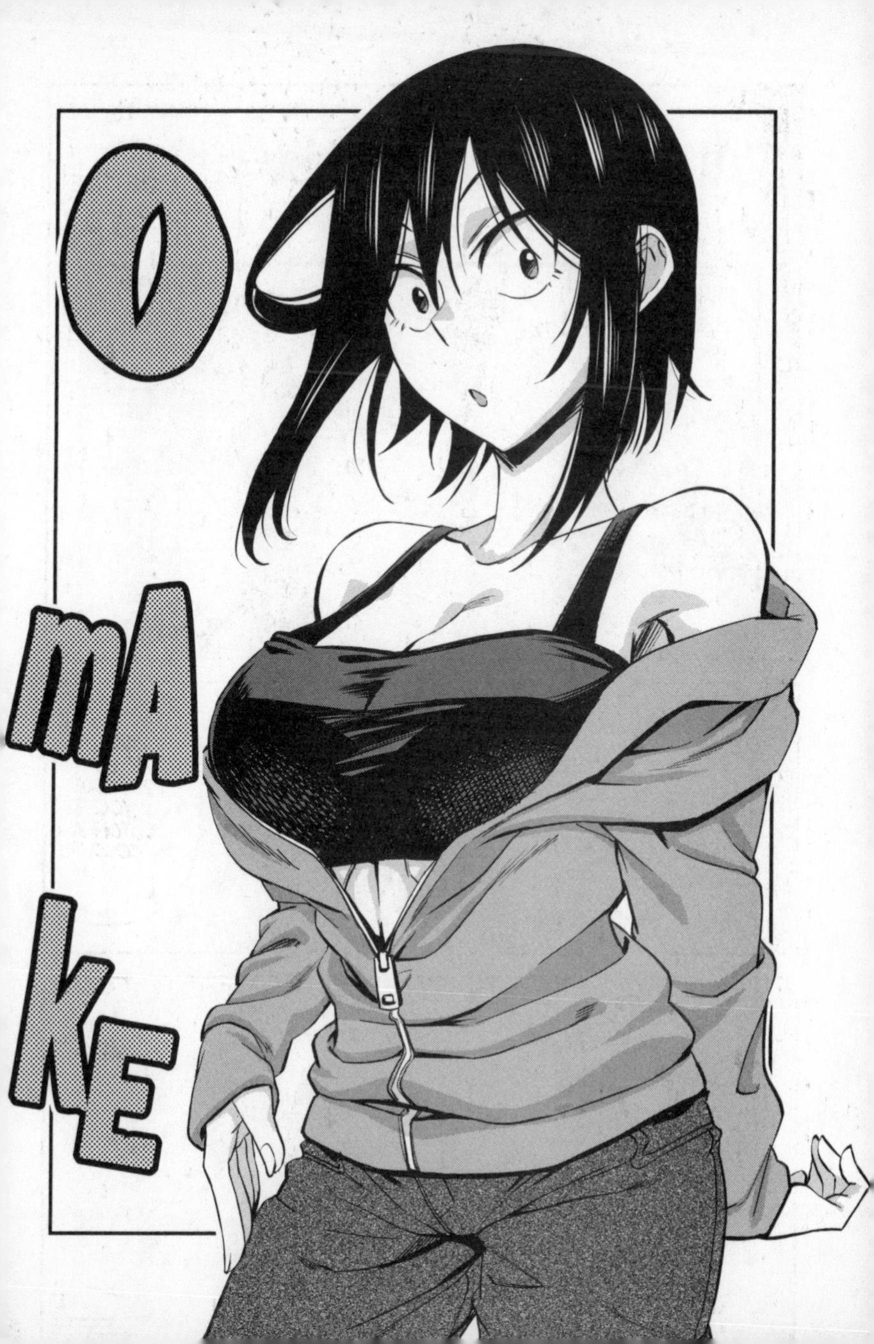
OMAKE

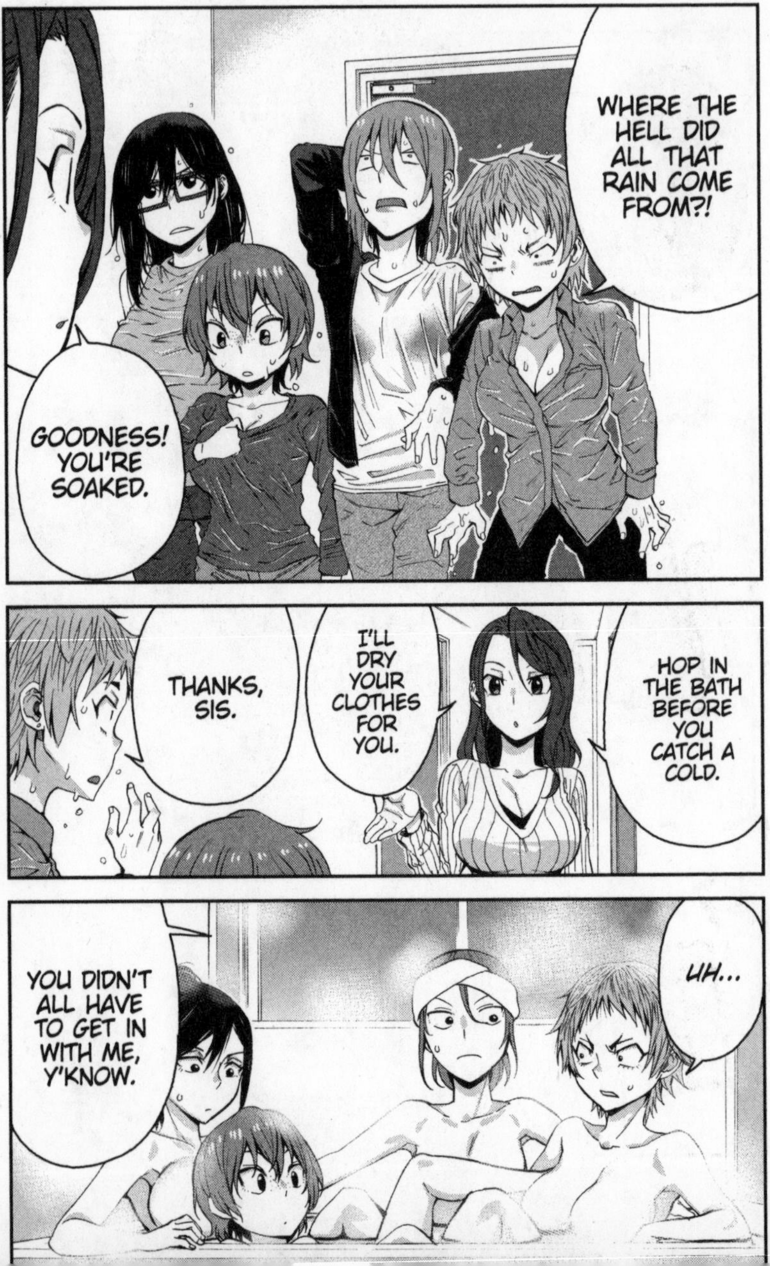
WHERE THE HELL DID ALL THAT RAIN COME FROM?!
GOODNESS! YOU'RE SOAKED.
HOP IN THE BATH BEFORE YOU CATCH A COLD.
I'LL DRY YOUR CLOTHES FOR YOU.
THANKS, SIS.
UH...
YOU DIDN'T ALL HAVE TO GET IN WITH ME, Y'KNOW.

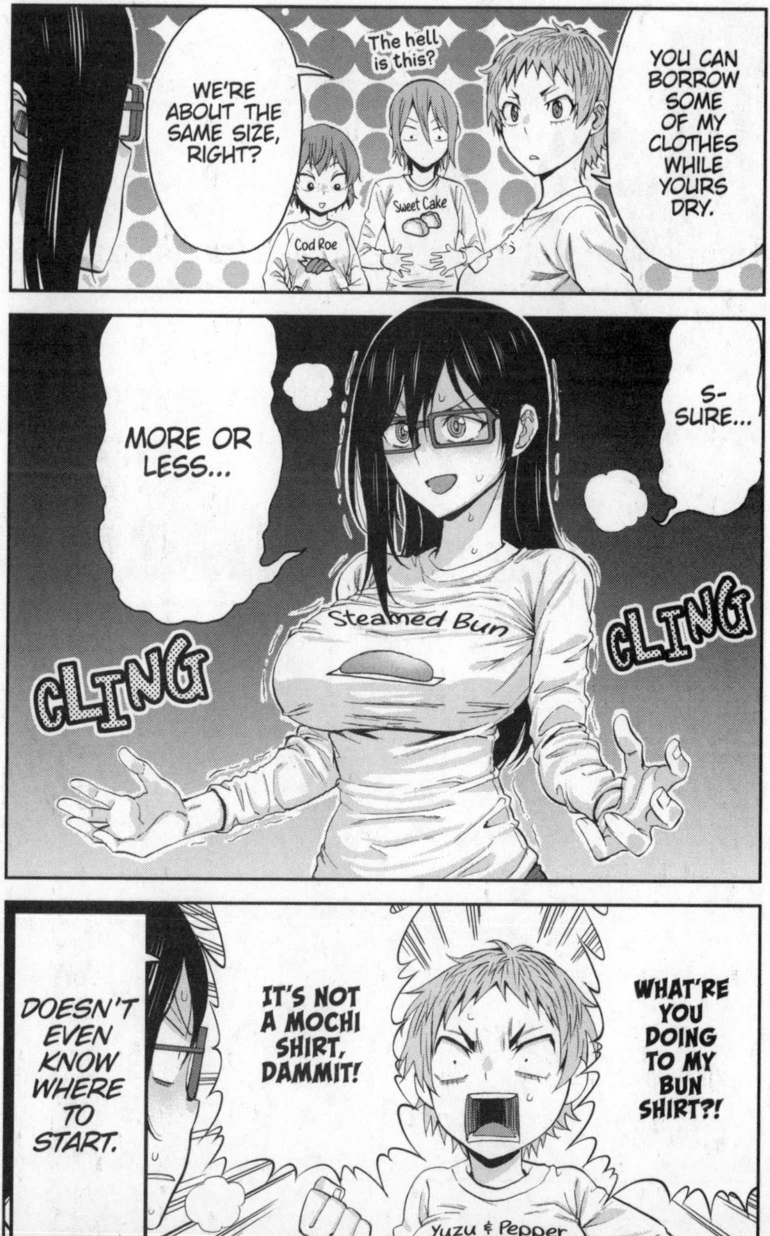
YOU CAN BORROW SOME OF MY CLOTHES WHILE YOURS DRY.
The hell is this?
Sweet Cake
WE'RE ABOUT THE SAME SIZE, RIGHT?
Cod Roe
S-SURE...
CLING
MORE OR LESS...
Steamed Bun
CLING
WHAT'RE YOU DOING TO MY BUN SHIRT?!
IT'S NOT A MOCHI SHIRT, DAMMIT!
Yuzu & Pepper
DOESN'T EVEN KNOW WHERE TO START.

Afterword

Thanks for reading Volume 7.

Somehow, Volume 1 seems like forever ago, but at the same time, like just yesterday.

Hitomi-chan and Usa-kun have known each other a year now, and things keep on changing, little by little. I was so glad to be able to give Usa-kun this chance to voice his feelings. Thanks to all the readers who've stayed with us up till now.

I'm looking forward to drawing a fun new Hitomi-chan and Usa-kun in Volume 8! Girls with powerful eyes really are the best.

Chorisuke Natsumi

夏海ちょりすけ

VEN SEAS ENTERTAINMENT PRESENTS

omi-chan is Shy With Strangers

Vol. 7

story and art by CHORISUKE NATSUMI

TRANSLATION
Avery Hutley

ADAPTATION
Patrick King

LETTERING
Carolina Hernández Mendoza

COVER & LOGO DESIGN
H. Qi

PROOFREADER
Tui Head

SENIOR EDITOR
Jenn Grunigen

PREPRESS TECHNICIAN
Melanie Ujimori
Jules Valera

PRODUCTION DESIGNER
Eve Grandt
Brennan Thome

PRODUCTION MANAGER
John Ramirez

MANAGING EDITOR
J.P. Sullivan
Shanti Whitesides

EDITOR-IN-CHIEF
Julie Davis

ASSOCIATE PUBLISHER
Adam Arnold

PUBLISHER
Jason DeAngelis

Hitomichan ha hitomishiri Vol. 7
© Chorisuke Natsumi 2022
Originally published in Japan in 2022 by Akita Publishing Co.,Ltd.
English translation rights arranged with Akita Publishing Co.,Ltd.
through TOHAN CORPORATION, Tokyo.

Seven Seas press and purchase enquiries can be sent to Marketing Manager Lianne Sentar at press@gomanga.com. Information regarding the distribution and purchase of digital editions is available from Digital Manager CK Russell at digital@gomanga.com.

Seven Seas and the Seven Seas logo are trademarks of Seven Seas Entertainment. All rights reserved.

ISBN: 978-1-68579-674-7
Printed in Canada
First Printing: December 2023
10 9 8 7 6 5 4 3 2 1

//// READING DIRECTIONS ////

This book reads from *right to left*, Japanese style. If this is your first time reading manga, you start reading from the top right panel on each page and take it from there. If you get lost, just follow the numbered diagram here. It may seem backwards at first, but you'll get the hang of it! Have fun!!

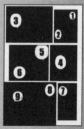

Follow us online: www.SevenSeasEntertainment.com

CONTENTS

[CHARACTER PROFILES]

TAKANO HITOMI

SECOND-YEAR. CLUMSY AND KIND-HEARTED, DESPITE HER SLIGHTLY TERRIFYING LOOKS.

USAMI YUU

THIRD-YEAR. "USA-KUN" FOR SHORT. BEFRIENDED HITOMI-CHAN AFTER A CHANCE ENCOUNTER.

USAMI KAORU

SECOND-YEAR. USA-KUN'S YOUNGER SISTER AND HITOMI-CHAN'S CLASSMATE. A REAL FREE SPIRIT.

HITOMI'S BROTHER

A FULL-TIME WORKER WITH A HUGE BUILD. A LITTLE ROUGH AROUND THE EDGES, BUT CARES DEEPLY FOR HITOMI-CHAN.

KARASUMA ANGELICA

TRANSFERRED FROM AMERICA INTO USA-KUN'S CLASS. HAS A TENDENCY TO GET CARRIED AWAY AROUND KAORU.

HIMARI

HAS A REAL KNACK FOR BUMPING INTO HITOMI-CHAN. SWEETER AND MORE SENSIBLE THAN HER DELINQUENT LOOKS CONVEY.

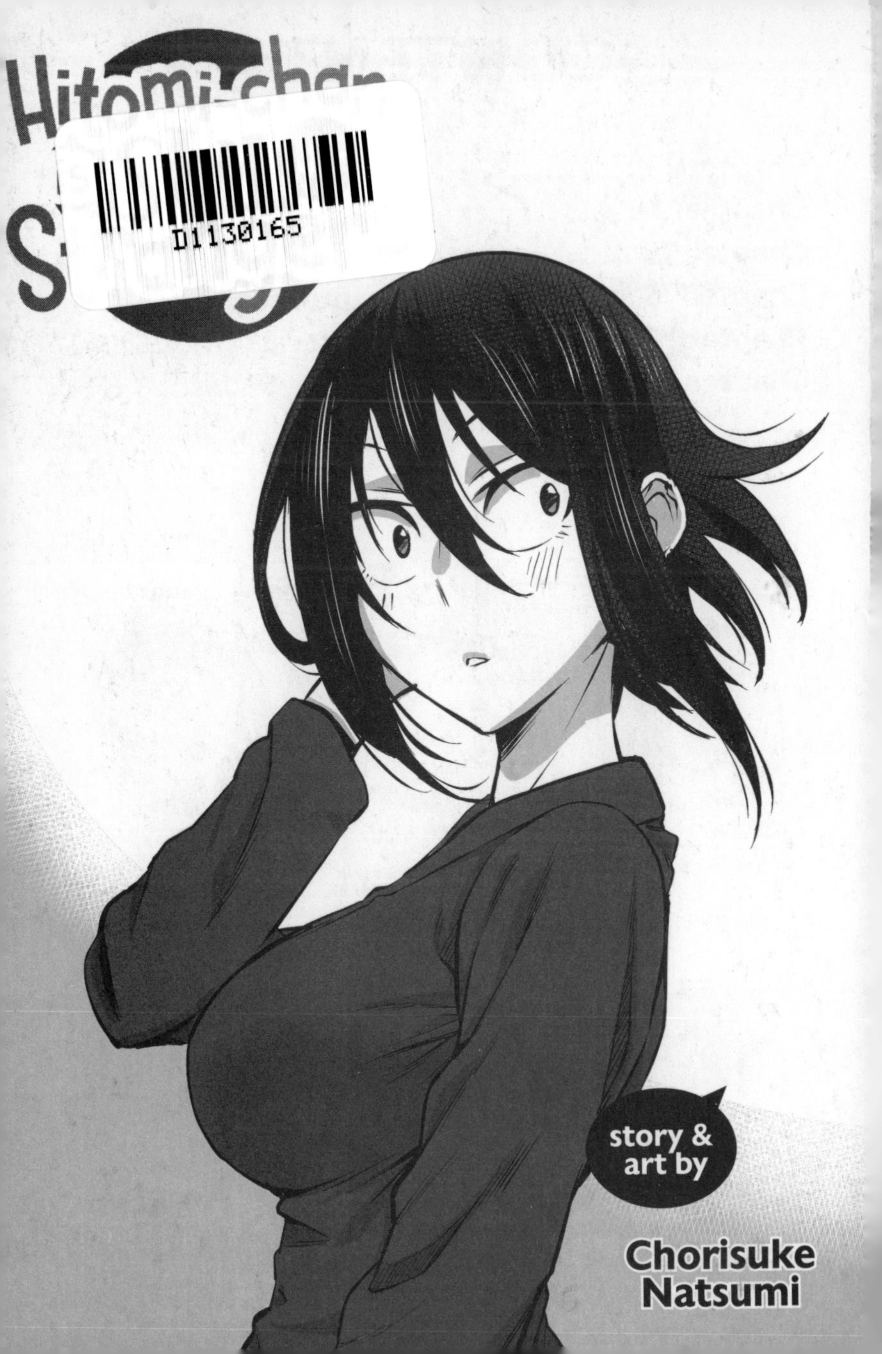
story &
art by
Chorisuke
Natsumi